D1710630

ELECTRONIC
CUSTOMER RELATIONSHIP
MANAGEMENT

Advances in Management Information Systems

Advisory Board

ELECTRONIC CUSTOMER RELATIONSHIP MANAGEMENT

JERRY FJERMESTAD
NICHOLAS C. ROMANO, JR.
EDITORS

ADVANCES IN MANAGEMENT
INFORMATION SYSTEMS
VLADIMIR ZWASS SERIES EDITOR

M.E.Sharpe
Armonk, New York
London, England

References to the AMIS papers should be as follows:

Bartolacci, M.R. and Meixell, M. Success Factors in online supply chain management and e-customer relationship
management. J. Fjermestad and N.C. Romano Jr., eds., *Electronic Customer Relationship Management. Advances
in Information Management Systems,* Volume 3 (Armonk, NY: M.E. Sharpe, 2006), 21–33.

ISBN 0-7656-1327-1
ISSN 1554-6152

Printed in the United States of America

The paper used in this publication meets the minimum requirements of
American National Standard for Information Sciences
Permanence of Paper for Printed Library Materials,
ANSI Z 39.48-1984.

BM (c)   10   9   8   7   6   5   4   3   2   1

**ADVANCES IN
MANAGEMENT INFORMATION SYSTEMS**

AMIS Vol. 1: Richard Y. Wang, Elizabeth M. Pierce, Stuart E. Madnick, and Craig W. Fisher
Information Quality
ISBN 0-7656-1133-3

AMIS Vol. 2: Sergio deCesare, Mark Lycett, Robert D. Macredie
Development of Component-Based Information Systems
ISBN 0-7656-1248-1

AMIS Vol. 3: Jerry Fjermestad and Nicholas C. Romano, Jr.
Electronic Customer Relationship Management
ISBN 0-7656-1327-1

Forthcoming volumes of this series can be found on the series homepage.
www.mesharpe.com/amis.htm

Editor-in-Chief
Vladimir Zwass

zwass@fdu.edu

CONTENTS

Part IV. CRM in Business-to-Consumer Commerce

SERIES EDITOR'S INTRODUCTION

VLADIMIR ZWASS, EDITOR-IN-CHIEF

It is the objective of the *Advances in Management Information Systems (AMIS)* to present our knowledge about the field of Information Systems (IS), but also to be an instrument in the expansion and in the deepening of this knowledge. The editors and the authors of the present volume worthily contribute to this goal by focusing our attention on enterprise strategies and information systems that aim to bind firms to their customers.

The expansion of the advancing market economies over the last three centuries has been greatly amplified by the recent accession of the large parts of the world to the market system. These are epochal changes, with their enactments and impacts *in statu nascendi*. This much is, however, clear: Over the last two decades, the choices and opportunities for the participants in global economies have expanded vastly. The inexorable competitive pressures of the marketplace have increased the pace of organizational and technological innovations, and have in turn been driven by these innovations. In particular, the ongoing globalization of the markets has expanded the choices of the buyer, the customer, be that a consumer or a firm.

Information has always been the lifeblood of the marketplaces. Computerized information systems of the last half-century have enabled new organizational forms, with the constellations of firms delivering their products as a virtual company, and with process specialists (think FedEx) emerging to serve across industries and across nation-states. Most products in today's marketplaces are either information-based, or are a part of package involving a physical good, information, and (information-based) service. Consider a customized computer system delivered by Dell, an electronic airline ticket priced by a yield-management system, or a slot machine that recognizes the returning customers and adjusts the game on offer to their inferred preferences. The total augmented product is far more responsive to the marketplace and to the customer than in the past.

The Internet-Web compound that is enabling—when not driving—this transformation today is certainly not the culmination of the change process. It is as certainly a major technological discontinuity, opening the world to transformative technologies, and submitting these technologies to the transformation attendant on their adoption in diverse contexts, all enacting their forces of change. With multiple options available to the customers in market economies, the competition for best customers becomes an engine of economic growth. The competition for customers occurs at the firm level (however, assisted-or hampered-may it be by governments). Firms need to focus all their activities on profitably serving their customers. This means, in turn, being able to continually identify, reach, and satisfy the customers with long-term profitability. Customer Relationship Management (CRM) is the strategy with precisely that aim.

A multifaceted effort, CRM has been defined in many ways, a number of them valid. We may consider CRM to be a business strategy to acquire and manage relationships with customers in order to maximize the long-term value of these relationships. Basically, the firm implementing

CRM aims to increase the loyalty of profitable customers and to increase the profitability of loyal customers. This is the point of view of the owner firm. In the customer's perception, an effective CRM program means that the firm satisfies the customer more completely than any competing supplier could. This engenders loyalty. Indeed, the foundational premise of CRM is the high level of financial return on customer loyalty. Customer equity is a crucial endowment of a firm (Rust, Zeithaml, and Lemon, 2000). Selecting and acquiring customers based on their lifetime value results in higher profits than seeking out customers based on other criteria (Venkatesan and Kumar, 2004). Metrics are available to actually project this return (Pfeifer and Farris, 2004). CRM is a significant development in the shift of the business and marketing orientation from the product focus (marketing the products) to the customer focus (satisfying or exceeding customer requirements over a long horizon of the relationship).

The immediately obvious aspects of CRM have then to be these: an integrated view of the customer and the customer's dealings with the firm; the primacy of the long, relational attitude toward the customer over the short-sighted, transactional view; increasingly more refined individualized approach to a customer over the span of the relationship; knowledge of the projected value of the existing customers to the firm over the long term; and a large degree of knowledge of non-customers and of what separates some of them from becoming desirable customers. This brief analysis of CRM tells us that the strategy is impossible without advanced and integrated information systems, centering on data warehouses for the longitudinal analysis of the total view of the customers and on integrated databases for the delivery of service to them. This is, of course, not enough. The organizational transformation into customer-focused culture, customer-oriented business processes, the customer-centric performance metrics, new incentive systems deriving from creating lasting customer relationships, are all necessary components of CRM. Such companies as Southwest Airlines come to mind.

Indeed, relationship marketing, the underlying premise of CRM, cannot be effective without an appropriate use of information technology (IT) (Zineldin, 2000). Today, customers are reached via multiple channels, integrating the Internet-based touch points of the Web and email, delivered also over mobile devices, with the direct marketing and brick-and-mortar-based sales. It is necessary to sustain consistent, unified interaction with the customer across all the touch points, from the Web to the store, and across all the company's units interacting with the customer, from sales to service (Pan and Lee, 2003). Moreover, integrated collaboration with channel partners such as distributors and retailers is necessary for a producer. Each interaction with the customer, be it a sale or a well-handled customer complaint, ought to have a positive effect on the relationship. As e-commerce becomes increasingly embedded in the physical world, we can no longer treat the Internet-Web based touch points in isolation (Zwass, 2002).

Hence, electronic CRM (eCRM) has come to signify the use of IT to reach and serve the desirable customers, as well as to increase their value to the vendor over the relationship's time. ECRM enables the company to manage customer relationships in real time, bringing to bear the necessary information to all the events in this relationship. Examples of success abound. Thus, Dell manages the demand for its customized products in real time, by modifying the offer terms across the customer touch points based on the current availability of the components. eCRM mobilizes the collective knowledge of the firm's employees, making it available to a Peat Marwick's consultant visiting the client's office, and marshals the collective knowledge of a virtual company, making it available to the client of Skandia's financial services (Vandermerwe, 2000). Harrah's Entertainment engenders surpassing loyalty in its casino clientele through the pervasive use of data mining (Loveman, 2003). The technology enables the company to get to understand the various microsegments of its customers, predict their long-term "worth" to the casino operator, and devise comprehensive incentives for the customers to indeed increase that worth. Harrah's is also using IT to measure their employees service performance based on extensive customer-oriented metrics. eCRM can provide informational "dashboards" that allow tracking the effects of various CRM initiatives weekly or even daily, as needed.

eCRM is being deployed in the consumer-oriented (B2C) and in the business-to-business (B2B) commerce. As one example from the B2C commerce, CRM needs to provide profitably the special levels of service for the special customers, as the charge cards and airlines do it, with several levels of special treatment. Several models of prosuming (combination of consumption with production) may be supported, with the customers taking increasingly more active role in shaping products (Klein et al. 2005). Customer participation in the product life cycle ranges from co-innovation in the product development to joint personalization and configuration during the acquisition, on to the feedback during the ongoing product support. The customer is a crucial element in a firm's innovation, since as the users of the vendor's products both consumers and firms are increasingly able to adapt the information-containing products to new contexts (von Hippel, 2005). In B2B commerce, CRM needs to ensure an integrated global view of the customer to the seller firm, and a uniform where needed and country-specific where desired service to the customer. With an effective eCRM, it should be possible to expand the existing relationships and pursue—profitably—a greater share of the customer's business (Anderson and Narus, 2003). eCRM is becoming a part of a Sense-and-Respond organization, with an IT-enabled capability of adaptation to a rapidly changing business environment (Kapoor et al. 2005). The company has to be classified by the customer as being easy to do business with, in the words of Kalakota and Robinson (2003). These authors parse the eCRM-supported functions into these verbs: target (market planning), engage (market), transact, retain (deploying analytics), and service (assist throughout product's lifetime). In various instances, the vendor also helps the customers to retire the product.

As several case studies in the volume will tell you, eCRM delivers results only after a purposive, comprehensive, and painstaking process of organizational change, as part of the overall CRM. Indeed, "too few companies are paying enough attention to the organizational challenges inherent in any CRM initiative" (Agarwal et al. 2005, p. 1), with the resulting disappointments. Examples of CRM failures abound as well. The economies of technology-driven initiatives are seductive. A facile comparison between the direct cost of the customer order taken by a qualified individual and that of the customer being sent into a touch-tone hell motivates CRM implementations doomed to fail. The owner firm will not learn from the interaction with the customer; in fact, the customer will likely look for another vendor. The customer expects access to the vendor at any time in the form preferred by the customer. Moreover, it is productive access that the customer expects, where the counterpart on the firm's side is fully informed and empowered to assist. Increasingly, in what is been called the support economy by Zuboff and Maxmin (2002), and may equally be called the concierge economy, the solution to the customer's problem goes beyond the corporate boundaries, with collaborative eCRM gaining in importance. If the customer contacts your firm, your partnerships need to come into play seamlessly, transparent to the customer. This is what extended enterprise means. Again, much can be learned from Dell. The total customer experience is likely to be based on your weakest link.

The volume's studies bring forth all three components of eCRM: analytical (based on the formal analysis of large stores of customer data, frequently involving data mining from data warehouses), operational (delivery of surpassing customer service in an integrated fashion across all touch points), and collaborative (coordinating the activities of all business partners in the delivery of customer service). The leading suppliers of CRM software, such as Siebel Systems,

SAP, Oracle, PeopleSoft, and Teradata, continually enhance their enterprise software, for example, by adding new process components. The relatively new model of on-demand CRM software, particularly attractive to smaller companies, has been forcefully promoted by salesforce.com. IT implementation has to be accompanied by the appropriate IT management practices, with the greater involvement of high-level IT personnel in corporate CRM policies and practices—else, the IT investment may go to waste (Karimi et al. 2001). Successful implementations of CRM generally require an incremental approach, yet with great attention paid to the data infrastructure and to the organizational change processes (Goodhue et al. 2002).

The volume makes clear that information technology is an enabler of CRM, but "getting closer to customer isn't only about an information technology system" (Gulati and Oldroyd, 2005, p. 101). CRM itself is no substitute for the general product and process innovation. Although these facts are known about all the organizational information systems, they should be particularly heeded when deploying IT in dealing with customers in the ever more competitive global marketplace. In the lyrical words of Georg Simmel, who did Adam Smith one better, market competition "achieves what usually only love can do: the divination of the innermost wishes of the other, even before he himself becomes aware of them" (Simmel 1908/1955, p. 62). It is the goal of eCRM to assist the competing firm in divining the divination of the competitive marketplace and to communicate that, well, love.

The editors of this *AMIS* volume, Jerry Fjermestad and Nicholas Romano, are who they should be—the leaders in establishing eCRM as an area of study in MIS. Their previous work has done much to deepen and systematize our understating of the role of eCRM in corporate success (Romano and Fjermestad, 2001–02 and Fjermestad and Romano, 2002–03). In their own introduction, they will present the domain and the included papers at a greater length, and to your benefit.

REFERENCES

Agarwal, A., Harding, D. P., and Schumacher, J.R. Organizing for CRM, *The McKinley Quarterly*, July (2004). Available at http://www.mckinsey.com/practices/marketing/ourknowledge/pdf/McKinsey_on_Marketing-Organizing_for_CRM.pdf (Accessed May 15, 2005).

Anderson, J.C. and Narus, J.A. Selectively pursuing more of your customer's business. *MIT Sloan Management Review*, 44, 3 (2003), 42–49.

Fjermestad, J. and Romano, N. C., Jr., eds. Advances in electronic commerce customer relationship management. Special section. *International Journal of Electronic Commerce*, 7, 2 (2002–03), 7–117.

Goodhue, D.L., Wixom, B.H., and Watson, H.J. Realizing business benefits through CRM: Hitting the right target the right way. *MIS Quarterly Executive*, 1, 2 (2002), 79–94.

Gulati, R. and Oldroyd, J. The quest for customer focus. *Harvard Business Review*, 83, 4 (2005), 92–101.

Kalakota, R. and Robinson, M. *Services Blueprint: Roadmap for Execution.* Boston: Addison-Wesley, 2003.

Kapoor, S., Bhattacharya, K., Buckley, S., Chowdhary, P., Ettl, M., Katircioglu, K., Mauch, E., and Phillips, L. A technical framework for sense-and-respond business management. *IBM Systems Journal*, 44, 1 (2005), 5–24.

Karimi, J., Somers, T. M., and Gupta, Y.P. Impact of information technology management practices on customer service. *Journal of Management Information Systems*, 17, 4 (2001), 125–158.

Klein, S., Köhne, F., and Totz, C. Extending customer's roles in e-commerce–Promises, challenges, and some findings. In M. J. Shaw, ed., *Electronic Commerce and Digital Economy*. Advances in Management Information Systems. Armonk, NY: M.E. Sharpe, 2006, pp. 75–90.

Loveman, G. Diamonds in the data mine. *Harvard Business Review*, 81, 5 (2003), 109–113.

Pan, S.L. and Lee, J-N. Using e-CRM for a unified view of the customer. *Communications of the ACM*, 46, 4 (2003), 95–99.

Pfeifer, P.E. and Farris, P.W. The elasticity of customer value to retention: the duration of customer relationship. *Journal of Interactive Marketing*, 18, 2 (2004), 20–31.

Romano, N. C., Jr., and Fjermestad, J., eds. Electronic commerce customer relationship management. Special Section. *International Journal of Electronic Commerce*, 6, 2 (2001–02), 7–113.

Rust, R.T., Zeithaml, V.A., and Lemon, K.N. *Driving Customer Equity: How Customer Lifetime Value Is Reshaping Corporate Strategy*. New York: Free Press, 2000.

Simmel, G. Competition. In *Conflict and the Web of Group-Affiliations*. New York: The Free Press, 1955 [1908], pp. 58–85.

Vandermerwe, S. The customer-connected company and the role of e-technology in making it happen. In *Defying the Limits: Reaching New Heights in Customer Relationship Management*. San Francisco: Montgomery Research, 2000, pp. 41–52.

Venkatesan, R. and Kumar, V. A customer lifetime value framework for customer selection and resource allocations strategy. *Journal of Marketing*, 68 (October 2004), 106–125.

von Hippel, E. *Democratizing Innovation*. Cambridge, MA: MIT Press, 2005. Available at http://web.mit.edu/evhippel/www/democ.htm (Accessed June 2, 2005).

Zineldin, M. Beyond relationship marketing: Technologicalship marketing. *Marketing Intelligence and Planning*, 18, 1 (2000), 9–23.

Zuboff, S. and Maxmin, J. *The Support Economy*. New York: Viking, 2002.

Zwass, V. The embedding stage of electronic commerce. In P.B. Lowry, J.O. Cherrington, and R.R. Watson, eds., *The E-Business Handbook*. Boca Raton, FL: St. Lucie Press, 2002, pp. 33–43.

ACKNOWLEDGMENTS

The editors wish to thank Vladimir Zwass, editor of the *Advances in Management Information Systems* series, and all of the authors who contributed to this volume, who worked so hard to prepare valuable chapters on electronic customer relationship management.

ELECTRONIC CUSTOMER RELATIONSHIP MANAGEMENT

CHAPTER 1

ELECTRONIC CUSTOMER RELATIONSHIP MANAGEMENT

An Introduction

NICHOLAS C. ROMANO, JR. AND JERRY FJERMESTAD

Abstract: This volume of Advances in Management Information Systems (AMIS) *underscores the growing importance of customer relationship management (CRM) in information systems (IS) practice and research, as evidenced over the past decade in conferences, journals, and practitioner publications. This introduction does more than just outline the chapters included in the volume; it surveys the state of research on CRM. Thus, we revisit and extend the series of articles the editors authored on CRM as a subfield of the IS discipline to explore whether or not it has matured or languished with the passage of time. We present evidence of continued growth of IS research into CRM up to this point, and then we introduce the chapters within this volume that illustrate the advances made and the issues and challenges that remain in the subfield for further study. We believe that this volume of* AMIS *sets the stage for continued research for some time to come.*

Keywords: Customer Relationship Management; Information Systems Research; Electronic Customer Relationship Management

INTRODUCTION

In the field of information systems (IS) the idea of considering the customer as an asset and a source of value is not a new one. Ives and Learmonth (1984) proposed the customer resource life cycle for use in IS, and later Ives and Mason (1990) described how information technology (IT) can be used to revitalize a firm's customer service. These early forays into the realm of customer relationship management (CRM) were not immediately followed by a large volume of published articles on the topic, let alone by practice in the IS field. As is often the case, somewhat visionary articles preceded mainstream research on the topic by several years. Although articles on CRM may have been published in other disciplines, particularly marketing, before or at the same time as these two seminal IS articles, these were the first we found in an extensive literature review of IS-CRM (Romano and Fjermestad 2001–2002). We have not replicated that extensive study, primarily because the continued and accelerated growth of literature into CRM in IS makes it impractical, but also because many of the suggestions we made there can be readily observed to have been implemented in the literature.

When we performed that study of IS-CRM, we recommended six lines of development that would promote and indicate the maturation of CRM as an MIS subfield of study: One, development of empirically testable CRM theories; Two, conducting of lab and field experiments to test

hypotheses based on theory; Three, development and use of valid instruments; Four, development of a cumulative tradition of research and replication, extension of theories, models, and
instruments, and development of standard constructs and metrics; Five, additional publication of
IS-CRM research in top MIS journals; and Six, development of new classification schemes for
rapidly changing terminology. Four years later, we believe it is meaningful to revisit the literature
and see whether our suggestions have been accepted or ignored.

In the remainder of this introduction we address, first, the state of IS-CRM research in terms of
each of our earlier recommendations for future research. Next we overview and introduce the
chapters in this volume on CRM advances and issues. Finally we suggest additional issues and
challenges that researchers and practitioners in CRM still face in terms of IS.

CRM AND ECRM

CRM has changed over the years from a customer service business unit loosely linked to marketing to an electronic dynamo attempting to maximize the value of existing customer relationships.
Dyché (2002) in her *CRM Handbook* suggests that CRM is the infrastructure that enables the
delineation of an increase in customer value, and the correct means by which to motivate valuable
customers to remain loyal—to buy again. The key words are *infrastructure* and *enables*. The
infrastructure consists of the people and processes that an organization has at its disposal to understand, motivate, and attract its customers. It is the technology that enables the organization to
improve customer service, differentiate customers, and deliver unique customer interactions.

For one company, Wal-Mart (Swift 2001), the infrastructure is an enterprise data warehouse.
This eCRM system enables the company to collect massive amounts of data to manage the ever-
changing needs of customers and the marketplace. Coupled with people and process, it permits
the integration of operational data with analytics, modeling, historical data, and predictive knowledge management to give its customers what they need and want at the right time.

CRM and eCRM are about firms capturing and keeping customers through the Internet in real time
(Greenberg 2002). CRM is about customers interacting with employees, employees collaborating
with suppliers, and every interaction's being an opportunity to maintain and improve a relationship.

THE STATE OF IS-CRM RESEARCH

In keeping with methodological literature (Keen 1980; Vogel and Wetherbe 1984; Alavi and Carlson
1992; Pervan 1998), implementation of our six recommendations (Romano and Fjermestad 2001–
2002) would indicate that IS-CRM research is maturing as a subfield of MIS. Here we discuss the
current status of each of these areas to determine whether the subfield is growing and maturing or
waning and failing to bear fruit.

Theory Development

In our study of IS-CRM (Romano and Fjermestad 2001–2002) we found only three theoretically oriented articles out of 369. Clearly one indicator that the IS-CRM subfield is beginning to mature would
be the development of meaningful theories or the use of relevant theories from reference disciplines that
logically lead to testable hypotheses. Specifically we put forth the following recommendation:

"First, there is clearly a need for empirically testable theories. While conceptual models,
frameworks, and overviews all provide an excellent start, testable theories can lead to mean-

ingful hypotheses that can be experimentally tested in the lab and the field to move research forward." (Romano and Fjermestad 2001–2002, p. 85)

Since 2001, a number of IS-CRM papers that specifically address employing useful theory have been published. We briefly review here some of the papers that have developed IS-CRM theoretical models. Susarla, Barua, and Whinston (2002) developed a theoretical framework that can be empirically tested. Madeja and Schoder (2003) investigated how eight concepts derived from the media characteristics of the World Wide Web (Web) impact corporate success in e-business if implemented as features of companies' Web sites, and they constructed a path model for testing their research hypotheses. Chen, Gillenson, and Sherrell (2004) expanded on the technology acceptance model (TAM) (Davis 1989) and innovation diffusion theory (Rogers 2003) to provide important theoretical contributions to the area of business-to-consumer (B2C) e-commerce. Komiak and Benbasat (2004) proposed a new theoretical trust model that differentiated between cognitive trust and emotional trust and defined customer trust in each type of commerce as cognitive trust and emotional trust in the various entities. They developed eight propositions and hypotheses for future researchers to test. These four excellent papers, among many similar ones we found, clearly illustrate that IS-CRM research is maturing in terms of theory development. We therefore believe that our first recommendation is being implemented by IS researchers within the literature.

In our study of IS-CRM (Romano and Fjermestad 2001–2002) we observed that few studies were based on existing theories, from either IS or its reference disciplines. Here we review a few of many studies that, while they have not extended existing theory or developed new theory, are theory based and employ existing theory. Chai and Pavlou (2002) apply the theory of planned behavior (TPB) (Ajzen 1991) to study behavioral intentions to transact in two dissimilar countries and develop a cross-cultural e-commerce adoption model. Levina and Ross (2003) analyze and interpret data from the case of vendor strategy and practices in one long-term successful applications-management outsourcing engagement using the economic theory of complementarity in organizational design (Milgrom and Roberts 1995), and from the standpoint of client-vendor relationship factors. They explain the IT vendors' value proposition and how vendors can offer benefits that client firms cannot readily replicate internally. These and many similar papers now being published further demonstrate that IS-CRM research is maturing in terms of its use of theory.

Hypothesis Testing

A second indicator that the IS-CRM subfield is maturing would be the emergence in the literature of hypothesis testing to develop support for IS-CRM theory. Specifically we made this recommendation:

> Second, once theories have been developed, there is a need for lab and field experiments to test hypotheses in order to find support for them and rule out other possible explanations. (Romano and Fjermestad 2001–2002, p. 85)

A quick scan of the current IS-CRM literature reveals that hypothesis testing is more often incorporated in studies now than during the period covered in our study. Madeja and Schoder (2003) also tested their research hypotheses on 224 companies that target consumers (B2C) and found that information- and functionality-richness (interactive character) and continuous updating of the Web site are key drivers of success for general companies. Chen et al. (2004) also tested four major hypotheses based on their proposed theoretical model and found that the model sub-

6 ROMANO AND FJERMESTAD

stantially explained and predicted consumer acceptance of virtual stores and also explained many of the factors that lead to the user's intention to use, and actual use of, a virtual store. Madeja and Schoder (2004) constructed a covariance structure (LISREL) model and tested three research hypotheses with a data set of 469 cases of general companies in the German-speaking market. They found that CRM is a critical success factor in electronic commerce, independent of how long the company has been on the Web, and that CRM is especially critical for B2C and small companies. These are three among many papers emerging in the literature that illustrate an increased use of hypothesis testing—providing evidence of the maturation of IS-CRM over time.

Instrument Validation

In our study only a very small percentage of the survey articles discussed instrument validation, and not all of these discussed reliability testing or validity in detail. We made the following recommendation:

> Third, there is a strong need for researchers to validate the instruments they employ and to explain these procedures in their articles in order to evoke confidence that the results are meaningful, interpretable, and reliable. Instrument development and validation must be carefully undertaken prior to use. Researchers in this new subfield need to explore referent disciplines, such as psychology, and use methods that validate instruments from a number of perspectives, including convergent validity, discriminate validity, construct validity, and reliability. (Romano and Fjermestad 2001–2002, p. 85)

In the current IS-CRM literature we were able to easily find articles that discuss instrument validation in greater detail than we found in our earlier study. Susarla et al. (2003) provide a detailed analysis of both discriminant and convergent validity as well as the reliability of the instrument they developed for their study. Croteau and Li (2003) also discuss both discriminant and convergent validity, and they used structural equation modeling (SEM) with partial least squares (PLS) to assess their model. Stefanou, Sarmaniotis, and Stafyla (2003) relied on previously developed instruments when possible and performed a detailed factor analysis and additional tests for reliability, sampling adequacy, and sphericity. Pennington, Wilcox, and Grover (2003) also discuss reliability, convergent validity, and unidimensionality of the instrument they used and adopt existing measures when possible. These papers illustrate how IS-CRM researchers have begun to seriously validate their instruments and discuss the results of these tests in their published studies, and they clearly demonstrate maturation in the IS-CRM subfield of MIS research.

Cumulative Tradition of Research

We also found that, although there were many papers on CRM, there was not a growing tradition of research or body of knowledge that was being cited. We made the following recommendation:

> Fourth, there is a need for a cumulative tradition of research in which replication, extension of theories, models, and instruments, and development of standard constructs and metrics define the subfield and give each new study contextual meaning within a common body of knowledge. There is a need for depth as well as breadth of research. (Romano and Fjermestad 2001–2002, p. 85)

This is the most difficult aspect of IS-CRM research to assess without doing a full co-citation analysis (Culnan 1987), which is beyond the scope of this chapter. To truly establish a tradition of research would require a much longer time frame—a decade or more. We have, however, been able to see—at least in the area of trust in IS-CRM—that there appears to be a growing body of knowledge that is leading to a tradition of research. Two of the leading IS researchers in this area, D. Harrison McKnight and Norman Chervany, have published a number of papers on the topic that are cited in the majority of papers on trust in e-commerce and trust in information systems (see McKnight 2000; McKnight and Chervany 2000; McKnight and Chervany 2001; McKnight and Chervany 2001; McKnight and Chervany 2001–2002; McKnight et al. 2002).

The AMCIS and HICSS papers were published in the CRM minitracks of these respective conferences, and the IJEC paper was published in the first special issue on CRM that the authors guest edited. These papers are frequently cited now in articles on trust both inside and outside the IS discipline, showing the emergence of a tradition of IS-CRM research on trust. We hope that over time other areas of IS-CRM research will also begin to develop traditions of research.

Publication of IS-CRM Research in Top MIS Journals

In our assessment of IS-CRM research (Romano and Fjermestad 2001–2002) we found that few articles had yet been published in the core MIS journals, such as *JMIS, ISR*, and *MISQ*, relative to other IS research topics. We made the following recommendation:

> There is a need for researchers in the ECCRM subfield to submit their work to the core MIS journals (*Journal of Management Information Systems, MIS Quarterly, Information Systems Research, Information and Management*) in order to increase the perception of its maturity within the MIS research community at large and make it a true subdiscipline of MIS. (Romano and Fjermestad 2001–2002, p. 85)

We explored the IS-CRM literature in IS journals by reviewing every paper published in the top-tier IS journals, based on past and recent published journal rankings (Gillenson and Stutz 1991; Holsapple et al. 1994; Walstrom et al. 1995; Hardgrave and Walstrom 1997; Walczak 1999; Whitman et al. 1999; Mylonopoulos and Theoharakis 2001; Walstrom and Hardgrave 2001; Peffers and Ya 2003; Lowry et al. 2004), also the second-tier journal *Information and Management,* and the top-ranked journal in e-commerce, *International Journal of Electronic Commerce*. The latter two had a relatively large number of IS-CRM articles in the initial study, so we thought they were likely to publish additional articles in this area. The criteria for inclusion in the count were that the main theme of the paper was IS-CRM, a secondary but substantial theme was IS-CRM, or the paper built on previous IS-CRM research. Table 1 shows the number of publications from 1984 to early 2002 and then from December 2001 to November 2004, illustrating that CRM publications in top-ranked IS and related journals continue to increase in number. The overlap in the dates has to do with the availability of papers at the time of the first and the present review of the literature.

The data in Table 1.1 show that IS-CRM articles continue to be published in top-tier IS journals at an apparently increasing rate. In the less-than-two-year period of the second review of the literature every journal published at least half as many articles on IS-CRM as it had in the previous 16–year time span of the first review. Overall, since the first study,

Table 1.1

Count of IS-CRM Articles Published in Top Journals

Journal Name	Number of IS-CRM Papers		
	1984–2001	2002–2004	%
Communications of the ACM	21	11	52
International Journal of Electronic Commerce	15	12	80
Decision Support Systems	10	7*	70
Information and Management	10	7	70
Journal of Management Information Systems	5	3	60
MIS Quarterly	4	3	75
Management Science	3	2	67
Decisions Sciences Journal	1	1	100
Information Systems Research	0	3	300
Total	69	49	71

*Several of these papers were in a special issue of *DSS* published in December 2001 and were unavailable at the time of the original introspective study; therefore they are included in this second count.
   See Appendix 1.1 for a complete listing of all publications by journal.

these journals published almost two-thirds the number of articles they had previously. We believe that this bodes well for IS-CRM research to continue to grow and mature as a subfield of MIS.

New Classification Schemes

One other aspect of IS-CRM—and in fact of much e-commerce literature that we noticed in our original study—was the evolution of new terminology that the traditional IS keyword classification scheme (Barki et al. 1988) did not support. Even the update to this classification (Barki et al. 1993) did not support common terms in the IS-CRM and e-commerce literature, such as "customer relationship management," "electronic commerce," "trust," "Internet," "World Wide Web," "auctions," "loyalty," and many others. For this reason we made the following recommendation:

> Sixth, since the new research topics that are being explored do not fit into previously defined classification schemes, there is a need to develop new schemes in order to analyze the topics addressed by this new research. (Romano and Fjermestad 2001–2002, p. 86)

We found only one new article that attempted to classify IS research, and it focused on IS diversity (Vessey et al. 2002). One of the five characteristics of diversity in this article was topic. Even this study, which spanned the years 1995 to 1999, did not list the topic e-commerce, let alone specific subsets like CRM or others. So there is still work to be done to create new classification schemes that include the emerging MIS research areas of e-commerce and CRM.

OVERVIEW OF CHAPTERS

Now we briefly introduce each of the chapters that follow.

Part I. The Role of CRM and eCRM

Chapter 2: Success Factors in Online Supply Chain Management and e-Customer Relationship Management, Michael R. Bartolacci and Mary Meixell

Bartolacci and Meixell discuss the interrelationships between eCRM and SCM. One complements the other, yet many firms have had difficulty implementing eCRM and SCM applications. These authors evaluate select critical success factors for eCRM and SCM implementation. They suggest that both online SCM and eCRM require a commitment from top management to be successful. In these ways, success for both eCRM and SCM is interrelated. Furthermore, they highlight a most important point for practitioners of both eCRM and online SCM: the need for integration between the respective systems. They discuss this and other factors related to technology and implementation success.

Chapter 3: Using Electronic Customer Relationship Management to Maximize/Minimize Customer Satisfaction/Dissatisfaction, Yoon Cho and Jerry Fjermestad

Cho and Fjermestad discuss the importance of customer loyalty in relation to eCRM. They highlight the major concerns of eCRM—increasing customer satisfaction and customer loyalty, minimizing customer dissatisfaction, resolving customer complaints, and increasing product/service quality. Theories applied to eCRM have been rooted in satisfaction/dissatisfaction, and theories for customer complaining behavior have been proposed by traditional marketers. The present study also investigates models for customer satisfaction and complaining behavior that examine factors affecting customer relationship management.

Part II. Organizational Success Factors of CRM

Chapter 4: Customer Relationship Management Success and Organizational Change: A Case Study, Carl-Erik Wikström

Wikstrom presents a case study of a company implementing a CRM system from inception to implementation. The findings suggest that firms have had mixed results in implementing CRM systems. The challenge of managing organizational change has been raised as a potential factor affecting the successful outcome of eCRM efforts.

Chapter 5: Success Factors in CRM Implementation: Results from a Consortial Benchmarking Study, Rainer Alt and Thomas Puschmann

Alt and Puschmann describe the results of a cross-industry benchmarking project, which combines a questionnaire sample with more detailed case studies. The results show that there is no 'unique' CRM project and that successful implementations are rarely based on technical excellence. This research proposes six critical success factors for CRM projects: stepwise evolution, straightforward implementation and long-term project scope, organizational redesign, integrated system architecture of standard components, change management, and top management support. The six successful practice companies illustrate how these critical success factors are applied.

Chapter 6: Collaborative Customer Relationship Management in Financial Services Alliances, Malte Geib, Lutz M. Kolbe, and Walter Brenner

Geib, Kolbe, and Brenner describe the challenges derived from an analysis of five financial services companies that formed different financial services alliances. The main inhibitors of a consistent approach toward customers are found in business processes and information systems that are not sufficiently integrated. The results suggest that partial standardization of eCRM systems in financial services alliances inhibits the exploitation of economies of scale as well as the integration of systems. Consequently, obtaining a comprehensive view of a customer relationship becomes complicated if the integration of systems containing knowledge of customers, such as operational and analytical eCRM systems as well as transaction systems, is limited. To illustrate how a state-of-the-art IT infrastructure for eCRM can be designed in financial services alliances, the authors present a case study of a leading financial services alliance in Germany.

Part III. Enhancing Performance of CRM

Chapter 7: Improving Customer Interaction with Customer Knowledge Management, Adrian Bueren, Ragnar Schierholz , Lutz M. Kolbe, and Walter Brenner

Bueren, Schierholz, Kolbe, and Brenner develop, integrate, and validate a customer knowledge management process model. Their approach enables companies to improve knowledge support of their customer-oriented business processes, aiming to improve the overall performance of the enterprise. The authors use very interesting process-oriented knowledge management models which focus on the characteristics of knowledge during its life cycle. They analyze the relationships and environmental variables that influence the processes of knowledge development, dissemination, modification, and use. The model is validated through four case studies.

Chapter 8: An Examination of the Effects of Information and Communication Technology on Customer Relationship Management and Customer Lock-In, Ja-Shen Chen and Russell K.H. Ching

In seeking new opportunities, many businesses have turned to eCRM to strategically compete in global electronic marketplaces. With greater emphasis being placed on the application of technology, Chen and Ching address the question: *Does the infusion of ICT influence a business's ability to retain its customers?* They surveyed the 1,000 largest Taiwanese companies benefiting from ICT to examine the impacts of three CRM elements (market orientation, IT investment, and mass customization) upon CRM performance, partnership quality, and customer lock-in, as measured by customer network effect and information sharing.

Their results suggest that the three elements have positive relationships with eCRM performance and partnership quality. The authors further discuss these findings in the light of eCRM.

Part IV. CRM in Business-to-Consumer Commerce

Chapter 9: What Makes Customers Shop Online? Na Li and Ping Zhang

Addressing the question of what makes customers shop online, the authors conducted an analytical review of the IS literature on consumer online shopping beliefs, affective reactions, attitudes, intentions, behaviors, and satisfaction. They developed a classification of research variables and a framework for online shopping to provide an overview of the state of the art in this area and to point out limitations and directions for future research. Their results suggest that there are ten types of variables: external environment, consumer demographics, personal characteristics, e-store characteristics, beliefs about online shopping phenomena, affective reactions, attitudes toward online shopping behavior, intentions to shop online, shopping behavior, and satisfaction. Important "external" factors and psychological constructs that may directly or indirectly impact customers' intention, behavior, and satisfaction are revealed in this chapter. These findings would help electronic store owners, e-commerce Web site designers, and other e-commerce shareholders to target more appropriate consumer groups, improve product and service quality, and design better e-commerce Web sites. This study also identifies possible gaps in the research stream and potential opportunities for future research.

Chapter 10: Toward Achieving Customer Satisfaction in Online Grocery Shopping: Lessons Learned from Australian and Swiss Cases, Sherah Kurnia and Petra Schubert

Kurnia and Schubert in their study of online grocers report that their e-commerce applications do not meet the expectations of their customers. They suggest that both Australia and Switzerland lack an acceptable degree of sophistication in Web site design. In order to increase the consumers' satisfaction level, the designers need to better understand consumers' expectations and improve the performance of their Web sites accordingly.

INFORMATION SYSTEMS CUSTOMER RELATIONSHIP MANAGEMENT: ISSUES AND CHALLENGES

As we complete the editing of this volume, we find that a fair number of issues and challenges remain for researchers and practitioners alike. Significant and important advances have been made. In this section we discuss some issues and challenges that have received little attention in academia and industry yet offer new directions for continued inquiry into eCRM. Among the many topics that could be discussed, we have selected the following: resistance and usability; integration of CRM with enterprise systems and processes; blending of the three areas of CRM; and the need for increased collaboration between IS-CRM research and other areas such as marketing.

Resistance and Usability

Rosen (2001) asserts that eCRM involves people, processes, and technology. Both people and processes are vital to success. How then should we design systems that focus on people and processes? Two sets of IS principles can aid in this regard: usability and resistance. We are surprised that more firms have not focused on these two important areas during eCRM implementations, in light of what Atkinson (1993) pointed out more than a decade ago—that in 80 percent of total quality management initiatives in the area of customer-supplier relationships, resistance to change was a key factor leading to failure to reap full benefits—and in light of the recent suggestion by AMR research analysts that poorly designed user interfaces and employee resistance are major factors leading to eCRM failures (McKenzie 2001). We believe that researchers and practitioners alike should consider usability frameworks (Gould and Lewis 1985; Nielsen 1992) and Markus's (1983) resistance model for eCRM implementations. We need to study whether and how resistance and usability (or lack there of) contribute to eCRM implementation failures and to develop and test methods to overcome these potential barriers to success (Fjermestad and Romano 2003).

Integration of CRM with Other Enterprise Systems

Bartolacci and Maxell (2005) start to address this issue in Chapter 2 of this monograph, but integration with enterprise systems is much larger in scope than what they discuss. Organizations will want to continue to reduce costs and lead times. A key objective of many Fortune 1000 companies is to build a "chain" of suppliers that will maximize customer value. This leads to the integration of all activities within and between enterprises, including:

- procurement of materials and services (purchasing, outsourcing-relationship management)
- transformation of materials and services into intermediate and final goods (production–MRP, ERP)
- delivery to customers (transportation)
- data collection, data transmission, storage and analysis (data warehousing, business intelligence, data mining, knowledge management).

In essence this is the concept of "mass customization" and e-commerce linked together. Zwass (2003) proposed an aspect-opportunity framework consisting of domain activities of commerce, collaboration, communication, connection, and computation. This commerce–customer–supply chain linkage can become a continual source of innovative products and services. Shaw (2000) also suggested that e-business is a threefold framework consisting of supply chain management, the back office (ERP), and CRM. The three functions are integrated and coordinated through infrastructure management, knowledge management, and channel management.

The issues that organizational management must deal with in terms of an integrated enterprise system include:

- Sufficient flexibility to react to sudden changes in parts availability, distribution or shipping channels, import duties, currency rates—agility;
- Ability to use the latest computer and transmission technology to schedule and manage the shipment of parts in and finished products out; and
- Staffing with local specialists to handle duties, trade, freight, customs, and political issues.

Integration of Analytical, Operational, and Collaborative CRM

Gefen and Ridings (2002) discussed three types of CRM: operational; analytical; and collaborative. Operational CRM attempts to create seamless integration between back-office transaction processing and customer interfaces to the firm (Gefen and Ridings 2002). Analytical CRM empowers organizations to analyze customer relationships through data and text mining (Gefen and Ridings 2002). Collaborative CRM enables organizations to intimately communicate with select customers, suppliers, and business partners (Kobayashi et al. 1998). Researchers have begun to explore all three of these areas independently. However, just as CRM applications must be integrated with other enterprise systems and processes, so too must these three types of CRM be integrated more seamlessly in order for the full potential of any one of them to be achieved. Presently, researchers in the three areas seldom collaborate. They publish their work in some of the same conferences and journals, but with a different focus that isolates rather than unifying them as CRM researchers. To our knowledge little research has explored how to integrate these three CRM application areas. We believe that development of conceptual models and overarching CRM architectures would be a first step toward integration of all three into a cohesive whole that addresses all of the organization's needs in this area.

Interfaces with Other Disciplines

Like many areas of IS research and practice, CRM attracts researchers and practitioners from multiple disciplines including computer science (CS), marketing, management, and even sociology and psychology. However, we do not believe there is significant CRM research project collaboration across the boundaries of these disciplines, especially among IS, marketing, and management, all of which are usually in the same college of business. This lack of concerted collaboration leads to some insularity in each discipline and impedes their progress toward the ultimate goal—that of helping firms do a better job establishing, developing, and maintaining profitable relationships with customers.

In order for CRM research to have the greatest impact on practice and future research, researchers from these various fields need to collaborate more closely. Newer journals that are not specifically targeted at any one field, such as the *International Journal of Electronic Commerce,* the *Journal of Electronic Commerce Research,* and the *Journal of Electronic Commerce in Organizations*, do publish articles by researchers from various fields, such as marketing, IS, CS and management, but the majority of those articles have authors all from the same field. We believe that articles authored by researchers in different disciplines will have the greatest potential for impact in all fields, as they draw from the experience of each. For example, two marketing researchers, Shapiro and Mittal, teamed up with an IS researcher, Romano, to explore the synergies between the two disciplines in their paper "Emergent internet technologies for relationship marketing: assessing the buyer's perspective," published in the *Journal of Relationship Marketing* (Shapiro et al. 2003). We hope to see more such multidisciplinary CRM papers in the near future.

SUMMARY

For today's organizations CRM is eCRM in every way, shape, and form. CRM is the people, processes, and technology necessary to assure that the organization is in touch with the customer and suppliers. CRM is the infrastructure and technology that enables the employees to communicate, sell, analyze, and collaborate with the firm's customers.

The present volume illustrates some of the advances that have taken place over the last five years, as the guest editors have been involved in chairing minitracks on CRM at the Americas Conference on Information Systems (2000, 2001, 2202, 2003, 2004, 2005), the Hawaii International Conference on System Sciences (2001, 2002, 2003, 2004, 2005), and the ISOneWorld Conference (2002, 2003), as well as guest editing special issues on the topic in the *International Journal of Electronic Commerce* (2001–2002 Winter; 2002–2003 Winter), the *Business Process Management Journal* (2003), the *Journal of Enterprise Information Management* (2004), and the *Journal of Organizational Computing and Electronic Commerce* (forthcoming 2005). It also highlights some of the many issues and challenges that remain to be addressed by researchers and practitioners in the growing area of IS-CRM. In this introductory chapter, our update on the status of the subfield provides evidence that IS research into the field of CRM is still growing and maturing. We have also introduced the collection of chapters in this volume that demonstrate both the breadth and the depth of IS-CRM research and some of the advances that have been achieved. Finally, we have highlighted some of the issues and challenges that we think are important for IS-CRM researchers to address in the near future, if the area is to continue to mature over time.

APPENDIX 1.1. PUBLICATIONS BY JOURNAL
(descending order by number of publications and journal title)

International Journal of Electronic Commerce

1. Cao, Y. T.; Gruca, S.; and Klemz, B.R. Internet pricing, price satisfaction, and customer satisfaction. *International Journal of Electronic Commerce*, 8, 2 (2003), 31–51.
2. Jukic, N.; Jukic, B.; Meamber, L.A.; and Nezlek, G. Implementing polyinstantiation as a strategy for electronic commerce customer relationship management. *International Journal of Electronic Commerce*, 7, 2 (2003), 9–30.
3. Khalifa, M. and Liu, V. Satisfaction with Internet-based services: The role of expectations and desires. *International Journal of Electronic Commerce*, 7, 2 (2003), 1–49.
4. Koufaris, M.; Kambil, A.; and Labarbera, P. A. Consumer behavior in web-based commerce: An empirical study. *International Journal of Electronic Commerce*, 6, 2 (2001), 115–138.
5. Luo, X. and Seyedian, M. Contextual marketing and customer-orientation strategy for e-commerce: An empirical analysis. *International Journal of Electronic Commerce*, 8, 2 (2003), 95–119.
6. McKnight, D.H. and Chervany, N.L. What trust means in e-commerce customer relationships: An interdisciplinary conceptual typology. *International Journal of Electronic Commerce*, 6, 3 (2001–2002), 35–60.
7. Pavlou, P.A. Consumer acceptance of electronic commerce: Integrating trust and risk with the technology acceptance model. *International Journal of Electronic Commerce*, 7, 3 (2003), 101–133.
8. Romano, N.C., Jr. Customer relationship management for the Web-access challenged: Inaccessibility of the Fortune 250 business Web sites. *International Journal of Electronic Commerce*, 7, 2 (2002–2003), 81–117.
9. Romano, N.C., Jr. and Fjermestad, J. Customer relationship management research: An assessment of research. *International Journal of Electronic Commerce*, 6, 3 (2001–2002), 61–114.
10. Schubert, P. Extended web assessment method (EWAM): Evaluation of electronic commerce applications from the customer's viewpoint. *International Journal of Electronic Commerce*, 7, 2 (2002–2003), 51–80.
11. Suh, B. and Han, I. The impact of customer trust and perception of security control on the acceptance of electronic commerce. *International Journal of Electronic Commerce*, 7, 3 (2003), 135–162.
12. Zhang, P. and von Dran, G.M. User expectations and rankings of quality factors in different website domains. *International Journal of Electronic Commerce*, 6, 3 (2001–2002), 9–34.

Communications of the Association for Computing Machinery

1. Bolton, R. N. E-services: Marketing challenges of e-services. *Communications of the ACM*, 46, 6 (2003), 43–44.
2. Brereton, P. The software customer/supplier relationship. *Communications of the ACM*, 47, 2 (2004), 77–81.

3. Brohman, M.K.; Watson, R.T.; Piccoli, G.; and Parasurama. A. E-services: Data completeness: A key to effective net-based customer service systems. *Communications of the ACM*, 46, 6 (2003), 47–51.
4. Hoffman, K.D. Marketing + MIS = e-service. *Communications of the ACM*, 46, 6 (2003), 53–55.
5. Fink, J.; Koenemann, J.; Noller, S.; and Schwab, I. The adaptive web: Putting personalization into practice. *Communications of the ACM*, 45, 5 (2002), 41–42.
6. Ganapathy, S.; Ranganathan, C.; and. Sankaranarayanan, B. Visualization strategies and tools for enhancing customer relationship management. *Communications of the ACM*, 47, 11 (2004), 92–99.
7. Pan, S.L. and Lee, J.-N. Using e-CRM for a unified view of the customer. *Communications of the ACM*, 46, 4 (2003), 95–99.
8. Russell, B. and Chatterjee, S. Relationship quality: The undervalued dimension of software quality. *Communications of the ACM*, 46, 8 (2003), 85–89.
9. Rust, R.T. and. Kannan, P.K. E-services: EA new paradigm for business in the electronic environment. *Communications of the ACM*, 46, 6 (2003), 36–42.
10. Siau, K. and Shen, Z. Building customer trust in mobile commerce. *Communications of the ACM*, 46, 4 (2003), 91–94.
11. Vatanasombut, B.; Stylianou, A.C.; and Igbaria, M. How to retain online customers. *Communications of the ACM*, 47, 6 (2004), 64–70.

Decision Support Systems

1. Bhattacherjee, A. An empirical analysis of the antecedents of electronic commerce service continuance. *Decision Support Systems*, 32, 2 (2001), 201–214.
2. Kannan, P.K. and Rao, H.R Introduction to the special issue: Decision support issues in customer relationship management. *Decision Support Systems*, 32, 2 (2001), 83–84.
3. Kim, Y. Toward a successful CRM: Variable selection, sampling, and ensemble. *Decision Support Systems* (Forthcoming). Corrected proof available online at www.sciencedirect.com.
4. Kohli, R.; Piontek, F.; Ellington, T.; Van Osdol, T.; Shepard, M.; and Brazel, G. Managing customer relationships through e-business decision support applications: A case. *Decision Support Systems*, 32, 2 (2001), 171–185.
5. Massey, A.P.; Montoya-Weiss, M.M.; and. Holcom, K. Re-engineering the customer relationship: Leveraging knowledge assets at IBM. *Decision Support Systems*, 32, 2 (2001), 155–170.
6. Verhoef, P.C. and Donkers, B. Predicting customer potential value: An application in the insurance industry. *Decision Support Systems*, 32, 2 (2001), 189–199.
7. Verhoef, P.C.; Spring, P.N.; Hoekstra, J.C.; and Leeflang, P.S.H. The commercial use of segmentation and predictive modeling techniques for database marketing in the Netherlands. *Decision Support Systems*, 34, 4 (2003), 471–482.

Information and Management

1. Chiou, J.-S. The antecedents of consumers' loyalty toward Internet service providers. *Information and Management*, 41, 6 (2004), 685–695.
2. Koufaris, M. and Hampton-Sosa, W. The development of initial trust in an online company by new customers. *Information and Management*, 41, 3 (2004), 377–397.
3. Lu, H. and Lin, J.C.-C. Predicting customer behavior in the market-space: A study of Rayport and Sviokla's framework. *Information and Management*, 40, 1 (2002), 1–10.
4. Negash, S.; Ryan, T.; and Igbaria, M. Quality and effectiveness in Web-based customer support systems. *Information and Management*, 40, 8 (2003), 757–768.
5. Ranganathan, C. and. Ganapath, S. Key dimensions of business-to-consumer web sites. *Information and Management*, 39, 6 (2002), 457–465.
6. Smith, M.A. and Kumar, R.L. A theory of application service provider (ASP) use from a client perspective. *Information and Management*, 41, 8 (2004), 977–1002.
7. Spiegler, I. Technology and knowledge: Bridging a "generating" gap. *Information and Management*, 40, 6 (2003), 533–539.

Information Systems Research

1. Lilien, G.L.; Rangaswamy, A.; Van Bruggen, G.H.; and Starke, K. DSS effectiveness in marketing resource allocation decisions: Reality vs. perception. *Information Systems Research*, 15, 3 (2004), 216–235.
2. McKinney, V.; Yoon, K.; and. Zahedi, F.M. The measurement of web-customer satisfaction: An expectation and disconfirmation approach. *Information Systems Research*, 13, 3 (2002), 296–316.
3. McKnight, D.H.; Choudhury, V.; and. Kacmar, C. Developing and validating trust measures for e-commerce: An integrative typology. *Information Systems Research*, 13, 3 (2002), 334–359.

Journal of Management Information Systems

1. Gefen, D. and Ridings, C.M. Implementation team responsiveness and user evaluation of customer relationship management: A quasi-experimental design study of social exchange theory. *Journal of Management Information Systems*, 19, 1 (2002), 47–69.
2. Kocas, C. Evolution of prices in electronic markets under diffusion of price-comparison shopping. *Journal of Management Information Systems*, 19, 3 (2002), 99–120.
3. Pennington, R.; Wilcox, H.D.; and Grover, V. The role of system trust in business-to-consumer transactions. *Journal of Management Information Systems*, 20, 3, (2003), 197–226.

MIS Quarterly

1. Albert, T. C.; Goes, P.B.; and Gupta, A. GIST: A model for design and management of content and interactivity of customer-centric web sites. *MIS Quarterly*, 28, 2 (2004), 161–182.
2. Chatterjee, D.; Grewal, R.; and. Sambamurthy, V. Shaping up for e-commerce: Institutional enablers of the organizational assimilation of web technologies. *MIS Quarterly*, 26, 2 (2002), 65–90.
3. Susarla, A.; Barua, A.; and Whinston, A.B. Understanding the service component of application service provision: An empirical analysis of satisfaction with ASP services. *MIS Quarterly*, 27, 1 (2003), 91–123.

Management Science

1. Anderson, E.T. Sharing the wealth: When should firms treat customers as partners? *Management Science*, 48, 8 (2002), 955–971.
2. Padmanabhan, B. and Tuzhilin, A. On the use of optimization for data mining: Theoretical interactions and eCRM opportunities. *Management Science*, 49, 10 (2003), 1327–1343.

Decision Sciences

1. Zahay, D. and Griffin, A. Customer learning processes, strategy selection, and performance in business-to-business service firms. *Decision Sciences*, 35, 2 (2004), 169–203.

REFERENCES

Ajzen, I. The theory of planned behavior. *Organizational Behavior and Human Decision Processes*, 50, 2 (1991), 179–211.
Alavi, M. and Carlson , P. A review of MIS research and disciplinary development. *Journal of Management Information Systems*, 8, 4 (1992), 45–62.
Atkinson, P.E. How to avoid TQ failure. *Management Services*, 37, (1993), 22–26.
Barki, H.; Rivard, S.; and Talbot, J. An information systems keyword classification scheme. *MIS Quarterly*, 12, 2 (1988), 299–322.
Barki, H.; Rivard, S.; and Talbot, J. A keyword classification scheme for IS research literature: An update. *MIS Quarterly*, 17, 2 (1993), 299–322.
Bartolacci, M.R. and Meixell, M.J. Success factors in supply chain management and e-customer relationship management. In J. Fjermestad and N.C. Romano Jr., eds., *Advances in Management Information Systems* (Armonk, NY: M.E. Sharpe, Inc., 2006), pp. 21–33.

Chai, L. and Pavlou, P.A. Customer relationship management: A cross-cultural empirical investigation of electronic commerce. In *Proceedings of the Eighth Americas Conference on Information Systems*, 2002, pp. 483–491.

Chen, L.-d.; Gillenson, M.L.; and Sherrell, D.L. Consumer acceptance of virtual stores: A theoretical model and critical success factors for virtual stores. *ACM SIGMIS Database*, 35, 2 (2004), 8–31.

Croteau, A.-M. and Li, P. Critical success factors of CRM technological initiatives. *Canadian Journal of Administrative Sciences*, 20, 1 (2003), 21–35.

Culnan, M. Mapping the intellectual structure of MIS, 1980–1985: A co-citation analysis. *MIS Quarterly*, 11, 3 (1987), 341–353.

Davis, F.D. Perceived usefulness, perceived ease of use, and user acceptance of information technology. *MIS Quarterly*, 13, 3 (1989), 319–340.

Dyché, J. *The CRM Handbook.* Boston: Addison-Wesley, 2002.

Fjermestad, J. and Romano, N.C. Electronic customer relationship management revisiting the general principles of usability and resistance: An integrative implementation framework. *Business Process Management Journal*, 9, 5 (2003), 572–591.

Gefen, D. and Ridings, C.M. Implementation team responsiveness and user evaluation of customer relationship management: A quasi-experimental design study of social exchange theory. *Journal of Management Information Systems*, 19, 1 (2002), 47–69.

Greenberg, P. *CRM at the Speed of Light.* New York: McGraw-Hill, 2002.

Gillenson, M. and Stutz, J. Academic issues in MIS: journals and books. *MIS Quarterly*, 15, 4 (1991), 147–452.

Gould, J.D. and Lewis, C. Designing for usability: Key principles and what designers think. *Communications of the ACM*, 28, 3 (1985), 300–311.

Hardgrave, B. and Walstrom, K. Forums for MIS scholars. *Communications of the ACM*, 40, 11 (1997), 119–124.

Holsapple, C.; Johnson, L.; Manakyan, H.; and Tanner, J. Business computing research journals: A normalized citation analysis. *Journal of Management Information Systems*, 11, 1 (1994), 131–140.

Ives, B. and Learmonth, G.P. The information system as a competitive weapon. *Communications of the ACM*, 27, 12 (1984), 1193–1201.

Ives, B. and Mason, R.O. Can information technology revitalize your customer service? *Academy of Management Executive*, 4, 4 (1990), 52–69.

Keen, P.G.W. MIS research: reference disciplines and cumulative traditions. In *Proceedings of the First International Conference on Information Systems*, 1980, pp. 8–18.

Kobayashi, M.; Shinozak, M.; Sakairi, T.; Touma, M.; Daijavad, S.; and. Wolf, C. Collaborative customer services using synchronous web browser sharing. In *Proceedings Conference on Computer Supported Cooperative Work.* New York: ACM Press, 1988, pp. 99–109.

Komiak, S.X. and Benbasat, I. Understanding customer trust in agent-mediated electronic commerce, web-mediated electronic commerce, and traditional commerce. *Information Technology and Management*, 5, 1–2 (2004), 181–207.

Levina, N. and Ross, J.W. From the vendor's perspective: Exploring the value proposition in information technology outsourcing. *MIS Quarterly*, 27, 3(2003), 331–365.

Lowry, P.B.; Romans, D.; and Curtis, A. Global journal prestige and supporting disciplines: A scientometric study of information systems journals. *Journal of the Association for Information Systems*, 5, 2 (2004), 29–80.

Madeja, N. and Schoder, D. Designed for success—empirical evidence on features of corporate web pages. In *Proceedings of the 36th Annual Hawaii International Conference on Systems Sciences.* Los Alamitos, CA: IEEE Computer Society, 2003, pp. 188–197.

Markus, M.L. Power, politics, and MIS implementation. *Communications of the ACM*, 26, 6 (1983), 430–444.

McKenzie, J. Serving suggestions. *Financial Management*, December (2001), 26–27.

McKnight, D.H.; Cummings, L.L.; and Chervany, N.L. Initial trust formation in new organizational relationships. *Academy of Management Review*, *23*, 3 (1998), 473–490.

McKnight, D.H. and Chervany, N. What is trust? A conceptual analysis and an interdisciplinary model. In H. M. Chung (ed.), *Proceedings of the Americas Conference on Information Systems.* Long Beach, CA: Omnipress, 2000, pp. 827–833.

McKnight, D.H.; Choudhury, V.; and Kacmar, C. Trust in e-commerce vendors: A two stage model. In W. Orlikowski, P. Weill, S. Ang, H. Krcmar, and J.I. DeGross, eds., *Proceedings of the Twenty-First International Conference on Information Systems.* Atlanta (2000), 532–536.

McKnight, D.H. and Chervany, N.L. Conceptualizing trust: A typology and e-commerce customer relationships model. In R.H. Sprague, Jr., ed., *Proceedings of the Thirty-Fourth Annual Hawai'i International Conference on System Sciences*, Maui, HI, USA, January 3–6 (Los Alamitos, CA: IEEE Computer Society Press, 2001).

McKnight, D.H. and Chervany, N.L. What trust means in e-commerce customer relationships: An interdisciplinary conceptual typology. *International Journal of Electronic Commerce*, 6, 2 (Winter 2001–2002), 35–59.

McKnight, D.H.; Choudhury, V.; and Kacmar, C. Developing and validating trust measures for e-commerce: An integrative typology. *Information Systems Research*, 13, 3 (2002), 334–359.

McKnight, D.H. and Chervany, N.L. While trust is cool and collected, distrust is fiery and frenzied: A model of distrust concepts. In D. Strong, Straub, D. and DeGross, J. I. (eds.). *Proceedings of the Seventh Americas Conference on Information Systems*. Madison, WI: Omnipress, 2001, pp. 883–888.

McKnight, D.H.; Choudhury, V.; and Kacmar, C. (2000). Trust in e-commerce vendors: A two-stage model. In *Proceedings of the International Conference on Information Systems* (ICIS-2000), Brisbane, Australia, December 11–13, pp. 532–537.

Milgrom, P. and Roberts, J. Complementarities and fit: Strategy, structure, and organizational change in manufacturing. *Journal of Accounting & Economics*, 19, 2–3 (1995), 179–208.

Mylonopoulos, N. and Theoharakis, V. On-site: Global perceptions of IS journals. *Communications of the ACM*, 44, 9 (2001), 29–33.

Nielsen, J. The usability engineering life cycle. *IEEE Computer*, 25, 3 (1992), 12–22.

Peffers, K. and Ya, T. Identifying and evaluating the universe of outlets for information systems research: Ranking the journals. *Journal of Information Technology Theory and Application*, 5, 1 (2003), 63–84.

Pennington, R.; Wilcox, H.D.; and Grover, V. The role of system trust in business-to-consumer transactions. *Journal of Management Information Systems*, 20, 3 (2003), 197–226.

Pervan, G. P. A review of research in group support systems: Leaders, approaches and directions. *Decision Support Systems*, 23, 2 (1998),149–159.

Rogers, E. M. *Diffusion of Innovations*, 5th ed. New York: The Free Press, 2003.

Romano, N.C., Jr. and Fjermestad, J. Customer relationship management research: An assessment of research. *International Journal of Electronic Commerce*, 6, 3 (2002), 61–114.

Rosen, K. Five myths of CRM. *Computerworld* (2001) (available at http://www.computerworld.com/softwaretopics/crm/story/0,10801,60972,00.html, accessed on December 30, 2004).

Schoder, D. and Madeja, N. Is customer relationship management: A success factor in electronic commerce? *Journal of Electronic Commerce Research*, 5, 1 (2004), 38–53.

Shapiro, J.; Romano, N.C. Jr.; and Mittal, B. Emergent internet technologies for relationship marketing: Assessing the buyer's perspective. *Journal of Relationship Marketing*, 2, 3/4 (2003), 85–108.

Shaw, M.J. Building an e-business from enterprise systems. *Information Systems Frontiers*, 2, 1 (2000), 7–17.

Stefanou, C.; Sarmaniotis, J. C.; and Stafyla, A. CRM and customer-centric knowledge management: An empirical research. *Business Process Management Journal*, 9, 5 (2003), 617–634.

Susarla, A.; Barua, A.; and Whinston, A.B. Multitasking and incentives in application service provider contracts for customer relationship management. In *Proceedings of the Eighth Americas Conference on Information Systems*, 2002, pp. 554–557.

Susarla, A.; Barua, A.; and Whinston, A.B. Understanding the service component of application service provision: An empirical analysis of satisfaction with ASP services. *MIS Quarterly*, 27, 1 (2003), 91–123.

Swift, R. *Accelerating Customer Relationships*. Upper Saddle River, NJ: Prentice Hall, 2001.

Vessey, I.; Ramesh, V.; and Glass, R.L. Research in information systems: An empirical study of diversity in the discipline and its journals. *Journal of Management Information Systems*, 19, 2 (2002), 129–173.

Vogel, D.R. and Weatherbe, J.C. MIS research: A profile of leading journals and universities. *Database*, 15, 3 (1984), 3–14.

Walczak, S. A re-evaluation of information systems publication forums. *Journal of Computer Information Systems*, 40, 1 (1999), 88–97.

Walstrom, K. and Hardgrave, B. Forums for information systems scholars. *Information and Management*, 39, 1 (2001), 117–124.

Walstrom, K.; Hardgrave, B.; and Wilson, R. Forums for management information systems scholars. *Communications of the ACM*, 38, 3 (1995), 93–102.

Whitman, M.; Hendrickson, A.; and Townsend, A. Research commentary—academic rewards for teaching, research and service: Data and discourse. *Information Systems Research*, 10, 2 (1999), 99–109.

Zwass, V. Electronic commerce and organizational innovation: Aspects and opportunities. *International Journal of Electronic Commerce*, 7, 3 (2003), 7–37.

PART I

THE ROLE OF CRM AND ECRM

CHAPTER 2

SUCCESS FACTORS IN ONLINE SUPPLY CHAIN MANAGEMENT AND E-CUSTOMER RELATIONSHIP MANAGEMENT

MICHAEL R. BARTOLACCI AND MARY MEIXELL

Abstract: Online customer relationship management (eCRM) and online supply chain management (SCM) have both come to the forefront of the Internet economy. eCRM complements SCM by supporting the analysis of business-to-business (B2B) online transactions to improve the organization's overall knowledge of demand. Furthermore, SCM planners can better plan for the fulfillment of online orders in an eCRM-enabled organization, as production and delivery processes are more easily customized with improved prediction from eCRM-derived demand knowledge. Many firms, however, have had difficulty implementing eCRM and SCM applications. In this chapter we discuss the relationship between eCRM and SCM and evaluate select critical success factors for eCRM and SCM implementation.

Keywords: Electronic Customer Relationship Management (eCRM), B2B, Supply Chain Management (SCM)

INTRODUCTION

Customer relationship management and supply chain management have been the focus of a great deal of practitioner interest and academic research over the last decade. Customer relationship management has allowed companies to spend more of their time and resources on valuable customers that make up the majority of their sales and profits. Customer identification/savings cards that are used during retail sales transactions are just one example of the use of CRM that allows companies to tailor their goods/services, marketing, and support appropriately. Such cards are common in consumer goods markets and have made their way into the entertainment service industry as well (Loveman 2003). Supply chain management has allowed companies to gain efficiencies as well as increased sales through reductions in inventories, lead times, and paperwork processing.

The tremendous growth of the Internet has led to the development of online versions of both customer relationship management and supply chain management. Electronic customer relationship management (eCRM) research is still in its initial stages and has focused primarily on the marketing aspects of online transactions (Romano and Fjermestad 2003). Likewise, research in online supply chain management (to be more generally defined as SCM for the remainder of this chapter) has come about only in recent years. This chapter uses a literature survey approach from a broad array of sources across the fields of supply chain management, marketing, information systems, and related areas in order to establish the important characteristics and qualities that SCM and eCRM share. Special attention is given to works that emphasize key business functions/processes or required conditions for the success of both. In order to analyze the critical success factors for these two related system types, a definition of success is provided in the next section.

An SCM application is effective, in the most general terms, when it produces efficiencies or increases sales for one or more members of the supply chain. For example, an online transportation exchange is effective when it successfully matches buyers of transportation services with providers in a profitable manner for all involved, including the shipper, the carrier, and the intermediary. An online collaborative forecasting application such as Collaborative Planning, Forecasting and Replenishment (CPFR) (McKaige 2001; White 1999) is effective when the cost and the responsiveness of the supply network improve because of the Internet-based collaboration.

In this chapter we adopt a broad definition of effectiveness or success to include both internally and externally focused performance metrics. A useful frame of reference is the set of effectiveness metrics advocated by the supply chain operations reference model: reliability, responsiveness/flexibility, cost, and asset management (Supply Chain Council 2003). These metrics define effectiveness in an operational sense directly to SCM, incorporating both productivity and customer-related concerns.

In the context of eCRM, effectiveness or success includes the ability to tailor the goods or services provided throughout the supply chain to the needs of each member using an analysis of ordering and related information. eCRM success may also be measured in a similar fashion with the supply chain operations reference model metrics. In the case of SCM, reliability can be defined as the ability to have stable lead times for products or materials managed online. For e-CRM, reliability can be defined as the ability to quickly identify and serve valuable customers in various online contexts. The other three metrics apply to both in a similar fashion. In this way, the performance of both SCM and eCRM can be measured in a multidimensional fashion. This is especially important, because the mission, strategy, and objectives of the firms participating in the online initiatives can vary considerably, based on the value of the product offered to customers (Keeney 1999).

This chapter first examines the nature of eCRM and SCM and then brings to light some of the factors that ultimately lead to success or failure. The similarities are especially auspicious, as eCRM and SCM are closely related in both goals as well as activities. Both contain the notion of catering to, and improving service for, the customer. Also, both utilize online technologies for the process of streamlining information gathering and exchange between suppliers and customers. While SCM focuses on the logistical nature of the transfer of goods or services, eCRM focuses on the tailoring of such goods or services to the customer's wants and needs, including the notion that some customers cannot be served profitably and should be dropped. Salmen and Muir make the case that "e-loyalty" is brought about through wise use of eCRM systems (2003). They also put forth that a eCRM system enables the systematic, active construction and maintenance of digital customer relations throughout the complete life cycle of customer relationships. One can argue that any SCM system achieves the same general goals involving both suppliers and customers with respect to the transfer of goods and/or services. In the sections that follow, both similarities and differences will be highlighted.

Nature of eCRM

The foundation of eCRM is the application of traditional CRM methodologies, techniques, and tools to data that is garnered via electronic commerce as opposed to traditional channels of distribution. Traditional CRM may be defined as a process that balances the use of corporate resources with the satisfaction of customer needs. Traditional CRM looks at outputs in terms of revenues and profits while taking customer value and motivation into account (Shaw 1999; Gebert et al. 2003).

Information technology is integral to successful application of CRM, and the definition of CRM may be extended to incorporate the significance of Internet-based technology in managing customer relationships. Plakoyiannaki and Tzokas (2002) formulate a model of the CRM process that revolves around this extended definition. They define the following tasks for the CRM process:

- Creating a corporate culture conducive to customer orientation, learning, and innovations
- Making customer value a key component of the corporate strategy and planning process
- Collecting and transforming customer data to aid strategic and operational decision making
- Appreciating, identifying, and nurturing knowledge creation, dissemination, and use within the organization
- Developing clear market segments and customer portfolios
- Defining, developing, and delivering the value proposition
- Using campaign and channel management as part of the value proposition
- Measuring performance at each stage of the process to navigate decision making.

eCRM accomplishes these same tasks with the benefit of electronically gathered information, and in such a way as to tailor the service level specific to each customer (Romano and Fjermestad 2003).

For example, logistical services may be tailored to better meet customer needs in profitable fashion, as outlined in Fuller, O'Conor, and Rawlinson (1993). In this pre-Internet article, the authors address the challenges of providing a level of service appropriate to the need of "logistically distinct businesses," which serve to cluster customers into categories so that the service creation can be provided most efficiently. In pre-Internet days, customers would be segmented by logistics requirements, followed by the establishment of a service standard for each segment, and a reconfiguration of the logistics pipelines so that each segment could be served efficiently, according to its newly identified and specially tailored level of service. Fuller et al. (1993) provide a telecom equipment manufacturer example. It highlights customers with distinctly different needs, including one who needs components for new system installation to be delivered as a complete order. The telecom manufacturer's use of a series of eight variables for segmenting products may disaggregate its customers into some 384 market "buckets."

The steps identified previously encompass a vision of the CRM process and represent a foundation on which to define eCRM. Gurau et al. (2003) propose descriptions of the transition from traditional forms of media associated with CRM to eCRM-based ones. eCRM involves the collection and mining of data involving online purchases and relationships. In many ways it can be thought of as a necessary tool for conducting SCM, as will be detailed in the next section. eCRM also involves using the knowledge gained to improve customer loyalty, expand sales, and improve customer service.

CRM and eCRM represent "relationship marketing," in direct contrast to traditional "marketing mix" approaches known as "transaction marketing." Gonroos (1994) defines transaction marketing to include minimal customer contact, while relationship marketing utilizes a broader customer interface. At the heart of traditional CRM is the collection of customer satisfaction data and other key business performance-related data. Business decisions must be supported by knowledge gleaned from processed sales transaction and related data. Benefits from CRM are realized only when key decisions are influenced by this knowledge store. Bose and Sugumaran (2003) put forth that true CRM is possible only through the integration of knowledge management systems and traditional customer tracking systems. "We observe in practice that customer relationship management and knowledge management have a considerable synergy potential. . . . While KM acts as a service provider for CRM, the interdependencies and mutual benefits between the two approaches result in a merger of equals" (Gebert et al. 2002).

Two main types of e-CRM exist: operational and analytical (Dyche 2001; Fjermestad and Romano 2003). Operational eCRM involves actual contact with the customer through electronic means such as an online Web form or fax. The processing of data collected through operational eCRM is analytical eCRM. This involves many of the same techniques as traditional CRM, such as data mining, to glean valuable information about current and potential customers. The definition of the "e" in eCRM does not limit the data collection and processing to the Internet. By definition, any electronic contact with a customer through which data can be gathered for further analysis can be considered a form of eCRM.

eCRM has the potential to take a quantum leap forward with the tremendous expansion of wireless networking across the globe. Third-generation cellular networks promise high-speed Internet connections, text messaging, and a host of other services such as location-based services which inform wireless users about goods and services available in their immediate area. Knowing the purchasing habits of customers and their cellular/wireless device numbers/network IDs can only lead to developing a more intimate relationship as they travel about. The ability to integrate location-based information about a company's goods or services with traditional e-CRM principles has the potential to even create a new form of eCRM.

The notion of a personal network (Niemegeers and Heemstra de Groot 2002) that surrounds and moves with each wireless user may become reality in the not-so-distant future. Such a network revolves around the location of the user and his/her wants and needs for information and support services. A personal network is just an extension of the notion of a personal area network, where a wireless user interacts in an ad hoc fashion, using very short distance networking technologies such as Bluetooth with local devices. The evolution of personal area networks into more generalized "personal networks" is an ongoing process, as more and more location-based services are introduced and as third-generation cellular networks and related wireless technologies proliferate. The ability of a company to conduct eCRM using personal networks is the challenge of tomorrow. A piece of information as simple as the location of a wireless user may provide an opportunity to market additional goods or services using online coupons or other means. There will be a delicate balance between conducting effective eCRM and creating Internet-like spam in this new form of eCRM. Shen and Lee (2000) suggest that people will feel unhappy if they get too many advertisements or useless messages after paying for these services; so transferring the proper message is the most important concern in this emerging area. Hackney, Ranchhod, and Hackney (2004) characterized the shift to wireless technologies for e-commerce as "U-commerce" or "ultimate commerce." They caution that such systems are impotent to the challenges of customer behavior, where technology alone will not provide for the perceived value proposition in commercial activities. Determining what kind of "message" to send wireless users will hinge on the type of data that is collected.

Once data is collected, the analytical part of eCRM must be undertaken in order to put it to use. Although data mining is not the focus of this chapter, its importance does warrant mention, since it provides the basis for the analytical part of eCRM. Without the ability to determine the wants and needs of customers (or potential customers), collected data is worthless in the context of CRM. Data mining involves the use of statistical software tools in order to determine patterns in data. These patterns are used to develop knowledge about customers and also provide the foundation for the ultimate use of CRM: developing better relationships with customers. The use of such knowledge must be well planned and follow a set of predetermined process steps aimed at enhancing customer interaction and sales.

The application of knowledge gained through data mining can take a myriad of directions. Knowledge management, therefore, takes on a critical function within the organization. Gebert and co-researchers (Gebert et al. 2003) propose a customer knowledge management model that seeks to exploit the data gathered from and about customers. Their model encompasses four goals (Gebert et al. 2003):

1. Knowledge transparency, which allows business processes to be executed with a customer knowledge basis in a transparent manner
2. Knowledge dissemination, which supports the process owners by defining who receives what customer knowledge
3. Knowledge development, which defines how knowledge is created and adapted
4. Knowledge efficiency, which deals with the selection process and how the correct or crucial knowledge is selected to support a business process

Knowledge management must be in place in order to allow data collection, whether it is done electronically or not, to ultimately lead to useful information for conducting eCRM.

Electronic coupons based on customer buying patterns are just one example of the use of eCRM data to foster better relationships with customers electronically. Such coupons are sent via e-mail and represent a cost-effective method for promoting loyalty and encouraging sales. Many "click-and-mortar" companies also have the added advantage of promoting both online and traditional sales through electronic coupons. Promotions, service enhancements, and product customizations are just a few examples of actions that can be taken following customer knowledge created through the use of data mining.

The goal of this description of CRM and eCRM is to provide the basis for comparison with supply chain management and its online equivalent. Supply chain management has evolved into its online equivalent in much the same way as CRM has evolved into eCRM. The next section will describe the nature of supply chain management in general and provide the setting for the examination of success factors for both eCRM and online SCM that is conducted later.

NATURE OF SUPPLY CHAIN MANAGEMENT AND ITS ONLINE EQUIVALENT

Online supply chain management (SCM) has evolved into an important tool for creating efficiencies in business operations. It is the natural evolution of traditional supply chain management that manages supply channels as well as distribution channels in order to reduce inventory and lead times and improve customer service as well as product quality. More formally, supply chain management is defined by the Council of Logistics Management Council (www.clm.org) as the systematic, strategic coordination of the traditional business functions and the tactics across these business functions within a particular company for the purposes of improving long-term performance of the supply chain as whole.

The functions most frequently involved in supply chain management are purchasing, operations, logistics, and transportation. For the telecom manufacturer involved in segmenting its customers into logistically distinct businesses, the functions would include transportation and warehousing. Online SCM extends the implementation of traditional supply chain management through the integration of business-to-business (B2B) electronic commerce to achieve the improved performance sought within the supply chain.

The SCM literature addresses two general categories of B2B online applications: market mediation and collaboration (Keskinocak and Tayur 2001). Market mediation mechanisms are those used either to generate new channels of distribution through e-marketplaces or to support existing channels with company Web sites. For example, Internet-based auctions for acquiring goods and services in the B2B environment improve supply chain performance by matching orders for goods and services with available capacity. Webster (2002) proposed that the expansion of real-time enterprisewide information systems and Internet-based markets portends a shift in the role that dynamic lead time, pricing, and capacity may play in the future economy.

Market mediation may be implemented on the Web with procurement-related applications. Chaudhury, Mallick, and Rao (2001) discuss the uses of the World Wide Web in the context of activity theory and the variety of business roles it supports: as an advertising channel, an ordering channel, a procurement channel, and a customer support channel. On one hand, buyers involved in procurement search out new suppliers or special deals with existing ones on the Internet, then execute the purchase via Internet-enabled ordering processes. The notion that the Web is a tool to carry out a plan seems to fit well with the goals of online SCM, although many authors admit "the Web has a long way to go before it becomes a full-fledged ordering channel" (Chaudhury et. al. 2001). eCRM may indeed support market mediation in SCM, as the buying firm may look toward its own selling organization to acquire knowledge concerning demand that will enable more efficient procurement of goods and services. Gebert et al. (2003) identify these as goals in their knowledge management model, relative to dissemination of knowledge to process owners, including supply and distribution planners. Thus, the market mediation process is inextricably related to eCRM.

The second category is Internet-based collaboration in the supply chain. This provides the mechanism to improve efficiency and responsiveness through enhanced information exchange between partners in the supply chain. Again, the use of Internet technology in this type of application improves transaction efficiency; but more importantly, it also improves supply chain performance by increasing visibility and enabling the supply chain to be managed as an integrated system rather than a set of individual production processes (Rayport and Sviokla 1995). An example of Internet-based collaboration between parties in a supply chain is Collaborative Planning, Forecasting, and Replenishment (CPFR) and its supporting technologies, which were developed under the auspices of a Voluntary Interindustry Commerce Standards committee (McKaige 2001; White 1999). Retailers and their suppliers have benefited by using this form of Internet-based collaboration that coordinates product planning and forecasting. Case studies reported on Internet-based collaboration (http://www.cpfr.org/) describe the benefits in terms of reduced inventory and increased sales due to improved in-stock rates. Another form of collaboration —e-planning in the supply chain—may include a notification system for sudden, unanticipated changes that are likely to affect partners (Czupryna 2000). Plakoyiannaki and Tzokas (2002) identify the use of CRM data in this way to aid in operational decision making. eCRM is valuable in collaboration processes as well, especially in demand planning and in the use of forecast information in the design of the production processes that enable efficient production of tailored products and services in a supply chain.

These applications of SCM continue to hold great promise, yet a shortfall exists between the opportunity and the actualization (Greengard 2001; Pyke et al. 2001). eCRM has its share of failures as well. The success or failure of both eCRM and SCM depends upon several related factors. We now outline these factors, as identified in previous research on their impact.

THE VALUE OF INFORMATION

The success of a SCM or CRM initiative, whether online or not, is determined to some extent by the degree to which the correct use of information drives an overall improvement in supply chain efficiency or marketing efforts. This is measurable using the evaluation attributes previously mentioned. In the case of SCM, research on the impact of improved demand information and the impact of reduced uncertainty on inventory systems addresses the value of information in the supply chain. A number of studies, both empirical and analytical, have investigated the relationship between providing information to suppliers and the benefits that can be attributed to the improved communication environment. For instance, Salmen and Muir (2003) reinforce the notion of "value-creating information" and its availability to customers in eCRM. Such information empowers customers and allows them to absorb what they want when they want it. Their work identifies two fundamental approaches for information dispersal (Salmen and Muir 2003):

1. Providing personalized purchasing and related information upon a customer's request
2. Retaining more general information about a customer that may be useful and providing it via a list or similar format

SCM has the same basic approaches for information dispersal, be it the ability to review agreed-upon lead times for individual raw components when dealing with a supplier, or to provide listings of ship dates for a customer's review.

One way that information in the supply chain improves performance is by making daily transactions more efficient. Sriram and Banerjee (1994) illustrate this with their work on the effects of electronic data interchange (EDI) implementations on purchasing policies. The authors surveyed the National Association of Purchasing Management and found that companies who placed routine orders electronically without approvals were more efficient, in part because they reduced supplier monitoring accordingly. This resulted in a reduction in the number of buyers needed and tended to promote a longer-term buyer–seller relationship between the companies. This study illustrates that providing information to suppliers may indeed reduce costs. It also revealed that suppliers often tend to encourage buyers to use EDI and not the other way around. There was also no significant difference in the impact of EDI between buyers who were encouraged by their suppliers and those who were not and adopted it on their own.

In addition to costs, responsiveness in supply chains can be improved when suppliers share information with suppliers. Richeson et al. (1995) illustrate this with an investigation into the correlation between manufacturer–supplier communication and overall improvement in just-in-time delivery performance. These authors find that when more information is provided to suppliers in an IT arrangement, communication enhances manufacturing performance. This study also finds that both routine and nonroutine communications are essential to a successful manufacturer-supplier relationship.

Tailored logistics also improves customer responsiveness in a supply chain, although the concept is limited, as described in Fuller et al. (1993). Without the information afforded by the Internet, and in particular the knowledge concerning specific customer needs for transportation and warehousing, suppliers place customers in relatively few categories. Such is the case of the telecom manufacturer previously mentioned, which used 384 market buckets to describe the needs of its customers. Suppliers can be most responsive to customer needs when the service level is defined on an individual basis. This level of customization is possible only through the customer knowledge gained via eCRM. In this case, eCRM is required for SCM to succeed. Other examples of eCRM as a foundation to SCM can be cited, such as the use of customer characteristics in supplementing demand information for a product in Internet-based collaboration.

The information acquired through eCRM applications may also aid in structuring the supply chain to meet each customer's individual need. Traditionally, logistics systems are built to be cost efficient through scale economies. At one point, for example, railroad companies were offering unit train service that transported goods for a single shipper on a specific origin–destination lane and thus offered the lowest possible freight rates.

Thus, the value of the information shared in the supply chain is a factor that influences success. Those applications with insufficient value will tend to fail, and those with significant value will be more often favored with success. Walton and Marucheck (1997) report that three limiting factors emerge from the analysis as important to supplier reliability: length of time the buying company has been using EDI with any supplier, type of data shared with suppliers (planned production or capacity information is useful), and EDI acquisition investment.

The literature also brings to light the importance of the interaction between parties in the information exchange to the success of both eCRM and SCM. The CPFR case studies address this issue relative to cross-enterprise forecast collaboration for SCM (VICS 1999). A partner who disagrees with a posted forecast proposes a change, which may be followed by a counterproposal from another partner. This proposal and counterproposal process may iterate numerous times. An online environment is especially well suited for this type of interactive task.

Obviously, this kind of interaction is neither easily accomplished, nor necessitated, in eCRM, but the intensity of the data gathering is important. eCRM tends to use unidirectional communication between parties for data collection purposes. Trust and/or some form of fulfillment should accompany this one-way communication. In other words, customers, or potential ones, must have a reason to trust the company or expect something in return and therefore to provide the desired information. In the case of SCM, there is a "collaboration effect," in direct contrast to the situation where data exchange is unidirectional. When a customer shares information with the supplier and receives feedback on the accuracy of the data, as in the case of forecast collaboration, we can say that a collaboration effect exists and is an important contributor to the performance improvement in a supply chain. The effective use of underlying technologies represents another success factor for both eCRM and SCM. We address technological aspects of success in the next section.

TECHNOLOGICAL ASPECTS OF ELECTRONIC COMMERCE

Ngai and Wat (2002) outline six categories of technological issues related to electronic commerce. These six categories—security, technological components, network technology/infrastructure, support systems, algorithm/methodology, and other technical issues—cover the entire IT spectrum. Of these, both SCM and eCRM rely heavily on security, network technology/infrastructure, and support systems for their day-to-day operations. eCRM, in particular, utilizes supporting systems for its overall success. The collection of customer information online presents several problems from an online marketing point of view. These problems include creating the proper Web interface to collect the information, determining how much information to collect, and properly validating and filtering information that is collected online. Berson and fellow researchers (2000) also assert that the way a company uses customer information is fundamental to the success of CRM. They also define the primary tools for processing information, such as marketing automation, data warehousing, and data mining, which work only as part of the larger business process.

Croteau and Li (2003) find that possessing knowledge management capabilities was the most significant critical success factor affecting CRM impact. They further state that the relationship between technological readiness and knowledge management capabilities is also significant. One can certainly make the case that SCM relies on such knowledge management technologies as well for its ultimate success. Judicious partnering with both suppliers and customers requires the management of both internal and external knowledge of the organizations involved. Kenyon and Vakola (2003) utilize a survey of businesses in the grocery retailing area to determine the importance of data collection and use for CRM. They find that this critical function ranked second in importance for overall success, trailing only "maintaining a competitive advantage." One can certainly argue that a company can maintain a competitive advantage through the collection of use of the right customer data. In fact, with the electronic version of CRM, its potential for building an advantage is greatly increased, owing to inherent efficiencies in data collection and dispersal.

A number of information technology/systems-related factors also influence the success of SCM, but technology cannot overcome poor communication. Arminas (2002) details "real-world" SCM problems due to communication problems. A major stumbling block for e-collaboration is described, involving a prime contractor and its first-tier suppliers and the poor communication between purchasers, engineering departments, and suppliers. This example points out the impact of poor communication on SCM, noting that the successful application of IT/IS cannot assure SCM success, but a poor application can most certainly achieve failure.

Another aspect of technology is technological drift. Ciborra (2000) defines "technological drift" as the gap between intent and outcome with respect to how a modern knowledge-based organization carries out its implementation of technology to manage itself. This term describes a common problem that must be overcome in the implementations of both SCM and eCRM. Ideally, eCRM, and CRM in general, propose three benefits for their implementation in a knowledge-based company (Bygstad 2003):

- gives each worker the tools to manage contacts, activities, documents, etc.
- provides a tool for dialog marketing, allowing the company to individualize marketing activities
- represents a synergic potential for the company, as information can lead to new products and markets

To achieve these intended outcomes, a company must struggle with the process of conflict and resolution between different actors, including the technology itself. Such a process is only partially controllable in a modern organization with empowered employees (Ciborra 2000; Bygstad 2003). A successful implementation of SCM faces the same conflict process. Angeles and Nath (2003) define the factors involved in this "technological drift" from their analysis of a survey related to EDI:

- strategic commitment of top management
- readiness for high-level EDI
- joint partnering
- communications
- EDI infrastructure
- trading partner flexibility

It should be obvious from this list that all involve some form of conflict, whether between top and middle management or between the partners in the supply chain. "Technological drift" aptly describes what an organization must deal with when choosing the appropriate level of technology for either SCM or eCRM. Often cost/benefit analyses do not readily lend themselves to the evaluation of such technologies, owing to the intangible benefits described earlier. With a dearth of "hard numbers" for such analyses, this conflict process results.

BEHAVIORAL ASPECTS OF ELECTRONIC COMMERCE

When examining the relevant literature related to success of both SCM and eCRM, one must also examine some of the behavioral aspects of online marketing and purchasing. Although the business-to-consumer (B2C) electronic commerce and information exchange that takes place in eCRM involves a somewhat different dynamic than the business-to-business (B2B) purchasing that occurs in SCM, it is still a worthwhile exercise to examine its nature and potential impact on success for both of them.

For the case of SCM, Steinfield et al. (1995) investigated the effects of such interorganizational data networks on buyer–seller relationships. One of their important conclusions was that the more firms used interorganizational networks, the greater the tendency to develop hierarchical relationships with their trading partners. This result shows that SCM develops naturally in an electronic environment. Their conclusion concerning smaller trading partners, however, appears to mitigate the effectiveness of this online trading environment. Electronic marketplaces may therefore be necessary to bring these smaller companies into the electronic trading arena. This result is also found in collaboration-oriented online systems. Small suppliers may not have the resources to implement the technology needed to share information in their supply chains, and so special consideration is often needed for smaller training partners.

Other work focuses on factors that influence consumer online behavior and applies to both SCM and eCRM (Steinfield et al. 1995; Hoffman et al. 1996; Novack et al. 2000). The concept of "flow," which originates in the field of organizational psychology, has been extended to an online environment and defined in this context as "a cognitive state experienced during online navigation that is determined by: (1) high levels of skill and control; (2) high levels of challenge and arousal; (3) focused attention; and (4) is enhanced by interactivity and 'telepresence.'" Novack et al. (2000) state that consumers who achieve 'flow' on the Web are so acutely involved in the act of online navigation that thoughts and perceptions not relevant to navigation are screened out. This allows the consumer to focus entirely on the interaction. Concentration on the navigation experience is so intense that little attention can be given to anything else, and other events occurring in the consumer's physical environment lose significance. As self-consciousness disappears, the consumer's sense of time becomes distorted, and the state of mind arising as a result of achieving flow on the Web is extremely gratifying. This phenomenon illustrates a key aspect of the online experience: that in the right circumstances a customer can brought into a unique state of high online interaction. Successful eCRM, and to a lesser extent SCM, might hinge upon gathering information when a current or potential customer is in such a state.

When discussing the behavioral aspects of eCRM and SCM, we must consider seller/customer relationships. As described earlier, eCRM represents a form of relationship marketing (Gronroos, 1994). The building of such relationships involves not only the supporting business processes, but also the elusive aspect known as "customer satisfaction." Gronroos (1994) points out that the temporal nature of customer satisfaction often is not known or is very weakly determined through surveys. In order to build a relationship, satisfaction must be monitored. Preis (2003) implies that customers compare prepurchase expectations with perceived actual performance, and make judgments about consumption experiences based on such comparisons. Satisfaction is portrayed as a nonlinear step function where small changes in perceived performance create little effect either way. Relationship building thus hinges upon a preconceived positive notion of performance to be fully or almost fully realized from the onset.

The ultimate success of both eCRM and SCM thus requires that all parties involved take action based on perceived benefits from the system being utilized. For instance, a supplier would not enter into a supply chain relationship with a customer via SCM if it did not envision efficiencies to be gained or additional sales revenues/profits. Work by Zank and Vokurka (2003) points out the positive influence that SCM has on the relationships between members of a supply chain. They utilized a survey of members of two specific industry associations, the International Association of Plastics Distributors and the Power Transmission Distributors Association, to determine the importance and impact of SCM conducted online. According to their survey, distributors, manufacturers, and customers all perceive benefits from e-business. As might be expected, the customer respondents, which included respondents from the purchasing area, rated issues tied to reducing costs as relatively more important.

Torkzadeh and Dhillon (2002) also utilize a survey to obtain empirical data on factors that influence the success of electronic commerce. Again, although this work was targeted at consumer behavior and the marketing aspects of B2C, it points out legitimate concerns for SCM and eCRM. The "fundamental objectives" that they point out, such as "It is important to minimize time to gather information," "It is important to maximize privacy," and "It is important to minimize the risk of product use," all have relevance in B2C and help to ultimately determine the success or failure of SCM and eCRM. Additional factors that potentially influence effectiveness are data gathering efficiency and security.

SUMMARY

Online customer relationship management (eCRM) and online supply chain management both involve the use of the Internet for managing relationships. eCRM focuses on the customer relationship, while online SCM further deals with suppliers and the transfer of goods between involved parties. SCM enables CRM through customization of goods and services needed when fulfilling orders for specific unique customers in a CRM-environment. Also, SCM planners are users of eCRM knowledge in the production and delivery processes required to tailor products and services.

Both online SCM and eCRM rely for their success on the underlying technology, the correct exchange of information, and the nature of the online experience/customer's online behavior. They both must overcome the problem of "technological drift," the gap between the intended use of technology and its implementation. This gap creates systems that are both underutilized and lacking in strategic advantage. One can certainly argue that both online SCM and eCRM, if properly designed and implemented, are systems of strategic importance. Both online SCM and eCRM also require a commitment from top management to be successful. In these ways, success for both eCRM and SCM is interrelated.

The information in this chapter is useful in pointing to key areas for management focus, since many firms are implementing both types of systems. Examination of the use of data mining and similar techniques for revealing interesting relationships between customers' buying patterns and suppliers' behavior (such as unexpected increases in lead times from suppliers during certain periods of heavy customer demand) would be a fruitful area for further work. The most important point for practitioners of both eCRM and online SCM is the need for integration between the respective systems.

Current software applications, whether in-house developed or commercial off-the-shelf, almost always focus on one or the other type of system. Such applications do not take into account the crucial CRM information that can be gleaned as an organization conducts its day-to-day SCM. Customer buying trends, at the very least, could be gleaned from SCM operations to aid production planning as well as marketing/customer relationship-building activities. Likewise, a CRM system would allow changes in customer preferences to be reflected in overall product forecasts, thereby affecting the aggregate planning and logistics that make up the keystone of the supply chain. Although Enterprise Resource Planning (ERP) application vendors have taken steps to develop modules for both eCRM and online SCM, a gap in availability still exists, since the bulk of applications supporting one or the other organizational function are from independent, vertical market-oriented software vendors.

REFERENCES

Angeles, R. and Nath, R. Electronic supply chain partnerships: reconsidering relationship attributes in customer-supplier dyads. *Information Resources Management Journal,* 16, 3 (2003), 59–84.

Arminas, D. E-collaboration ruined by poor communication skills. *Supply Management,* 7, 25 (2002), 11.

Berson, A.; Smith, S.; and Thearling, K. *Building Data Mining Applications for CRM.* New York: McGraw-Hill, 2000.

Bose, R. and Sugumaran, V. Application of knowledge management in customer relationship management. *Knowledge and Process Management,* 10, 1 (2003), 3–17.

Bygstad, B. The implementation puzzle of CRM systems in knowledge-based organizations. *Information Resources Management Journal,* 16, 4 (2003), 33–45.

Chaudhury, A.; Mallick, D.; and H. Rao, H. Web channels in e-commerce. *Communications of the ACM,* 1 (2001), 99–104.

Ciborra, C. *From Control to Drift.* New York: Oxford University Press, 2000.

Croteau, A. and Li, P. Critical success factors of CRM technological initiatives. *Canadian Journal of Administrative Sciences,* 20, 1 (2003), 21–34.

Czupryna, E. Putting e-planning to work. *IIE Solutions,* 8 (2000), 32.

Dyché, J. *The CRM Handbook: A Business Guide to Customer Relationship Management.* Boston: Addison-Wesley, 2001.

Fjermestad, J. and Romano, N.C .Electronic customer relationship management revisiting the general theories of usability and resistance: An integrative implementation framework. *Business Process Management Journal,* 9, 5 (2003), 572–591.

Fuller, J.; O'Conor, J.; and Rawlinson, R. Tailored logistics: The next advantage. *Harvard Business Review,* May–June (1993), 87–98.

Gebert, H.; Geib, M.; Kolbe, L.; and Brenner, W. Knowledge-enabled customer relationship management: Integrating customer relationship management and knowledge management concepts. *Journal of Knowledge Management,* 7, 5 (2003), 107–23.

Gebert, H.; Geib, M.; Kolbe, L.; and Riempp, G. Towards customer knowledge management: Integrating customer relationship management and knowledge management concepts. In *Proceedings of the 2nd International Conference on Electronic Business,* Tapei, Tawain, 2002, pp. 296–298.

Greengard, S. The hope and hype of online exchanges. *Business Finance Magazine,* March 2001.

Gronroos, C. From marketing mix to relationship marketing: Towards a paradigm shift in marketing. *Management Decision,* 32, 2 (1994), 4–21.

Gurau, C.; Ranchhod, A.; and Hackney, R. Customer-centric strategic planning: Integrating CRM in online business systems. *Information Technology and Management,* 4 (2003), 199–214.

Hackney, R.; Ranchod, A.; and Hackney, M. Marketing strategies through customer attention: Beyond technology-enabled customer relationship management. Working paper presented at the *AMCIS Conference,* August 6, 2004.

Hoffman, D. and Novak, T. Marketing in hypermedia computer-mediated environments: Conceptual foundations. *Journal of Marketing,* 60 (1996), 50–68.

Keeney, R. The value of internet commerce to the customer. *Management Science,* 45, 4 (1999), 533–542.

Kenyon, J. and Vakola, M. Customer relationship management: A viable strategy for the retail industry. *International Journal of Organization Theory and Behavior*, 6, 3 (2003), 329–353.

Keskinocak, P. and Tayur, S. Quantitative analysis for Internet-enabled supply chains. *Interfaces*, 2 (2001), 70–89.

Loveman, G. Diamonds in the data mine. *Harvard Business Review*, May (2003), 109–113.

McKaige, W. Collaborating on the supply chain. *IIE Solutions*, 3 (2001), 34–37.

Ngai, E. and Wat, F. A literature review and classification of electronic commerce research. *Information and Management*, 39 (2002), 415–429.

Niemegeers, I. and Heemstra de Groot, S. From personal area networks to personal networks: A user oriented approach. *Wireless Personal Communications*, 26 (2002), 175–186.

Novack, T.; Hoffman, D.; and Yung, Y. Measuring the customer experience in online environments: A structural modeling approach. *Marketing Science*, 19, 1 (2000), 22–42.

Plakoyiannaki, E. and Tzokas, N. Customer relationship management: A capabilities portfolio perspective. *Journal of Database Marketing and Customer Strategy Management*, 9, 3 (2002), 228–237.

Preis, M. The impact of interpersonal satisfaction on repurchase decisions. *Journal of Supply Chain Management*, 39, 3 (2003), 30–38.

Pyke, D.; Johnson, M.; and Desmond, P. E-fulfillment: It's harder than it looks. *Supply Chain Management Review*, January–February (2001), http://www.manufacturing.net/scl/scmr/scm0118/efulfillmentprint.html.

Rayport, J. and Sviokla, J. Exploiting the virtual value chain. *Harvard Business Review*, 73, 6 (1995), 75–85.

Richeson, L.; Lackey, C.; and Starner, W. The effect of communication on the linkage between manufacturers and suppliers in a just-in-time environment. *International Journal of Purchasing and Materials Management*, 1, (1995), 21–28.

Romano, N. and Fjermestad, J. Electronic commerce customer relationship management: Research agenda. *Information Technology and Management*, 4, (2003), 233–258.

Salmen, S. and Muir, A. Electronic customer care: The innovative path to e-loyalty. *Journal of Financial Services Marketing*, 8, 2 (2003), 133–144.

Shaw, R. *Measuring and Valuing Customer Relationships*. London: Business Intelligence Ltd., 1999.

Shen, K. and Lee, D. WAP mail service and short message service for mobile CRM. *Proceedings of the International Symposium on Multimedia Software Engineering (ISMSE 2000)*, December 11–13, 2000, Taipei, Taiwan, pp. 201–207.

Sriram, V. and Banerjee, S. Electronic data interchange: does its adoption change purchasing policies and procedures? *International Journal of Purchasing and Materials Management*, 1 (1994), 31–40.

Steinfield, C.; Kraut, R.; and Plummer, A. The impact of inter-organizational networks on buyer-seller relationships. *Journal of Computer Mediated Communication*, 1, 3 (1995) http://www.ascusc.org/jcmc/v011/issue3/steinfld.html.

Supply Chain Council, Supply Chain Operations Reference Model. (1993), http://www.supply-chain.org.

Torkzadeh, G. and Dhillon, G. Measuring factors that influence the success of internet commerce. *Information Systems Research*, 13, 2 (2002), 187–204.

(VICS) Voluntary Interindustry Commerce Standards Association, CPFR Roadmap: The Case Studies. (1999), http://208.143.22.52/cpfr_pdf/

Walton, S. and Marucheck, A. The relationship between EDI and supplier reliability. *International Journal of Purchasing and Materials Management*, 3 (1997), 30–35.

Webster, S. Dynamic pricing and lead-time policies for make-to-order systems. *Decision Sciences*, 33, 4 (2002), 579–599.

White, A. The value equation: Value chain management, collaboration and the Internet. (1999) http://www.cpfr.org/WhitePapers/The_Value_Equation.doc

Zank, G. and Vokurka, R. The Internet: Motivations, deterrents, and impact on supply chain relationships. *S.A.M. Advanced Management Journal*, 68, 2 (2003), 33–40.

CHAPTER 3

USING ELECTRONIC CUSTOMER RELATIONSHIP MANAGEMENT TO MAXIMIZE/MINIMIZE CUSTOMER SATISFACTION/DISSATISFACTION

YOON CHO AND JERRY FJERMESTAD

Abstract: *Electronic customer relationship management (eCRM) has attracted the attention of managers and academic researchers for the past several years. Issues of eCRM have varied from marketing to information technology. While there are many concerns and efforts for successful management of customer relationship in the online environment, this chapter posits that the major components of eCRM include increasing customer satisfaction and customer loyalty, minimizing customer dissatisfaction, resolving customer complaints, and increasing product/service quality. It reviews the major eCRM issues of customer satisfaction and dissatisfaction, as well as the aspects of customer loyalty and complaints that are consequences of customer satisfaction and dissatisfaction. It implies for both researchers and businesses that a hybrid approach from the marketing and information system perspectives leads successful eCRM.*

Keywords: *Electronic Customer Relationship Management (eCRM), Customer Satisfaction/Dissatisfaction, Complaining Behavior, Customer Loyalty*

INTRODUCTION

Electronic commerce relies on customer interactions via a computer and telecommunications infrastructure for the purpose of advertising, promoting, and selling products and services online. Electronic commerce replicates most of the physical activities that take place in the marketplace, to the point where increasing use of electronic commerce is shifting companies to new market spaces. The traditional marketplace emphasizes "customer satisfaction" as a way to earn consumer loyalty and attract new customers. Therefore this chaper examines the firm's approach to customer relationship management in order to account for the new realities of market spaces. To be successful in a market space, a firm must be responsive to its virtual customers' wants, needs, and desires and manage interactions with them properly in order to arrive at a win/win outcome. Marketing considers that interactions between customers or potential customers and the firm arrive at a win/win outcome, in either a marketplace or a market space, when: (i) such interactions lead to the sale of a given item(s); and/or (ii) such interactions lead to an increased likelihood that a sale of the same or other item(s) will happen in the near future to the satisfaction of both parties. Win/win means the customer wins through a satisfying purchase of a product or service and the firm wins by selling this product or service. Increased customer satisfaction will augment the likelihood that the customer will purchase again and/or induce other potential customers to buy, through either testimonials or word-of-mouth effects. Under this scenario, moving from the marketplace to the market space poses new challenges to the firm. Many years of experience have enabled them to manage a marketplace, but market space is the result of a recent phenomenon (the Web), which is about twenty years old.

In addition to the new realities of the market space, the constant development of the Web as a new environment medium opens significant challenges to marketers, which they may not be well prepared to face. The key new element is the dynamic nature of the interactive system used by customers to gain access to a firm's Web site, and what happens after the Web site has been reached. Under this scenario, three important questions must be answered: (i) How does a firm attract potential customers to its own Web site? (ii) Once customers enter the firm's Web site, how can the Web site "cooperate with the customer" in order to arrive at a win/win situation? (iii) How must the firm adjust its marketing information systems to ensure that proper information and feedback is obtained from market space interactions for better management decision making?

These three questions are not independent; i.e., the satisfaction experienced by potential customers reaching a firm's Web site will depend on the prior experience and expectations that they build along the way (both in the past and in this particular Web session) and the design of the Web site, which may or may not handle those expectations in a "cooperative" manner. Management will not have a clue as to what happened if proper arrangements are not made to capture the customers' satisfaction with the overall process. Because a market space is a unique blend of marketing activities in a "virtual," interactive electronic environment, this chapter will track the issue of customer satisfaction/dissatisfaction both from the traditional marketing viewpoint and in terms of the more recent information technology views about interactive systems. In particular, given the importance of "cooperation" between the firm and its customers, current knowledge of user satisfaction with collaborative environments will also be included. All these aspects will help the future formulation of a "hybrid model of customer satisfaction" using the Web that accounts for all the components of market space, under the win/win mandate of the "marketing principle."

Based on the foregoing, the purpose of this chapter is to review the state of art for eCRM by examining issues raised by researchers during the past several years, underlying theories and models of eCRM which are rooted in both consumer satisfaction and dissatisfaction in marketing, and other future research issues. This study also reviews consequences of customer satisfaction/dissatisfaction, such as customer loyalty and complaints.

DEFINING ELECTRONIC CUSTOMER RELATIONSHIP MANAGEMENT

eCRM has attracted the attention of e-business managers and academic researchers who are interested in increasing repeat business and customer loyalty (Julta, Craig, and Bodorik 2001). Various researchers have defined the eCRM according to different aspects. Based on the review by Jukic, Jukic, Meamber and Nezlek (2002–2003), eCRM is a business strategy that utilizes the power of technology to tie together all aspects of a company's business with the goal of building long-term customer loyalty. Jukic et al. (2002) also stressed that eCRM, in practical terms, is the management of customer interactions at all levels, channels, and media. Hansen (2000) sees eCRM as "*a process of acquiring, retaining and growing profitable customers. It requires a clear focus on the service attributes that represent value to the customer and that create loyalty.*" A review by Romano and Fjermestad (2001–2002) emphasized that eCRM involves attracting and keeping economically valuable customers while repelling and eliminating economically unvaluable ones. On the market space, eCRM is to build and maximize the value of the relationship with the customer and to improve customer retention rates (Jukic et al. 2002; Cho, Im, Hiltz, and Fjermestad 2002).

Issues of eCRM have been developed from relationship marketing, which is to establish, maintain, and enhance relationships with customers and other partners, at a profit, so that the objectives of the parties involved are met (Grönroos 2000). At the lowest level of a relationship, marketers build a financial bond with customers by using pricing strategies (i.e., periodic e-mail notification of price discounts to individual users) (Strauss, El-Ansary, and Frost 2003). At a level-two relationship, marketers stimulate social interaction with customers. Managing online community is one of the strategies for a level-two relationship. For a deeper-level relationship, e-businesses rely on creating structural solutions to customer problems. Offering customization service is a good example of level-three relationship (Strauss, El-Ansary, and Frost 2003).

Among various levels of relationship marketing, online companies have been paying attention to making stronger relationships in order to retain existing or create future customers. For example, customization of online communities has been used to maintain a strong relationship with customers. While the Internet services are getting popular, one of the most important challenges is to achieve customer satisfaction and maintain customer loyalty. Julta, Craig, and Bodorik (2001) note that customer metrics affect eCRM; they include customer retention, satisfaction, acquisition, and profitability. Another side of eCRM includes how to minimize customer dissatisfaction and complaints. Cho, Im, Hiltz, and Fjermestad (2002) posit that minimizing customer dissatisfaction and complaints is a key to successful eCRM. Therefore, this study defines eCRM as an e-business strategy that interacts with customers to maximize customer satisfaction, to build customer loyalty, and also to attract potential customers to the firm's Web site.

MAXIMIZING/MINIMIZING CUSTOMER SATISFACTION/ DISSATISFACTION AS MAJOR COMPONENTS OF ECRM

Various researchers have proposed a framework for eCRM studies. A previous review on eCRM in information system research by Romano and Fjermestad (2003) suggested the frameworks for CRM research, including eCRM within markets, eCRM business models, eCRM knowledge management, e-CRM technology issues, and e-CRM human issues. From about the early 1990s until now, studies on eCRM have addressed issues regarding (i) factors affecting customer satisfaction and loyalty; (ii) factors affecting customer dissatisfaction and complaints; (iii) effectiveness of the Web site; (iv) the impact of online communities on eCRM; (v) supply chain management; and (vi) knowledge management, and so on. Cho, Im, Hiltz, and Fjermestad (2002) note that the major eCRM components to be discussed include: (i) maximizing customer satisfaction/minimizing customer dissatisfaction; (ii) increasing customer loyalty; (iii) increasing product/service quality; and (iv) resolving customer complaints. This chapter will review issues of customer satisfaction/dissatisfaction, including theories and models that have been frequently applied to eCRM. It will also review issues of customer loyalty and complaints that are consequences of customer satisfaction/dissatisfaction.

Satisfaction is defined as a judgment that a product or service feature, or the product or service itself, provided (or is providing) a pleasurable level of consumption-related fulfillment, including levels of under- or over-fulfillment (Oliver 1981). According to Surprenant (1977), satisfaction leads to desirable consequences, such as repeat purchase, acceptance of other products in the line, brand loyalty, store patronage, and, ultimately, higher profits and increased profit share. According to Tse and Wilton (1988), satisfaction is the consumer's response to the evaluation of the perceived discrepancy between prior expectations and the actual performance of the product as perceived after its consumption.

Maximizing customer satisfaction and maintaining customer loyalty have become objectives for eCRM. In an effort to provide a positive contrast for the new against the old, this chapter first discusses the issue of customer satisfaction and customer loyalty as being at the center of successful brick-and-mortar physical business exchanges. The authors focus more on customer satisfaction, because it provides clues as to what managerial changes might have induced different and more desirable behaviors, raising the issue of customer loyalty myopia. This myopia stems from believing that consumer behavior can be created and sustained in and by itself without careful regard to its underlying basis on the customer satisfaction side, reviving the long-standing marketing dilemma of attitude and behavioral measures, and the degree to which attitudes influence or predict behavior.

The level of detail goes beyond the customer satisfaction concept and much more deeply into the underlying theories and models that attempt to explain why people may or may not be satisfied. Given the recent dismal performance of most e-commerce stars—e.g., amazon.com lost 70 percent of its market value in 2000—the authors are forced to admit that customers' purchasing behaviors are rather sticky and that most e-commerce innovations will be absorbed gradually when customers prove their worth beyond the initial trial phase. This question's importance transcends the domain of the enterprise and goes into society at large, because shopping exchanges are a key element of the social order and economic growth.

Although customer satisfaction has been identified as a key component of eCRM (Cho, Im, Hiltz, and Fjermestad 2002), the question of how to minimize online customer dissatisfaction has not received much attention. As with any transaction, online customer satisfaction/dissatisfaction is largely determined by how much the customer's expectations differ from the product's or service's actual performance—what traditional marketers refer to as the degree of disparity resulting from a customer's disconfirmation of expectations (Anderson 1973; Tse and Wilton 1988). According to the model of online customer complaining behavior proposed by Cho, Im, Fjermestad, and Hiltz (2001a and b), online customer dissatisfaction results from unmet expectations about a product, technology issues, and/or Web assessment factors (Schubert and Selz 1999), which include information content, customized product information, convenient after-sales support, privacy issues, fast and accurate delivery, and the like. Similarly, according to customer metrics by Julta and Bodorik (2001), online customer satisfaction primarily depends on lead time, delivery speed, product or service introduction, and convenience.

Researchers in the customer satisfaction/dissatisfaction (CS/D) area posited that the fulfillment of expectations is a determinant of consumer satisfaction. Most of the definitions of satisfaction or dissatisfaction that have been proposed contain some mention of "expectation" or a synonym (Gilly 1979). Bearden and Teel (1980) posit that the intensity of complaint behavior was often hypothesized to be directly proportional to the customer's degree of dissatisfaction.

THEORIES APPLIED TO ECRM STUDIES

Researchers on eCRM have applied various theories of customer satisfaction developed by marketing researchers. In this chapter, the authors cover in depth the most commonly accepted theories relating human factors to the satisfaction level and effective use of computer-mediated communications (CMC). The viewpoint is that current CMC techniques applied to e-commerce have grown out of different application domains, where the needs and benefits sought may have been different from what is required for successful business applications.

Various satisfaction/dissatisfaction theories have applied consumers' judgment on satisfaction with product/service. Most of the early studies focused on the approach to products only, comparing consumers' expectations with their experience of product performance. Expectation and disconfirmation have been used as proxies to predict satisfaction and significant variables in a satisfaction function. If the performance is above the (predicted) expectations (i.e., if positive disconfirmation occurs), increases in satisfaction are expected, while if the performance is below expectations (if negative disconfirmation occurs), increases in dissatisfaction are expected.

Satisfaction/dissatisfaction theories frequently cited include cognitive dissonance theory (Festinger 1957), contrast theory (Engel and Blackwell 1982; Howard and Sheth 1969; Cardozo 1965), assimilation-contrast theory (Oliver 1997), expectation-disconfirmation theory (Oliver and Desarbo 1988), generalized negativity theory (Yi 1990), level-of-aspiration (LOA) theory (Yi 1990), and adaptation-level theory (Helson 1948, 1959, and 1964). Other theories, such as equity theory and value-percept disparity theory, have been applied to explain the expectation-disconfirmation paradigm.

According to *cognitive dissonance theory,* disconfirmed expectations create a state of dissonance or psychological discomfort (Festinger 1957). The theory (Festinger 1957) states that dissonant or inconsistent states may exist and are a source of psychological tension to the person perceiving them. This tension will lead to efforts to reduce dissonance and restore consistency. Mechanisms to reduce dissonance include changes in behavior or attitudes or selective distortion of perceptions (Festinger 1957). The *contrast theory* presumes that when product expectations are not matched by actual performance, the contrast between expectation and outcome, or the surprise effect, will cause the consumer to exaggerate the disparity (Engel and Blackwell 1982; Howard and Sheth 1969; and Cardozo 1965). Similarly, *assimilation-contrast theory* (Oliver 1997) found that expectation and disconfirmation were independently related to the postexposure ratings.

Another support for eCRM is the *adaptation-level theory* (Helson 1964), which posits that one perceives stimuli only in relation to an adapted standard (Yi 1990). Adaptation-level theory says that if the original expectations were to change, the customer would still be free to compare unfavorably the product received with better ones (Helson 1964). The *generalized negativity theory* states that any disconfirmation of expectations is perceived as less pleasant than a confirmation of expectations (Yi 1990). Yi (1990) restated that disconfirmation of expectations results in a hedonically negative state, which is generalized to objects in the environment. If consumers expect a particular performance from a product, and a discrepant performance occurs, they will judge the product less favorably than if they had not had prior expectations. The elements and the process may be viewed as analogous to the *level-of-aspiration (LOA) theory*'s description of the evaluation of differences between expected and actual performance and the perception of "success" or "failure" (Yi 1990). Combining this idea from *LOA theory,* from Thibaut and Kelly, and from Sherif, one may suggest a model that calls attention particularly to some factors critical to the measurement of satisfaction.

Theories such as Hirshman's (1970) *exit-voice theory* related customer complaints to customer satisfaction and loyalty. *Exit-voice theory* explained that the immediate consequences of increased customer satisfaction are decreased customer complaints and increased customer loyalty (Fornell and Wernerfelt 1987). When dissatisfied, customers have the option of exiting (e.g., going to a competitor) or voicing their complaints in an attempt to receive compensation. An increase in overall customer satisfaction should decrease the incidence of complaints. Instead, overall customer satisfaction should also increase customer loyalty. Loyalty is the ultimate dependent variable in the model because of its value as a proxy for profitability (Reichheld and Schefer 2000).

Table 3.1

Theories Applied on eCRM Studies

Study	Major variables	Publication	Suggested theory
Khalifa and Liu	Consumer satisfaction	HICSS* (2002)	Expectation disconfirmation theory
Ho and Wu	Consumer satisfaction	HICSS * (1999)	Expectation disconfirmation theory
Cho, Im, Hiltz, and Fjermestad	Customer complaints	HICSS * (2002)	Cognitive dissonance theory, Hirschman's theory of exit, voice, and loyalty
Zhang and Dran	User satisfaction/website quality	HICSS * (2001)	Herzberg's theory; SERVUAL***
Krishnan et al.	Overall customer satisfaction	*Management Science* (1999)	Bayesian approach
Lee, Kim and Moon	Trust, transaction cost, and customer loyalty	CHI** (2000)	No suggested theory
Dutta and Segev	Customer relationship	HICSS * (1999)	A theory of cyber-transformation****
Li, Kuo, & Russell	Consumer online buying behavior	*Journal of Computer-Mediated Communication* (1999)	Channel theory
Cho and Ha	Utility	*Journal of Business & Economics Research* (2004b)	Von Neumann-Morgenstern utility theory
Goodwin and Ross	Complaining behavior	*Journal of Services Marketing* (1990)	Equity theory
Cho and Ha	E-satisfaction and behavioral intention to use websites	*Journal of Business & Economics Research* (2004a)	Uses and gratification theory; theory of reasoned action
Kimery and McCord	Intention to purchase	HICSS * (2002)	Exchange theory, theory of reasoned action and planned behavior
Cho, Im, Hiltz, and Fjermestad	Propensity to complain	*Advances in Consumer Research* (2001)	Hirschman's theory of exit, voice, and loyalty
Cho, Im, Hiltz, and Fjermestad	Propensity to complain	*Business Process Management Journal* (2003)	Dissonance theory

*Hawaii International Conference on System Sciences.
**Conference on Human Factors in Computing Systems.
***The study applied organizational behavior theories to IS and Marketing.
****The study introduced the market-space model.

Various researchers address the importance of customer satisfaction in the studies of electronic customer relationship management (eCRM: Table 3.1). Studies by Khalifa and Liu (2002–2003) and Ho and Wu (1999) apply the *expectation-disconfirmation theory* developed in marketing on their research model. Cho and Ha (2004a and b) apply various theories, such as uses and gratification theory and theory of reasoned action. *Uses and gratification theory* (Herzog 1944;

McGuire 1974; Luo 2002) has been frequently applied in this study to explain users' attitudes toward movie-related Web sites and consumer satisfaction. Another study by Cho and Ha (2004b) applies the *von Neumann-Morgenstern utility theory* that is applied by Hauser and Urban (1979) to explain the application of utilities to the method of decision analysis.

Another interesting theory that explains customer dissatisfaction and complaining behavior is *equity theory* (Blodgett, Granbois, and Walters 1993). According to previous studies (Blodgett, Granbois, and Walters 1993; Goodwin and Ross 1990), the way in which individuals involved in conflicts or disputes perceive justice has been explained by *equity theory*. Complaint-handling incidents, which are rated favorably, include compensation in line with the perceived costs experienced by the customer (Kelly and Davis 1994), thus supporting an equity-based evaluation of complaint outcomes (Blodgett, Granbois, and Tax 1997). A study by Tax, Brown, and Chandrashekaran (1998) and Goodwin and Ross (1990) addressed the concept of *justice* as a comprehensive framework to explain people's reactions to conflict situations. Three justice dimensions were discussed to explain complaint handling when customers encounter service failure (Blodgett, Granbois, and Tax 1997; and Tax, Brown, and Chandrashekaran 1998). Dimensions include *distributive justice, procedural justice,* and *interactional justice.*

MODEL OF CUSTOMER SATISFACTION/DISSATISFACTION

Traditional marketing researchers have suggested various models for customer satisfaction/dissatisfaction. Recently suggested models for eCRM have been developed from traditional customer satisfaction/dissatisfaction models. Those models have investigated how variables affect customer satisfaction/dissatisfaction. Traditional models for customer satisfaction/dissatisfaction include the *expectation-disconfirmation model, perceived-performance model, norms-based model, multiple-process models, attribution models, affective model, equity model, the American Customer Satisfaction Index model* (ACSI), and *complaint behavior model.*

Various researchers have measured the level of satisfaction/dissatisfaction and complaints by considering the difference between expectations and disconfirmation. Erevelles and Leavitt (1992) posit that the *expectancy-disconfirmation* (ED) paradigm has dominated consumer satisfaction/dissatisfaction research since its emergence as a legitimate field of inquiry in the early 1970s. According to this paradigm, consumers are believed to form expectations about a product before they purchase it (Oliver 1980). The ED paradigm can be derived from expectancy theory (Tolman 1932), and, especially, the notion of expectations is generally defined as consumers' beliefs that a product has certain desired attributes (Erevelles and Leavitt 1992). Bearden and Teel (1983) also considered expectations disconfirmation in the model to examine the antecedents and consequences of customer satisfaction/dissatisfaction. Oliver (1980) established a process to describe how satisfaction is produced in this expectation-disconfirmation framework. Before making a purchase, buyers form expectations of the products or service. Consumption of the product or service reveals a level of perceived quality (which itself can be influenced by expectations). The perceived quality either positively confirms expectations or negatively disconfirms them. Expectations serve, in Oliver's model, as an anchor or baseline for satisfaction, the positive confirmation or negative disconfirmation either increasing or decreasing the customer's resulting satisfaction (Vavra 1997).

A traditional model of satisfaction by Oliver (1980: Figure 1) is related to the The American Customer Satisfaction Index (ACSI), which was developed by Fornell (1992), and roughly emulates a national measure conducted in Sweden, the Swedish Customer Satisfaction Barometer. Fornell's model expresses satisfaction as the result of three elements: perceived (ex-

Figure 3.1 **The American Customer Satisfaction Index (ACSI) Model**

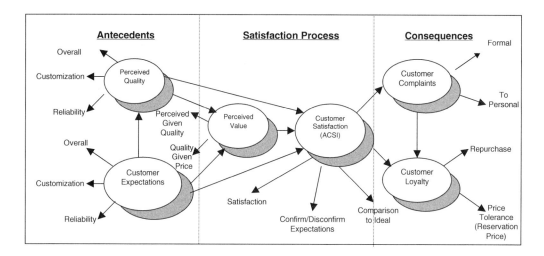

Source: American Society for Quality Research.

perienced) quality, expectations, and perceived value. Customer satisfaction models (Figure 3.1) have considered three components: antecedents (prepurchase), satisfaction process, and consequences (postpurchase). Prior experience is the most important antecedent of satisfaction. The model explains influences, such as demographics, word of mouth, personal expertise, evolution of technology, nature of competition, advertising and PR that affect customer expectations and performance. Further, the model explores how the satisfaction process subsequently influences complaining (or complementing) behavior as well as customer loyalty (Fornell 1992). Models are also embedded in the system of cause-and-effect relationships (as shown in Figure 3.1), which makes the model the centerpiece in a chain of relationships running from the antecedents of overall customer satisfaction—voice and loyalty (Bateson and Hoffman 1999).

Table 3.2 summarizes variables applied for the study of eCRM. Cho, Im, Hiltz, and Fjermestad (2001b) examined how differences in degree of dissatisfaction may occur, for many reasons, between online and offline customers. The major reasons include problems associated with different customer service center approaches (e.g., lack of an information or help desk during the order process, slow feedback response time, poor after-sales support), general terms and conditions (e.g., guarantees, guidelines for returning products), delivery issues (e.g., late or no delivery, product damage during delivery), security and privacy issues, failure of information quality, and system performance (e.g., slow Web sites, broken links to other pages).

Studies by Schubert (2002–2003) and Gehrke and Turban (1999) measured Web site effectiveness and also considered it an important dependent variable for eCRM. Various studies applied customer satisfaction as a dependent variable that affects eCRM (Cho and Ha 2004a). A suggested eCRM model by Lee, Kim and Moon (2000) applied customer loyalty as a dependent variable. The majority of studies examined Web site effectiveness including page loading speed, navigation efficiency (Gehrke and Turban 1999), information quality (Cho and Ha 2004a; Kim and Moon 2000; Schubert 2002–2003), product expectation (Cho, Im, Hiltz, and Fjermestad

Table 3.2

Models/Variables Applied on eCRM Studies

Study	Major Dependent Variable(s)	Publication	Suggested Factors Affecting Customer Satisfaction/Dissatisfaction	Comments
Hoxmeier and DiCesare	Response time	Americas Conference on Information Systems (2000)	Ease of use, satisfaction,*** system power, and reuse	—
Rumpradit and Donnell	Speed, accuracy, confidence, and satisfaction	HICSS* (1999)	Learning style preferences and user Interface with command/action techniques	—
Cho and Ha	E-satisfaction and behavioral intention to use websites	Journal of Business & Economics Research (2004a)	Information quality, convenience, technology, community, entertainment, price, and brand name factor	The study applied Fishbein and technology acceptance models.
Cho, Im, Hiltz, and Fjermestad	Customer complaints	HICSS* (2002)	Expectation of product and technology, Web assessment factors such as information, settlement, and agreement factors	The study investigated customer complaints by reviewing negative feedback system.
Cho, Im, Hiltz, and Fjermestad	Propensity to complain	Advances in Consumer Research (2001)	Degree of dissatisfaction, importance of purchase, perceived benefits from complaining, personal characteristics, and situational influences	The study examined the impact of propensity to complain to complaint behavior.
Zhang and Dran	User satisfaction/website quality expectations	HICSS* (2001)	Visual design, accuracy of info, site responsiveness, easy to navigate, clear layout of info, timely info, etc.	The study applied the Kano model to website quality model.
Lee, Kim, and Moon	Customer loyalty	CHI** (2000)	Comprehensive information, shared value, communication, uncertainty, number of competitors, and specificity	The study used a multi-phased model of customer loyalty.
Lowengart and Tractinsky	Importance of perceived characteristics of the stores	Journal of Electronic Commerce Research (2001)	Product value, shopping experience, service quality, and risk	The study applied a choice model, called multinominal logit (MNL) model.

(continued)

Cho, Im, Hiltz, and Fjermestad	Propensity to complain	Business Process Management Journal (2003)	Perceived price, information search effort, and ego involvement, the degree of dissatisfaction	The study applied product category (non-sensory vs. sensory product) in the online environment.
Dutta and Segev	Customer relationship	HICSS* (1999)	Interactivity, connectivity, product, price, promotion, and placement	—
Li, Kuo, & Russell	Online consumer behavior	Journal of Computer-Mediated Communication (1999)	Communication, distribution, and accessibility utilities, and four types of shopping orientation	Suggested a conceptual model on consumer online buying behavior.
Cho and Ha	Utility and willingness to purchase	Journal of Business & Economics Research (2004b)	Information quality, price sensitivity, quality of the website, customer service, and brand name familiarity	Applied product category and different levels for each factor.
Gehrke and Turban	Effectiveness of website	HICSS* (1999)	Page loading speed, business content, navigation efficiency, security, and marketing/customer focus	The study examined experts' recommendations of how to create an effective website.
Schubert and Dettling	Website effectiveness	HICSS* (2002)	Information, agreement, settlement, and after-sales phase, community components, and final section.	The study applied Fishbein and technology acceptance models.****
Kimery and McCord	Intention to purchase	HICSS* (2002)	Attention to assurance seals, trust in e-retailer, perceived risk, and attitude toward e-retailer	The exploratory research model has been applied in this study.

*Hawaii International Conference on System Sciences.
**Conference on Human Factors in Computing Systems.
***Satisfaction has been used as a predictor rather than a dependent variable in this study.
****The study has been developed from the previous study by Schubert and Selz (1999).

Figure 3.2   **Key Components of eCRM**

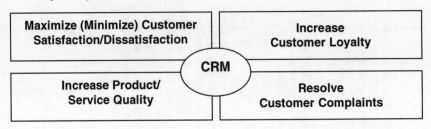

Source: Cho et al. 2002.

2001a and 2002; Lowengart and Tractinsky 2001), brand familiarity (Cho and Ha 2004a and b), and trust (Kimery and McCord 2002; Kim and Moon 2000). While many studies on CRM measured customer satisfaction, few studies (Cho, Im, Hiltz, and Fjermestad 2001a, 2002, and 2003) measured customer complaints or dissatisfaction as a dependent variable.

CONSEQUENCES OF CUSTOMER SATISFACTION/DISSATISFACTION

Traditional marketers (e.g., Oliver 1980; Fornell 1992) postulate that satisfaction subsequently influences complaining (or complementing) behavior as well as customer loyalty (Figure 3.1). A study by Cho, Im, Hiltz, and Fjermestad (2002) introduced components for the eCRM framework, such as maximizing customer satisfaction, minimizing customer dissatisfaction, resolving customer complaints, and improving product quality/customer service (Figure 3.2). This study posits that improving customer loyalty and minimizing customer complaints are major ways to increase/decrease customer satisfaction/dissatisfaction.

Customer Loyalty as a Consequence of Customer Satisfaction

Traditional researchers (e.g., Clark, Kaminski, and Rink 1992) have addressed the issue that brand switching as a result of dissatisfaction represents lost future sales to the customer, with losses potentially large if dissatisfaction is widespread, or if the product is frequently purchased or is a large-ticket item. Customer loyalty is also the additional consideration of proxy for customer satisfaction. It is defined as a combination of both commitment to the relationship and other overt loyalty behaviors (Bhote 1996).

With the development of e-businesses, "e-loyalty" has been receiving more attention recently. According to Reichheld and Schefer (2000), the Internet is a potentially powerful tool for strengthening relationships between firms and their customers. Various researchers found that the Web is actually a very sticky space in both the business-to-consumer and the business-to-business spheres (Reichheld and Schefer 2000). Researchers also argue that the Web is the medium with high interactivity (Hoffman, Novak, and Chatterjee 1995). A study by Reichheld and Schefer (2000) also argued that today's online customers exhibit a clear proclivity toward loyalty, which can be reinforced by the proper use of Web technology. A traditional marketing study by Gardial, Clemons, and Woodruff, Schumann, and Burns (1994) stated that establishing effective relationships results in greater customer loyalty and improved data on customer usage.

Various researchers have suggested factors that affect online customer loyalty. eCRM Researchers (e.g., Lee, Kim, and Moon 2000) suggest that managing communication between buyers and sellers is a means to maintain customer loyalty and increase retention rate. Studies by Cho, Im, Hiltz, and Fjermestad (2001a) and Levesque and McDougall (1996) encourage the use of complaints to improve communication channels between buyers and sellers in general, and as a specific means of turning dissatisfied customers into loyal repeat customers. A study by Figuiredo (2000) states that creating virtual communities is a strategy that attracts repeat purchasers and engenders repeat visits. Figuiredo (2000) also suggests that customer loyalty programs, such as frequent-flyer miles, are sufficient to foster consumer loyalty in the online environment. The importance of customization has been stated by Schafer, Konstan, and Riedl (1999) by addressing the role of a recommender system. According to Schafer, Konstan, and Riedl (1999), recommender systems are a key way to automate mass customization for e-commerce sites and to maintain the long-term value of the customer of Web sites. Reichheld and Schefer (2000) also posit that the Internet offers companies unprecedented opportunities for getting to know their customers in depth and for customizing offerings to meet their preferences.

MANAGING CUSTOMER COMPLAINTS AS A CONSEQUENCE OF CUSTOMER DISSATISFACTION

In traditional markets, customer complaints are considered an important source of information (Tse and Wilton 1988). Since complaint management is recognized as being central to customer satisfaction, any measure of complaint behavior should consider the degree and quality of the underlying customer satisfaction (Cho, Im, Hiltz, and Fjermestad 2001b and 2003). Research by Singh and Wilkes (1996) has shown that effectively handling customer complaints has a dramatic impact on customer retention and loyalty. Although e-marketers or e-researchers have addressed the importance of customer satisfaction and customer retention, the issues of customer dissatisfaction and complaints in the Web environment have rarely been investigated. Few studies have examined factors affecting online customer complaints. Clark, Kaminski, and Rink (1992) stated that defensive marketing is the way to retain dissatisfied customers and argued that it has been neglected as an area of marketing study.

Both traditional and eCRM studies have examined factors that affect customer complaints. Previous studies of customer complaining behavior have provided insights to businesses regarding which changes should be made to remedy customer problems or make restitution for purchase- or usage-related problems (Yi 1990). Researchers have frequently investigated how customer complaints are affected by individual customer characteristics, customers' perceptions of the sources of their dissatisfaction, outcome expectancies, product type, and the costs associated with complaining (Yi 1990; Singh and Howell 1985). A study by Keaveney (1995) identified causal factors that trigger dissatisfaction, including pricing, inconvenience, core service failures, service encounter failures, employee responses to service failure, and ethical problems.

Few researchers, however, have addressed the issues of online customer complaints. Studies by Cho, Im, Hiltz, and Fjermestad (2001a, 2001b, and 2003) proposed the model of online customer complaining behavior, developed from previous models by Bearden, Crockett, and Graham (1979), Landon (1977), Richins (1982), and Schubert and Selz (1999). Studies by Cho, Im, Hiltz, and Fjermestad (2001a and b) also investigated such technology factors as system performance, Web assessment factors, and other media characteristics as a primary cause of customer complaint behavior. Web assessment factors (Schubert 2002–2003) include information, agreement, and settlement components, all of which can be used to evaluate online customer complaints and to measure the effectiveness of electronic commerce sites that transcend traditional marketing paradigms. Another study by Cho, Im, Hiltz, and Fjermestad (2002) found several factors that affect customer complaints and suggest effective ways of handling customer complaints, particularly with different product types. A study by Cho, Im, Hiltz, and Fjermestad (2003) measured the impact of factors such as the degree of dissatisfaction, ego involvement, perceived price, and information search effort upon propensity to complain.

A study by Kelly and Davis (1994) has addressed the importance of the effective complaint management that has a dramatic impact on customer retention, deflects potential word-of-mouth damage, and improves profitability. Several researchers have stated the importance of complaint management for eCRM. In the early days of e-commerce, Barbara (1985) suggested looking at complaint management as an important aspect of online strategic marketing, having such potential benefits as maximizing customer satisfaction and loyalty, creating favorable publicity, and reducing the overall number of complaints. Sterne (1996) cites www.burke.com as an example of an online business that is considered a leader in e-CRM and improved relationships with online customers. Cho, Im, Hiltz, and Fjermestad (2001b) stated that complaint management is recognized as being central to customer satisfaction, and any measure of complaint behavior should consider the degree and quality of the underlying customer satisfaction. Cho, Im, Hiltz, and Fjermestad (2001b) posit that online customer complaints show how e-businesses handle customer complaints—a reflection of how much they value their customers. A study by Edvardsson and Roos (2004) also noted the impact of customers' complaint and switching behavior on building long-term and profitable relationships.

A study by Wang and Day (2001) described how online service quality is generated from feedback mechanisms that serve as intermediaries for Web-based information markets—in other words, how online product or service quality is used to evaluate online businesses. For example, customers can use online feedback systems to share their evaluations of product/service quality, including online transactions. In their simplest form, these systems result in increased sales when product or service quality is reported as satisfactory or better, and in decreased sales when customer complaints persist. Cho, Im, Hiltz, and Fjermestad (2002) also stated that online customer complaints, as a Web-enabled market feedback, have illuminated the origins and causes of online customer dissatisfaction. The qualitative components of this study focus on customer complaints gathered from public/nonprofit feedback Web sites and online customer service centers. This study also found that major online customer complaints and dissatisfaction have been generated from the problems with Web customer service centers. This result provides implications for how e-businesses' customer service centers should manage customer complaints effectively. The lack of research on online customer complaint management is surprising in light of the identification of this topic as a key eCRM issue by several leading e-businesses, including the Institute of International Research (http://www.iir-ny.com).

Based on the review of studies addressing the importance of online customer complaints, this study readdressed that the proper management of online complaints has a direct effect on customer retention. Complaint management refers to the strategies used to resolve disputes and to improve ineffective products or services in order to establish a firm's reliability in the eyes of customers (Tax, Brown, and Chandrashekaran 1998). Complaint data have been a key component in the process of problem correction and increased performance (Tax, Brown and Chandrashekaran 1998). It is believed that successful management of customer complaints will contribute to improved eCRM by emphasizing its value to e-businesses—that is, how complaint management can affect customer retention and profitability.

CONCLUSION

In an effort to provide a positive contrast of the new against the old, this chapter addressed the issue of customer satisfaction and dissatisfaction as being at the center of successful e- business exchanges. Further, the authors stressed the importance of customer loyalty and complaints as consequences of customer satisfaction and dissatisfaction. The authors reviewed theories and models that have been applied by e-commerce customer relationship management. Theories applied to eCRM have been rooted in satisfaction/dissatisfaction theories and theories for customer complaining behavior that have been proposed by traditional marketers. This chapter also investigated models for customer satisfaction and complaining behavior that examine factors affecting customer relationship management.

This chapter focused on how to maximize/minimize customer satisfaction/dissatisfaction for successful eCRM, because it provides clues as to what managerial changes might have induced different and more desirable behaviors, raising the issue of customer loyalty myopia. This myopia stems from believing that consumer behavior can be created and sustained in and by itself without careful regard to its underlying basis on the customer satisfaction side, reviving the long-standing marketing dilemma of attitude and behavioral measures, and the degree to which attitudes influence or predict behavior. This chapter also examined studies that address the importance of customer complaints that also go beyond the customer satisfaction concept and much more deeply into the underlying theories and models that attempt to explain why people may or may not be satisfied. This chapter suggested ways to maximize/minimize customer satisfaction/dissatisfaction, such as improving customer loyalty and resolving customer complaints.

This chapter provides implications for both academics and practitioners. Future study will be needed to investigate modes of online customer satisfaction that are proposed by Fournier and Mick (1999), including satisfaction-as-contentment, satisfaction-as-pleasure, and dissatisfaction-as-surprise. Future research exploring consumer satisfaction of pure-play vs. multichannel is also likely to be fruitful. Other issues that increase the level of relationship between or within online customers and businesses will also be subjects of future research.

Based on the review, this chapter found that little attention has been paid to issues of customer dissatisfaction and complaints in the online environment, and it found opportunities to measure online customer dissatisfaction and complaints both qualitatively and quantitatively. This chapter also recommended that e-businesses develop a defensive marketing strategy and use complaint management as an excellent competitive tool for customer relationship management (Cho, Im, Hiltz, and Fjermestad 2002). Taking complaint management seriously affects such factors as product/service quality, Web site design, and optional policies. The author believes that managing customer dissatisfaction and complaints facilitates repeat business and customer loyalty. Efforts toward the effective resolution of customer problems serve as the basis for long-term product/service quality and successful eCRM.

REFERENCES

Anderson, R.E. Consumer dissatisfaction: The effect of disconfirmed expectancy on perceived product performance. *Journal of Marketing Research*, February (1973), 38–44.

Barbara, S. Consumer complaint handling as a strategic marketing tool. *Journal of Consumer Marketing*, 2, 4 (Fall 1985), 5–17.

Bateson, J.E. and Hoffman, K.D. *Managing Services Marketing* (Fort Worth: The Dryden Press, 1999).

Bearden, W.; Crockett, O.M.; and Graham, S. Consumers' propensity-to-complain and dissatisfaction with automobile repairs. H. Keith Hunt and Ralph L. Day, eds., *Refining Concepts and Measures of Consumer Satisfaction and Complaining Behavior.* Bloomington: Indiana University, 1979, pp. 35–43.

Bearden, W. and Teel, J.E. Selected determinants of consumer satisfaction and complaint reports. *Journal of Marketing Research*, 20 (February 1983), 21–28.

Bearden, W. and Teel, J. E. An investigation of personal influences on consumer complaining. *Journal of Retailing*, 56, 3 (1980), 3–20.

Bhote, K. *Beyond Customer Satisfaction to Customer Loyalty*. (AMA Management Briefings). New York: American Management Association, 1996.

Blodgett, J.G.; Granbois, D.H.; and Walters, R.G. The effects of perceived justice on negative word-of-mouth and repatronage intentions. *Journal of Retailing*, 69 (Winter 1993), 399–428.

Blodgett, J.G.; Granbois, D.H.; and Tax, S.S. The effects of distributive, procedural, and interactional justice on postcomplaint behavior. *Journal of Retailing*, 73, 2 (1997), 185–210.

Cardozo, R.N. An experimental study of customer effort, expectation, and satisfaction. *Journal of Marketing Research*, 2 (August 1965), 244–249.

Cho, Y. and Ha, J. Users' attitudes towards movie-related websites and e-satisfaction. *Journal of Business & Economics Research*, March (2004a) n.p.

———. Consumer choice behavior on the Web: The effects of product attributes on willingness to purchase. *Journal of Business & Economics Research*, October (2004b), 75–87.

Cho, Y.; Im, I.; Fjermestad, J.; and Hiltz, R. An analysis of online customer complaints: Implications for Web complaint management. *Proceedings of the 35th Hawaii International Conference on System Sciences*, Big Island, Hawaii (2002).

Cho, Y.; Im, I.; Fjermestad, J.; and Hiltz, R. Causes and outcomes of online customer complaining behavior: Implications for customer relationship management (CRM). *Proceedings of the 2001 Americas Conference on Information Systems*, Boston (August 2001a).

Cho, Y.; Im, I., Hiltz, S.R.; and Fjermestad, J. The effects of post-purchase evaluation factors on online vs. offline customer complaining behavior: Implications for customer loyalty. *Advances in Consumer Research*, 29 (2001b), 318–326.

Cho, Y.; Im, I.; Fjermestad, J.; and Hiltz, S.R. The impact of product category on customer dissatisfaction in cyberspace. *Business Process Management Journal*, 9, 5 (2003), 635–651.

Clark, G.L.; Kaminski, P.F.; and Rink, D.R. Consumer complaints: advice on how companies should respond based on an empirical study. *Journal of Consumer Marketing*, 9, 3 Summer (1992), 5–14.

Edvardsson, B. and Roos, I. Customer complaints and switching behavior: A study of relationship dynamics in a telecommunication company. Working paper (2004).

Engel, J.F. and Blackwell, R.D. *Consumer Behavior*, 4th ed. New York: Holt, Rinehart and Winston, 1982.

Erevelles. S. and Leavitt, C. A comparison of current models of consumer satisfaction/dissatisfaction. *Journal of Consumer Satisfaction, Dissatisfaction. and Complaining Behavior*, 5 (1992), 104–114.

Festinger, L. *A Theory of Cognitive Dissonance*. Stanford, CA: Stanford University Press, 1957.

Figueiredo, J.M. de. Finding sustainable profitability in electronic commerce. *Sloan Management Review*, Summer (2000), 41–52.

Fornell, C.A. National customer satisfaction barometer: The Swedish experience. *Journal of Marketing*, 56 (1992), 6–21.

Fornell, C.A. and Wernerfelt, B. Defensive marketing strategy by customer complaint management: A theoretical analysis. *Journal of Marketing Research*, 24, November (1987), 337–346.

Fournier, S. and Mick, D.G. Rediscovering satisfaction. *Journal of Marketing*, 63, 4 (1999), 5–23.

Gardial, S.F.; Clemons, D.S.; Woodruff, R.B.; Schumann, D.W.; and Burns, M.J. Comparing consumers' recall of prepurchase and postpurchase product evaluation experiences. *Journal of Consumer Research*, 20 (1994), 548–560.

Gehrke, D. and Turban, E. Determinants of successful website design: Relative importance and recommendations for effectiveness. HICSS, *Proceedings of the 31st Hawaii International Conference on System Sciences*, Hawaii (1999).

Gilly, M.C. Complaining consumers and the concept of expectations. In H. Keith Hunt and Ralph L. Day, eds., *Refining Concepts and Measures of Consumer Satisfaction and Complaining Behavior.* Bloomington: Indiana University School of Business, 1979, 35–43.

Goodwin, C. and Ross, I. Consumer evaluations of responses to complaints: What's fair and why. *Journal of Services Marketing*, 4, 3, (1990), 53–61.

Grönroos, C. *Service Management and Marketing—A Customer Relationship Management Approach*, 2nd ed. Chichester, UK: Wiley, 2000.

Hanson, W. *Principles of Internet Marketing.* Mason, OH: South-Western College Publishing, 2000.

Hauser, J.R. and Urban, G.L. Assessment of attribute importances and consumer utility functions: Von Neumann-Morgenstern theory applied to consumer behavior. *Journal of Consumer Research*, 5, March (1979), 251–262.

Helson, H. Adaptive-level as a basis for a quantitative theory of frames of reference. *Psychological Review*, 55 (1948), 297–313.

Helson, H. *Adaptation-Level Theory in Psychology: A Study of a Science*, 1, Sigmund Koch, ed. New York: McGraw-Hill, 1959.

Helson, H. *Adaptation-Level Theory*. New York: Harper & Row, 1964.

Herzog, H. *What Do We Really Know About Day-Time Serial Listeners?: Radio Research*. Paul F. Lazarsfeld and Frank N. Stanton, eds. New York: Duel, Sloan and Pearce, 1944.

Hirschman, A.O. *Exit, Voice, and Loyalty*. Cambridge, MA: Harvard University Press, 1970.

Ho, C. and Wu, W. Antecedents of customer satisfaction on the Internet: An empirical study of online shopping. *Proceedings of the 32nd Hawaii Conference on System Sciences* (1999).

Hoffman, D.L.; Novak, T.; and Chatterjee, P. Commercial scenarios for the Web: Opportunities and challenges, *Journal of Computer-Mediated Communication*, 1, 3 (1995).

Howard, J.A. and Sheth, J.N. *The Theory of Buyer Behavior*. New York: John Wiley & Sons, 1969.

Jukic, N.; Jukic, B.; Meamber, L.; and Nezlek, G. Implementing polyinstantiation as a strategy of electronic commerce customer relationship management. *International Journal of Electronic Commerce*, 7, 2 (2002–2003), 9–30.

Julta, D.; Craig, J.; and Bodorik, P. Enabling and measuring electronic customer relationship management readiness, *Proceedings of the 34th Hawaii International Conference on System Sciences*, Hawaii, January (2001).

Keaveney, S.M. Consumer switching behavior in service industries: An exploratory study. *Journal of Marketing*, 59, April (1995), 71–83.

Kelly S.W. and Davis, M.A. Antecedents to customer expectations for service recovery. *Journal of the Academy of Marketing Science*, 22 (Winter 1994), 52–61.

Khalifa, M. and Liu, V. Satisfaction with Internet-based services. *International Journal of Electronic Commerce*, 7, 2 (2002–2003), 31–49.

Kimery, K.M. and McCord, M. Third-party assurances: The road to trust in online retailing." *Proceedings of the 35th Hawaii International Conference on System Sciences*, Big Island, Hawaii (2002).

Landon, E.L. A model of consumer complaining behavior, consumer satisfaction, dissatisfaction and complaining behavior. *Papers from a Marketing Research Symposium*, Ralph L. Day, ed. Bloomington: Indiana University, 1977.

Lee, J.; Kim, J.; and Moon, J. What makes Internet users visit cyber stores again?: Key design factors for customer loyalty. *CHI*, April (2000).

Levesque, T.J. and McDougall, G.H.G. Customer dissatisfaction: The relationship between types of problems and customer response. *Canadian Journal of Administrative Sciences*, 13, 3 (1996), 264–276.

Lowengart, O. and Trantinsky, N. Differential effects of product category on shoppers' selection of Web-based stores: A probabilistic modeling approach. *Journal of Electronic Commerce Research*, 2, 4 (November 2001), 142–156.

Luo, X. Uses and gratifications theory and e-consumer behaviors: A structural equation modeling study. *Journal of Interactive Advertising*, 2, 2 (Spring 2002). Available at www.jiad.org/vol2/no2/luo/index.htm. (Accessed December 2005.)

Mcguire, W. J. *Psychological Motives and Communication Gratification: The Uses of Mass Communications*. Jay G. Blumler and Elihu Katz, eds. (Beverly Hills, CA: Sage Publications, 1974).

Oliver, R. L. A cognitive model of the antecedents and consequences of satisfaction decisions. *Journal of Marketing Research*, 17 (1980), 460–469.

Oliver, R.L. Measurement and evaluation of satisfaction processes in retail settings. *Journal of Retailing*, 57 (1981), 25–48.

Oliver, R.L. and DeSarbo, Wayne S. Response determinants in satisfaction judgments. *Journal of Business Research*, 14 (March 1988), 495–507.

Oliver, R.L., *Satisfaction: A Behavioral Perspective on the Consumer*. New York: Irwin/McGraw-Hill, 1997.

Reichheld, F F. and Schefer P. E-loyalty: Your secret weapon on the Web. *Harvard Business Review* (July–August 2000), 105–113.

Richins, M.L. An investigation of consumers' attitudes toward complaining. *Advances in Consumer Research*, 9 (1982), 502–506.

Romano, N.C. Jr. and Fjermestad, J. Customer relationship management research: An assessment of research. *International Journal of Electronic Commerce*, 6, 2 (2001–2002), 59–111.

Romano, N.C. Jr. and Fjermestad, J. Electronic commerce customer relationship management: A research agenda. *Information Technology and Management*, 4 (2003), 233–258.

Schafer, B.J.; Konstan, J.; and Riedl, J. Recommender systems in e-commerce. *Proceedings of the 1st ACM Conference on Electronic Commerce* (1999), 158–166.

Schubert, P. and Selz, D. Web assessment—Measuring the effectiveness of electronic commerce sites going beyond traditional marketing paradigms. *Proceedings of the 32nd Hawaii International Conference on System Sciences*, Hawaii, January (1999) n.p.

Schubert, P. Extended Web Assessment Method (EWAM)—Evaluation of e-commerce applications from the customer's viewpoint. *International Journal of Electronic Commerce*, 7, 2 (2002–2003), 51–80.

Singh, J. and Howell, R.D. Consumer complaining behavior: A review and prospectus. *Proceedings of the Conference on Consumer Satisfaction/Dissatisfaction and Complaining Behavior.* Ralph Day and Keith Hunt, eds. Bloomington: Indiana University, 1985.

Singh, J. and Wilkes, R.E. When consumers complain: A path analysis of the key antecedents of consumer complaint response estimates. *Journal of the Academy of Marketing Science*, 24 (1996), 350–365.

Sterne, J. *Customer Service on the Internet.* New York: John Wiley and Sons, 1996.

Strauss, J.; El-Ansary, A.; and Frost, R. *E-Marketing*, 3rd ed. Upper Saddle River, NJ: Prentice Hall, 2003.

Suprenant, C. Product satisfaction as a function of expectations and performance. Consumer satisfaction, dissatisfaction and complaining behavior. *Papers from a Marketing Research Symposium*, R.L. Day, ed. Bloomington: Indiana University, 1977, pp. 36–37.

Tax, S.S.; Brown, S.W.; and Chandrashekaran, M. Customer evaluations of service complaint experiences: Implications for relationship marketing. *Journal of Marketing*, 62, April (1998), 60–76.

Tolman, E.C. *Purposive Behavior in Animals and Men.* New York: Appleton-Century, 1932.

Tse, D.K. and Wilton, P.C. Models of consumer satisfaction formation: An extension. *Journal of Marketing Research*, 25 (1988), 204–212.

Vavra, T.G. *Improving Your Measurement of Customer Satisfaction.* Milwaukee, WI: ASQ Quality Press, 1997.

Wang, J. and Day, R. Feedback mechanisms as intermediaries for Web information market: An exploratory study. *Proceedings of the 34th Hawaii International Conference on System Sciences*, Hawaii (January 2001).

Yi, Y. A critical review of consumer satisfaction. In *Review of Marketing*, V.A. Zeithaml, ed. Chicago: American Marketing Association, 1990, 68–123.

Online Resources

http://www.iir-ny.com

PART II

ORGANIZATIONAL
SUCCESS FACTORS OF CRM

CHAPTER 4

CUSTOMER RELATIONSHIP MANAGEMENT SUCCESS AND ORGANIZATIONAL CHANGE

A Case Study

CARL-ERIK WIKSTRÖM

Abstract: A major change agent in companies recently has been the shift from a product-oriented to a customer-focused business strategy. Many companies have invested heavily in technologies enabling a customer-focused relationship marketing strategy. However, firms have had mixed results in implementing customer relationship management systems. The challenge of managing organizational change has been raised as a potential factor affecting the successful outcome of CRM efforts. Our argument is that the proposed relationship between CRM success and organizational change should be made more explicit in order to thoroughly investigate this challenge. The present chapter contributes by presenting the results of an exploratory case study. In the case organization we identified several change events on different observational levels. Our research results show that it is beneficial to apply complementary methods in analyzing organizational change. We have shown that previous research into CRM success has failed to take into account emergent change events, and we suggest that when implementing CRM, a proper risk management procedure would help organizations to prepare better for environmental change events, such as changes in competition and in demand.

Keywords: Information Systems, Organizational Change, Customer Relationship Management, IS Success

INTRODUCTION

Relationship building and management, or what has been labeled as relationship marketing, is one of the leading approaches to marketing (Grönroos 1994). Practitioners as well as academics suggest that customer relationship management (CRM) provides an actual platform for the operational manifestation of relationship marketing (Plakoyiannaki and Tzokas 2002; Goodhue et al. 2002).

Recent studies show that the movement to customer relationship management is gaining momentum (Goodhue et al. 2002; Morris et al. 1998; Romano and Fjermestad 2001–2002), but still, after several years of implementing information technology to support relationship marketing, up to 55 percent of all CRM projects do not produce results (Rigby et al. 2002; Starkey et al. 2003).

The high risk of failure has motivated many researchers to study CRM success (Bose 2002; Bhatia 1999; Yu 2001; Peppard 2000; Abbott et al. 2001; Fjermestad and Romano 2003; Chin et al. 2003). Some studies suggest that in order to succeed in one's CRM effort, one should hit multiple targets at the same time. In their recent survey, Goodhue, Wixom, and Watson (2002) found three important targets: applications, infrastructure, and transformation. The authors maintain that "organizational transitions are the most disruptive and difficult CRM targets to reach." According to another survey by CRM Forum (Rigby et al. 2002), the majority of responders pinned the failure of their CRM programs on the lack of adequate change management. These studies suggest that if a company fails in transforming the organization and its processes (marketing, sales, and customer service) to become more "customer focused," the investment in the CRM system might not pay back in the long run. Gartner, Inc. predicted that worldwide spending on CRM would reach $76.5 billion in 2005, up from 23.26 billion in 2000 (in Starkey et al. 2003). Consequently a high financial risk is involved in a CRM effort.

Even though managers of CRM should lead and execute intentional change, the feasibility of "managing change" is increasingly being questioned (Balogun and Jenkins 2003). Change cannot be reified as something "done" to individuals, since individuals play intrinsic roles in shaping change outcomes. It is the assumption about controllability that informs perhaps the most enduring of organizational change management metaphors, that of unfreeze-change-refreeze (Lewin 1952). According to change management perspective, change is treated as a discrete event to be managed separately from the ongoing process of organizing. Focusing only on change management issues would leave out the issues of change emerging from the unpredictable interaction between IT and its human and organizational users (Markus and Robey 1988). We argue that it is as important to investigate issues of change that emerge unpredictably as it is to investigate those that have been planned ahead. We therefore decided to explore the phenomenon of change in the context of CRM in more detail. Our research question is: Which kinds of both emergent and planned change events may occur in an organizational context during a CRM implementation? Furthermore, we are interested in how the organization in our case dealt with the various change events in order to secure a successful outcome of their CRM effort.

In order to get deeper insight into organizational change, we chose to investigate the phenomenon qualitatively and selected one case company for a thorough investigation. Instead of selecting a more positivist research method, we believe that an exploratory approach would help bring forth factors of change that otherwise might not be revealed.

The chapter is organized as follows. First, we develop the theoretical background for our research. We define the core concepts and describe the results of earlier research into IS supporting relationship marketing and into organizational change. Based on our literature review we introduce a research framework, which we have used as lenses in analyzing the results of our empirical findings. We then describe our case and the research methodology undertaken in detail. Finally we present our research results, conclusions, and implications for future research.

PRIOR RESEARCH INTO CRM AND ORGANIZATIONAL CHANGE

Relationship Marketing

During the past five to ten years there has been a growing interest in studying the economics of long-lasting customer relationships (Romano and Fjermestad 2001–2002). Long-term relationships where both parties over time learn how to best interact with each other lead to *decreasing relationship costs* for the customer as well as for the supplier or service provider. Grönroos (1994) defines relationship marketing as follows: "Marketing is to establish, maintain, and enhance relationships with customers and other partners, at a profit, so that the objectives of the parties involved are met. This is achieved by mutual exchange and fulfillment of promises." Copulinsky and Wolf (1990) define relationship marketing from a different angle, stressing the role of IT as a "process where the main activities are to create a database including existing and potential customers, to approach these customers using differentiated and customer-specific information about them, and to evaluate the life-term value of every single customer relationship and the costs of creating and maintaining them." This definition includes the role of IT in supporting the relationship marketing processes.

Customer Relationship Management

Starkey and Woodcock (2002) define customer relationship management as being a business philosophy: "CRM is an IT-enhanced value process, which identifies, develops, integrates and focuses the various competencies of the firm to the 'voice' of the customers in order to deliver long-term superior customer value, at a profit, to well identified existing and potential customer segments." In the definition by Rigby, Reichheld, and Schefter (2002), "CRM aligns business processes with customer strategies to build customer loyalty and to increase profits over time," the words *technology* and *software* are absent. However, evidently CRM is seen as the bundling of customer strategy and processes, supported by the relevant software, for the purpose of improving customer loyalty and, eventually, corporate profitability. In this definition, which we have adopted for our research, we can observe the underlining of the alignment of all three components: business strategy (i.e., relationship marketing strategy), processes which support this strategy, and IT.

The IT component of CRM or the CRM technical architecture can include many applications, performing both analytical and operational functions. In our study we have adopted the CRM technical architecture from Goodhue et al. (2002).

On the analytical side, a data warehouse typically maintains historical data that support generic applications, such as reporting, queries, online analytical processing, and data mining, as well as specific applications, such as campaign management, churn analysis, propensity scoring, and customer profitability analysis. On the operational side, data must be captured, integrated, and stored from all in-bound touch points, including the Web, call centers, sales force, and ATMs. This data may be augmented with external demographic data. Current data can be maintained in an operational data store that supports operational applications, such as email, direct mail, telemarketing, and customer support. An additional example of an operational application is sales pipeline management. The purpose of a sales pipeline is to manage all sales activities, especially those related to sales opportunities and offers. A sales pipeline helps sales management to forecast the probability of future sales. It produces data to the analytical side as well.

Identified Problem Areas of CRM Success

There are many practitioner-oriented reports (Rigby et al. 2002; Starkey et al. 2002; Plakoyiannaki and Tzokas 2002; Yu 2001; Bose 2002) as to why CRM fails. However, very little academic research has been published on factors affecting the success of CRM. The study of 13 cases conducted by Fjermestad and Romano (2003) showed that organizations need to design and implement CRM systems to review and apply the principles of usability and resistance. The authors maintain that "the key reasons for successful CRM implementations were that the organizations focus on people and iterative, incremental approaches." According to a recent account of problem areas in CRM success, Rigby, Reichheld, and Schefter (2002) list four problem areas out of which two, "the implementing of CRM system before a business strategy has been created" and "rolling out CRM before changing the company's organization," relate directly to organizational change issues.

Table 4.1

CRM Success Factors and Potential Risks of Failure

Paper	Details of CRM Success Factors and Potential Risks of Failure
Fjermestad and Romano (2003)	Usability Resistance
Rigby, Reichheld, and Schefter (2002)	Implementing of CRM system before a business strategy has been created Rolling out CRM before changing the company's organization Assuming that more CRM technology is better Relationships are two-way streets
Corner and Hinton (2002)	Politics and vested interests Need for mobility Inadequate funding
Colgate and Danaher (2000)	Importance of internal marketing Employee empowerment Profitable target segments Business strategy emphasizing service Sufficient levels of involvement High experience or credence qualities Ability to calculate relationship performance
Plakoyiannaki and Tzokas (2002)	Lack of learning and market orientation capabilities Lack of integration capabilities Lack of analytical capabilities Lack of operational capabilities Lack of direction capabilities

According to a survey by CRM Forum (in Rigby, Reichheld, and Schefter 2002), 87 percent of the interviewees pinned the failure of their CRM programs on the lack of adequate change management. Corner and Hinton (2002) examined the implementation risks and relationship dynamics in a case company and found that politics and vested interests, the need for mobility, and inadequate funding were the most common risk categories. To avoid the risk of failure, Colgate and Danaher (2000) point out the importance of internal marketing and employee empowerment, profitable target segments, a business strategy emphasizing service, sufficient levels of involvement, high experience or credence qualities (greater risk and uncertainty), and the ability to calculate relationship performance.

Based on our analysis of the literature on CRM success, we chose to select organizational change as the main focus of our empirical investigation. Organizational change in the CRM context has not been widely investigated empirically in studies that we analyzed. Chin et al. (2003) do investigate change in the CRM implementation context using a positivist approach. They describe CRM implementation as a change process and show it to be of a teleological nature (see Van de Ven and Poole 1995). In the following section we introduce relevant previous research into organizational change.

Research into Organizational Change

Research into organizational change has a long history in organization science (Markus and Robey 1988; Van de Ven and Poole 1995; Clemons et al. 1995; Orlikowski 1995; Feldman 2000; Tsoukas and Chi, 2002; Munkvold 2001). Van de Ven and Poole (1995) introduce four basic theories for explaining processes of change in organizations: life cycle, teleology, dialectics, and evolution. These four theories represent different sequences of change events that are driven by different conceptual motors and operate at different organizational levels. Van de Ven and Poole have defined the core concepts of change processes as follows: *process* is the progression of events in an organizational entity's existence over time; *change*, one type of event, is an empirical observation of difference in form, quality, or state over time in an organizational entity; *entity* may be an individual's job, a work group, an organizational strategy, a program, a product, or the overall organization.

Tsoukas and Chia (2002) set out to offer an account of organizational change on its own terms—to treat change as a normal condition of organizational life. Buchanan (2001) considers the methodological implications arising from competing narratives of an organizational change process and demonstrates polyvocality of organizational change research.

Henderson and Venkatraman (1993) have formulated the well-known and much-referred-to model of strategic alignment. The authors argue that the inability to realize the value of IT investments is due partly to the lack of alignment between the business and IT strategies of organizations. Strategic alignment is not an event, but a process of continuous adaptation and change. Another interesting and recent way of conceiving organizational change management has been to see the change process as a process of knowledge generation (Balogun and Jenkins 2003).

Orlikowski (1995 and 1996) examined the use of a groupware technology and found that the customer support department realized many organizational changes that altered the nature and distribution of work, forms of collaboration, utilization and dissemination of knowledge, and coordination with internal and external units. Orlikowski (1996) outlined a perspective on organizational transformation which proposes change as endemic to the practice of organizing and hence as enacted through the situated practices of organizational actors as they improvise, innovate, and adjust their work routines over time.

Markus and Robey (1988) discussed how the so-called technological and organizational imperative perspectives have dominated research related to the development and implementation of IT and the related organizational change. These perspectives delineate clear cause-effect relationships between technology and organization. Technology is, according to the technological imperative perspective, viewed as an exogenous force, which determines or strongly constrains the behavior of individuals and organizations (Markus and Robey 1988). The view that "human actors design information systems to satisfy organizational needs for information" again represents the organizational imperative perspective. However, during later years there has been an increasing focus on different variants of the emergent perspective, viewing the organizational change as emerging from the unpredictable interaction between IT and its organizational users (Munkvold 2001).

An important example of a 'different' voice is Czarniawska and Sevon's (1996) analysis of change as translation or the materialization of ideas into objects and practices. Drawing on what they describe as Scandinavian institutionalism, their explicit aim is to transcend the conventional oppositions between stability and change; planned and emergent (adaptive) change; or imitation (old) and innovation (new). Change is seen as the result of intentions, random events, and institutional norms. Attention is focused on the construction (or translation) of meaning, as in the translation of ideas to fit problems, regardless of their form (see Sturdey and Grey 2003).

As an approach to studying the processes of organizational change, organizational discourse analysis has gained popularity in recent years (see Doolin 2003). Within this approach to organizational change are a number of streams: functional, interpretive, and critical perspectives on

Figure 4.1   **A Framework for Studying Organizational Change and CRM Success**

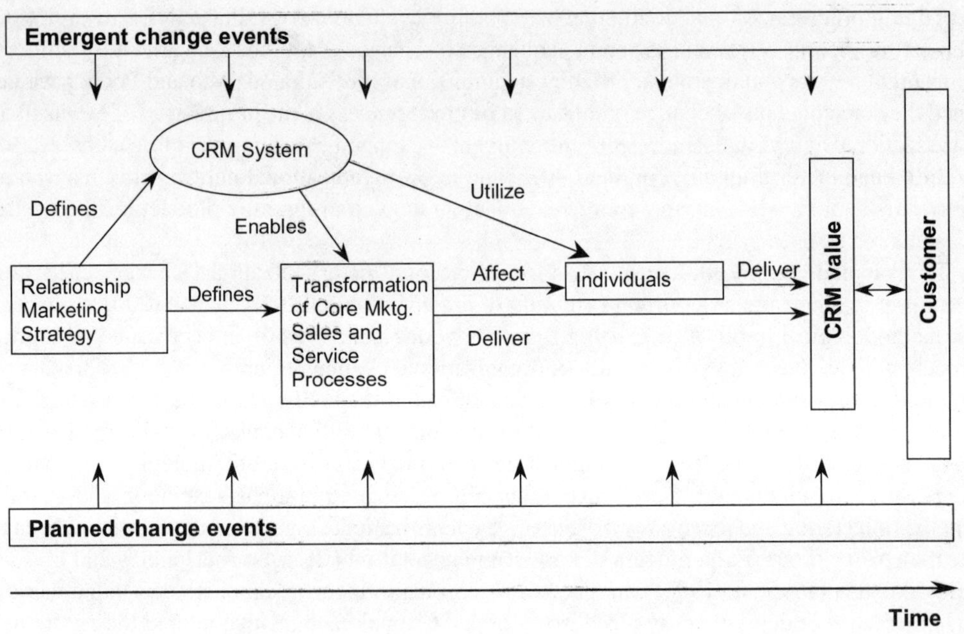

discourse (Doolin 2003). The functional perspective focuses on the instrumental use of language-based communication by social actors. The interpretive stream of discourse analysis sees language as a symbolic medium through which social reality is constructed. Czarniawska (1996) is one of the advocates of this interpretive perspective. The critical form of organizational discourse analysis is concerned with power, and explores how individual actors are constituted as subjects through the reproduction of discourses that have deep political implications.

Inspired by Markus and Robey (1988), we chose to observe both planned and emergent change events, and analyzed the change phenomenon at three levels: the environmental (markets, competition, societal issues like legislation), organizational, and individual levels. Furthermore, mainly based on Doolin (2003), we applied the interpretive method and observed the potential stories, metaphors, and humor expressed by the interviewees in order to help in constructing meaning in organizational change.

Organizational Change and CRM Success: A Research Framework

Goodhue et al. (2002) note that "in general, changing the technology without transforming the organization often leads to less-than-optimal results. Companies may need to develop a customer-centric culture, hire personnel with the vision and skills needed to implement and practice CRM and change business processes, organizational structures and reward systems." If, for instance, the sales people, as a result of inadequate training, unsatisfactory reward system, or incomplete restructuring of sales processes, refuse or are unable to use the CRM system, customer knowledge acquisition might suffer significantly. The company might therefore fail in gaining an up-to-date customer database, which would contain all the transactions that salespeople would otherwise have stored as a result of their personal interactions with customers. Ultimately the customer database might degrade and become practically useless.

In order to help in analyzing the research results, we constructed a research framework (Figure 4.1), which is mainly based on the research findings by Rigby et al. (2002), Starkey and Woodcock (2002), and Wigand (1997).

Our research framework contains the presumption that a company first needs a clear relationship marketing strategy to become customer focused. In order to be able to implement this strategy, a company needs to transform its core marketing, sales, and customer service processes. This transformation of processes again has effects on individuals (changes in reward system, changes in job division). As an enabler to these new customer-focused processes there is the CRM system, which will be implemented in coordination with the transformation of processes and utilized by organizational actors (sales people, marketing professionals). Along the way of implementing this new strategy, the organization is likely to face emergent as well as planned change events (triggered by putting the relationship marketing strategy into action).

The framework implies some causal relationships between various entities, but our main purpose here is not to search for evidence on whether some of these relationships do or do not exist in our case company. The motivation is to give the reader a clearer view of the potential change entities. We use this framework as lenses when we try to find answers to questions like: What types of organizational change events, both intentional and emergent, may occur in a CRM implementation? How in practice have these change events been dealt with in our case company? How did our case company succeed in the transformation of its key marketing, sales, and customer service processes? In the next two sections we shall introduce our case company and present the research methodology.

RESEARCH SETTING AND METHODOLOGY

Site

We selected Tieto-X Plc for our study for three reasons. First, the company operates very closely with its customers. Tieto-X is Finland's leading contract work solutions company specializing in IT expertise.

Most of its revenue comes from contract work services supplied by software designers and programmers, who often work inside the customer's premises, and who participate in the customer's IT development project as if the customer firm had employed them. It is therefore crucial that the customer also has access to Tieto-X's operational system in order to follow up the progress of an IT project, control its task-related transactions, and have access to all other information connected to the history of the cooperation with Tieto-X. Second, Tieto-X has over 120 Finnish companies and organizations as customers, including industry leaders from various business sectors—for example, from finance, public administration, trade and industry, telecom and media. Many of them, such as Nokia, have a demand for advanced electronic interconnection with their IT suppliers. They are willing to participate in the development of new and innovative technologies to streamline and enhance supplier–customer interaction in general. Third, by selecting Tieto-X for the study, we gained the opportunity, in the case company, to take on the role of actors in the implementation process of a new CRM solution. We acted as a consultant to Tieto-X's project group and we were also nominated to the steering group of the implementation project. This gave us the unique opportunity to observe in a more insightful way the multifaceted phenomenon of organizational change.

Tieto-X's turnover in 2002 was EUR 17.3 million and its operating profit EUR 2 million. The entire turnover was generated in Finland. Tieto-X has its headquarters in Helsinki and six local offices in other regions of Finland. The number of personnel is close to 270. Tieto-X was listed on the HEX Helsinki Exchanges NM-list in the autumn of 1999. Since Tieto-X's founding in 1995 (the first year's turnover was 0.59 million EUR) it has grown as fast or even faster than many other global and domestic IT companies. Tieto-X reached its best year—in terms of revenue figures—in 2001, when the turnover reached 21.39 million EUR. For Tieto-X, as well as for many other IT companies worldwide, year 2002 brought a slowdown due to a decrease in demand for IT services both globally and locally. The company's turnover declined by 19 percent. None-theless, Tieto-X has retained its profitability.

DATA COLLECTION AND ANALYSIS

We chose to conduct a single case study "which focuses on understanding the dynamics present within a single setting" (Eisenhardt 1989). Related to the differences in research approaches rep-resented by Deetz (1996), we leaned toward the *local/emergent approach*. We first constructed a research protocol. We then chose to focus on gathering data of organizational change events related to both the project of the CRM application implementation and the process of implement-ing a relationship-marketing strategy. We used various methods and sources for data gathering. We conducted person-to-person interviews and interviewed members of the business manage-ment (CEO), marketing people (chief marketing executive, key account managers), members of the sales organization (salespeople, sales assistants), as well as IT experts (CRM project manager, CIO, members of the CRM software vendor's project group). We used documents extensively (annual company reports, process descriptions, CRM project requirements definition reports, CRM implementation project memoranda) and utilized our own side notes.

We interviewed persons, asking mostly questions related to the phenomenon of change. We followed the logic of first asking an open-ended question, "Have you experienced any changes during the CRM systems implementation project?" If the answer was "Yes," we asked for some clarification with more detailed questions, such as: "Would you please describe in more detail the changes on the individual level, which you mentioned you have experienced?" All interviews were recorded and transcribed. A total of twelve interviews were conducted during the period of December 2002 through September 2003. Each interview lasted from 30 to 120 minutes. Several meetings and recheckings with the interviewees were conducted during the process, in order to clarify our understanding of the topics that arose when we analyzed the material. In this research we chose to operationalize the definitions of *process, change events,* and *entity* from Van de Ven and Poole (1995).

First, we used our framework in order to connect all the different change events found in the material to the respective entities in our framework. An example of an answer that led us in this analysis to locate a change event is: "Well, in the situation in the autumn of the year 2000, and in the winter of the year 2001, you could see that the big things were over, and now you had to sort of turn around the whole sales organization from being a recruiting organization, which just needed to recruit more IT experts, to become a customer-oriented sales organization working on the front line." These types of answers led us to categorize this particular change event to be emergent by its nature and to belong to both process and individual entities in our framework.

In order to be able to distinguish minor from major change entities we compared the answers of different individuals, and when we could determine that several of the interviewees had men-tioned the same change entity, we interpreted it as a major change event and listed it in Table 4.2. Then we arranged the observed change events of these entities into chronological order and lo-cated them on some of the observational levels (environmental, organizational, and individual).

In Table 4.2 we have gathered the results of our inquiry by listing the change events and the observational level at which they were identified. The table also includes the notion of whether the event was by its nature an emergent or a planned one.

Second, we analyzed the recorded interviews in order to find any discursive elements such as stories, metaphors, and humor that might help us in constructing meaning in organizational change.

Results

In the year 2000 a project group was established in Tieto-X to evaluate the present systems portfolio and to define systems requirements for the total renewal of both financial and operational systems. The main reason for starting a total systems renewal process was rapid growth, due mainly to several acquisitions during the years 2000–2002. In the year 2000 alone, three major IT expertise companies were merged with Tieto-X. Tieto-X did not have applications flexible enough to meet the growing need for future development and growth. A project leader, who was formerly a partner in one of the IT companies that Tieto-X had bought, and who had long experience in systems development on financial, human relations, and operational systems areas, led the IT development group. The group received commissioning from the company's board of directors. The growth through mergers brought differing company cultures into Tieto-X's organization. The development group therefore decided to go through a total concept and process redefinition endeavor, the aim being to unify the disperse concepts and business processes derived from the merged companies.

A major enabler for the growth of Tieto-X during the late nineties was the market factor of the Year 2000 modification effort. Most of the Year 2000 problems tackled old legacy systems (e.g., Cobol or RPGII based). Many of the merged companies had precisely this expertise. Another environmental market factor supporting growth was the fact that Finland became a member of the European monetary union (EMU) in 2002. This secured a high demand for Tieto-X's services.

Due to the rapid growth through acquisitions, Tieto-X did not have a central, unified customer repository. All information on a customer relationship was dispersed in Excel files or files used by stand-alone applications. Most importantly, the information on customer contracts was not readily available in the "front end" (for those servicing and contacting the customer). The CRM solution was bought as a packaged software. Tieto-X chose to buy a program called "Major Blue Marketing" from the Finnish software vendor Major Blue Ltd. The CRM package was integrated with both the HRM and financial systems in order to streamline competence and customer data management.

The customer relationship management system was scheduled to be implemented in the beginning of 2002 and targeted to be in production use by early 2003. The CRM project was started by requirements definition in 2001, continuing through 2002. Existing marketing processes were identified and described. Sales process ("customer acquisition and customer retention") and customer development process ("customer relationship growth process") were identified as key processes. Management of IT expertise/competence information process and operational customer relationship management process (invoicing and sales reporting) were defined as supporting processes. Compared with the CRM technical architecture described in Figure 4.1, Tieto-X brought the operational requirements of a new CRM system to the fore. The analytical functionality was to be designed in the second development cycle.

An important requirement for the new CRM system was the sales pipeline management. Sales pipeline included data from the stock of orders as well as from the stock of offers. To get online data from a stock of orders/contracts required the new CRM system. All customer contracts would be stored in this new customer repository instead of in the old offline Excel files. The manage-

Table 4.2

Change Events on Different Observational Levels

Environmental change event	E = emergent P = planned	Organizational change event	E = emergent P = planned	Individual change event	E = emergent P = planned
Year 2000 phenomenon	E	Firm mergers and merging of different company cultures	P	Change in job descriptions	P
Finland joining EMU caused increase in demand for IT services	E	Change of business strategy to become customer-focused	P	New division of tasks	P
Intensified competition by foreign companies	E	New product/service portfolio was developed	P	Increase in turnover of salespeople	E
		New incentive program was introduced	P	Demand for new competencies	E
		Turnover of members of top management	E		
		CRM implementation	P		

ment of the stock of offers required the new CRM system, too. Salespeople now had to store all their offers in the new CRM system. A pipeline sales report was tailored to report total sales value of contracts on stock, sales estimates, and a timeline, and to calculate quarterly sales figures. A comparison with figures from the corresponding period of the previous year was also calculated. In addition to the customer basic data, a CRM database was designed to provide a history of all customer transactions, both inbound and outbound, such as sales and service contacts, offers, contracts, and past sales history.

Most of the change at the environmental level was connected to the "Year 2000" phenomenon, and the fact that Finland joined EMU. Both of these change events offered the company many opportunities for increased business. At the same time, they, together with the company's planned strategy for increasing growth, were the seeds for planned organizational change. Intensified competition, which was due to foreign companies entering the Finnish market, was an additional emergent change event.

However, in the autumn of 2000 and early 2001, demand for expertise regarding the Year 2000 and especially EMU modifications declined. This compelled the management of Tieto-X to change their business strategy from a product-oriented to a customer-oriented one. Formerly Tieto-X had been a recruiting organization. In the late nineties the focus had been on finding resources to fill the ever-increasing demand. Now, when demand declined, a transformation of the organization from an order-intake organization to a customer-centric one was inevitable. The change agent in these planned change events was the declining demand—another emergent market factor external to the company.

In the winter of 2000 four companies were bought and merged with Tieto-X. This meant an increase of 90 employees, and it also meant that the different company cultures and ways of doing things had to be unified and aligned. At the same time, triggered by the decline in demand, the management started a planned change project to transform the organizational structure to become more customer focused. Organization was divided into business units, each focusing on a particular customer segment. Each salesperson received dedicated customer relationships to manage, as well as dedicated branches of industry to serve. A new product/service portfolio was developed. In addition to the contract work services supplied by software designers and programmers, the company is currently developing new software subcontracting services and IT personnel outsourcing services.

As an agent in these planned change events, there is first of all the increase in competition. Contract work services offerings did not satisfy the need for growth, due to foreign companies starting to establish their presence in Finland. The chosen strategy to strengthen customer relationships toward "partnerships," which demands broader IT expertise and service portfolio, was another change agent. The management reacted to the emergent events by several planned ones. The management reconstructed the division of tasks and sales processes. Also, the incentive program for salespeople was changed. Formerly, the salespeople were rewarded on the amount of revenue they generated from their customers. If somebody had a long-lasting customer relationship with, for example, Nokia, and the customer had to invest in the year 2000 and the EMU modifications of its legacy systems, the salesperson could rely on a steady income without needing to put much effort into customer acquisition or even retention activities. This old reward model and the existing market situation did not motivate one to work more actively at the "customer front end."

Another emergent change event was top management turnover. During the past two years all members of the company's top management have left the company. Their positions have been filled with new people—most of them from the acquired companies. This personnel turnover has been seen to have speeded up the transformation process, although some failures in recruiting new members to the top management had some opposite effects.

The planned organizational change has affected the salespeople's job descriptions. The salespeople no longer manage the recruiting of new experts. This was delegated to the human relations management department. The salespeople have now been urged to be more active contacting new and old customers, generating new contracts with both instead of relying solely on the old customer base and long-lasting contracts. However, the strengthening of old customer relationships was also important. This enforced the new partnership strategy. The salespeople have to more openly store information on all their customer contacts into the new CRM database. The reason is that the new sales pipeline reporting requires both numerical data and probability value data of offers on stock. If the pipeline report does not show satisfactory estimation of future sales, the salespeople are not awarded an advance payment of future bonuses. It is estimated that 70 percent of all salespeople are going to commit themselves to the new, planned relationship marketing strategy and will become motivated to act accordingly, and that that the other 30 percent will sooner or later leave the company.

A new division of tasks and changes in job descriptions, especially task division between salespeople and sales assistants, was a planned change event. Earlier, the sales assistants had the responsibility of managing both customer contracts and offers. Change in the customer relationship strategy, change in the way customer contacts are managed, and change of incentive programs are the most important planned agents for changes in the individual salesperson's job descriptions.

The introduction and implementation of the new CRM system was itself a major change event, a purposeful and planned managerial action to support the process of becoming a customer-focused organization. In the latter part of the year 2002 the salespeople as well as the managers received initial user training. However, due to some delays in finalization of the pipeline report, most of the users could not start using the system until spring of 2003. By September 2003 all but one of the business units had the system in full production use, and management was relying fully on the automated sales pipeline reporting for in its sales forecasting.

Nowadays Tieto-X has to take a bigger share of the business risk involved in partnerships with customers. Customers' buying power has increased, and they demand that more risk be carried by the service vendor. The operational data store of the CRM system has now become the only location where all transactions about customer relationships are stored. This helps in managing the customer relationship in the times of increasing customer buying power.

After conducting the discourse analysis of the interviews, we found several interpretive elements. When describing the situation in the organization before the transformation began, the project manager observed: "The situation before the CRM implementation was simply a chaos." These words clearly describe how he felt about the way things were before the implementation of the CRM system. One interviewee's description of how a particular assistant felt about the new CRM system—"She is waiting for the new CRM system like a little child waiting for Santa Claus"—shows that expectations before the planned transformation were very positive.

Statements such as, "We wanted the salespeople to leave their cottages and go out to meet the customer," and "We are transforming from an order-intake organization to a more dynamic one, an organization which operates on the customer front line," show the direction toward which managers wanted to turn their ship—toward the customer. In this way the sales organization was given a clear direction. Expectations were now focused on increased the number of sales activities aimed at the customers and no longer on recruiting activities aimed at finding more of the scarce resources of competent systems analysts and programmers.

After the CRM implementation and after the sales processes had been transformed, one man-

Table 4.3

CRM Success Factors and Potential Risks of Failure in Relation to the Findings at Tieto-X

Paper	Details of CRM Success Factors and Potential Risks of Failure	Relation to Success Factors at Tieto-X
Fjermestad and Romano (2003)	Usability	M
	Resistance	S
Rigby, Reichheld and Schefter (2002)	Implementing of CRM system before a business strategy has been created	S
	Rolling out CRM before changing the company's organization	S
	Assuming that more CRM technology is better	–
	Relationships are two-way streets	–
Corner and Hinton (2002)	Politics and vested interests	–
	Need for mobility	–
	Inadequate funding	–
Colgate and Danaher (2000)	Importance of internal marketing	M
	Employee empowerment	M
	Profitable target segments	–
	Business strategy emphasizing service	M
	Sufficient levels of involvement	M
	High experience or credence qualities	–
	Ability to calculate relationship performance	–
Plakoyiannaki and Tzokas (2002)	Lack of learning and market orientation capabilities	S
	Lack of integration capabilities	M
	Lack of analytical capabilities	–
	Lack of operational capabilities	–
	Lack of direction capabilities	–

S = strongly related.
M = moderately related.
– = not related.

ager used a metaphor: "Now we have got the orchestra tuned up to a level where even outsiders dare listen to it play," to show that the company had succeeded in achieving the planned transformation. After the implementation the project manager used the expression, "We are looking for several supporting legs, so that even if one leg gives way, the whole basket does not fall," to indicate how the organization should in the future be more prepared for emergent environmental change events, such as intensifying competition or the growing buying power of customers.

From the brief discourse analysis above, we can see how different metaphors acted as a resource for the managers in their conducting of the planned change. Our findings of the CRM implementation get support from Orlikowski (1992), who noted that "in the early adoption of a technology, cognitive and structural elements play an important role in influencing how people think about and assess the value of the technology." A cognitive element in our case was the salespeople's old mind-set of taking in orders and not working actively "on the front line." An example of a structural element that was also changed was the old reward system.

IMPLICATIONS AND CONCLUSIONS

In order to clarify our findings, we have estimated the priority of the change events which emerged in our case in relation to the potential CRM success factors presented in Table 4.1. See Table 4.3.

In the case company, change has evolved to a large extent the way Rigby, Reichheld, and Schefter (2002) have suggested it should. The relationship marketing strategy was adopted first, and a new technology—the CRM application—was implemented only after the reengineering of sales, marketing, and customer service processes was started. Moreover, the change process is clearly a teleological one (Van de Ven and Poole 1995). The introduction of the relationship marketing strategy was a planned goal stated by the management. The change process, which was initiated after the goal specification, was an action to reach the end state: a customer-focused organization and "a way of doing things."

Emergent factors such as the decline in demand for services and intensifying competition were the major agents for more change processes. In this respect our findings are similar to those of Chin et al. (2003). As Orlikowski (1995) notes in her paper on the implementation of a new incident-tracking support system in the customer service department at Zeta: "Changes in the environment put pressure on management to improve the customer service, but it was also management's receptivity to, and appreciation of, those changes that ultimately determined the precise organizational response." We found in our case company similar management reactions to exogenous events. However, we were not able to observe any change events emerging from the situational practices and enacted by the organizational actors themselves (see Orlikowski 1996). Such an analysis would need a longitudinal and a research-in-action approach.

Our results, which suggest focusing on change events from several observational levels, receive support from the findings of the extraordinary case study of "The Colorado Department of Revenue" (Bhattacherjee 2000), where, as in our case, the initial change agent was to become customer-centric. However, even though two of the cases in the study were successes, the third one failed to align business strategy (organizational event) with IT infrastructure, and at the same time lacked proper project management (individual event). Discourse analysis helped us to reach another view of the phenomenon of organizational change: it helped us to understand the bodies of knowledge, language, and associated practices that the organizational actors use to make sense of and to control their world.

First of all, our analysis shows that in the case organization the management had decided to change the company's business strategy from product/service-oriented to a customer-oriented one. This finding offers support to our framework and to the results of previous studies, which indicate that in order to succeed, a company should first change its strategy to become customer focused before implementing a CRM system.

Second, our findings give support to our overall framework, which suggests that to succeed in a CRM effort, one should also change the processes to produce CRM value, while individuals are affected in terms of changes in job descriptions and division of tasks. In our case organization the change of strategy had major effects on CRM processes. Before we entered the field, the management had already taken several actions to manage the change. They had reorganized the sales organization to become more customer focused. Each customer had a dedicated salesman. Particular customer segments had been allocated to each salesperson, too. The company had identified the key business processes related to sales and customer relationship management. One way of managing the change of processes was the introduction of a new incentive program. Another key element was the implementation of the new CRM application. All these changes culminated in changes in employees' job descriptions and in the division of daily tasks. Tieto-X did succeed in transforming the organization and the processes to become customer oriented.

Third, we have learned that if one tries to manage change, one should first identify the change events that are "manageable." In our case, the management reacted to emergent change events by several planned actions: growth through mergers, new product development, new incentive programs, and the decision to implement a CRM system.

One should understand that, at the same time one is trying to manage planned change of selected entities, there are ongoing emergent change processes. These processes might have consequences that affect the events being "managed." Our fourth conclusion therefore is that more attention should be drawn to the role of risk management in CRM implementation context. A proper risk management procedure would help organizations to be more prepared for environmental change events, such as changes in competition and changes in demand.

We have shown that in order to investigate organizational change thoroughly, one should use several methods. We analyzed managerial, processual, and discursive elements of change. We strongly suggest that future research use several complementary approaches in analyzing change events. We also suggest that researchers refine our CRM success framework and validate its relevance empirically.

ACKNOWLEDGMENTS

We would like to thank the members of Tieto-X Plc who participated in this research, and especially Juho Karjalainen and Asko Vainionpää for their valuable support.

REFERENCES

Abbott, J.; Stone, M.; and Buttle, F. Customer relationship management in practice—A qualitative study. *Journal of Database Marketing*, 9, 1 (September 2001), 24–34.

Balogun, J. and Jenkins, M. Re-conceiving change management: A knowledge-based perspective. *European Management Journal*, 21, 2 (2003), 247–257.

Bhatia, A. A roadmap to implementation of customer relationship management (CRM) (available at http://crm.ittoolbox.com/peer/docs/crm_abbhatia.htm, accessed on 9/14/2004).

Bhattacherjee, A. Customer-centric reengineering at the Colorado Department of Revenue. *Communications of AIS*, 3, 16 (June 2000).

Bose, R. Customer relationship management: Key components for IT success. *Industrial Management and Data Systems*, 102, 2 (2002), 89–97.

Buchanan, D.A. Getting the story straight: Illusions and delusions in the organizational change process. Leicester Business School, Occasional Paper, 68 (2001), 23.

Chin, C.Y.; Ding, M.S.; and Unnithan, C.R. Organizational transformation through CRM implementation: A descriptive case study. Working paper, School of Information Systems, Deakin University (April 2003).

Clemons, E.K.; Thatcher, M.E.; and Row M.C. Identifying sources of reengineering failures: A study of the behavioral factors contributing to reengineering risks. *Journal of Management Information Systems*, 12, 2 (Fall 1995), 9–36.

Colgate, M.R. and Danaher, P.J. Implementing a customer relationship strategy: The asymmetric impact of poor versus excellent execution. *Journal of the Academy of Marketing Science*, 28, 3 (2000), 375–387.

Copulinsky, J.R. and Wolf, M.J. Relationship marketing: Positioning for the future. *Journal of Business Strategy*, 11 (July–August 1990), 16–20.

Corner, I. and Hinton, M. Customer relationship management systems: Implementation risks and relationship dynamics. *Qualitative Market Research: An International Journal*, 5, 4 (2002), 239–251.

Czarniawska, B. and Sevon, G., eds., *Translating Organizational Change*. Berlin: Walter de Gruyter, 1996.

Deetz, S. Describing differences in approaches to organization science: Rethinking Burrell and Morgan and their legacy. *Organization Science*, 7, 2 (March–April 1996), 191–207.

Doolin, B. Narratives of change: Discourse, technology and organization. *Organization*, 10, 4 (2003), 751–770.

Eisenhardt, K.M. Building theories from case study research. *Academy of Management Review*, 14, 4 (1989), 532–550.

Feldman, M.S. Organizational routines as a source of continuous change. *Organization Science*, 11, 6 (2000), 611–629.

Fjermestad, J. and Romano, N.C. Jr. Electronic customer relationship management. Revisiting the general principles of usability and resistance—an integrative implementation framework. *Business Process Management Journal*, 9, 5 (2003), 572–591.

Goodhue, D.L.; Wixom, B.H.; and Watson, H.J. Realizing business benefits through CRM: Hitting the right target in the right way. *MIS Quarterly Executive*, 1, 2 (June 2002), 79–96.

Grönroos, C. From marketing mix to relationship marketing: Towards a paradigm shift in marketing. *Management Decision*, 32, 2 (1994), 4–20.

Henderson, J.C. and Venkatraman, N. Strategic alignment: Leveraging information technology for transforming organizations. *IBM Systems Journal*, 32, 1 (1993), 4–16.

Lewin, K. Group decision and social change. In Newcombe and Hartley, eds., *Readings in Social Psychology*. New York: Henry Holt, 1952.

Markus, M.L. and Robey, D. Information technology and organizational change: Causal structure in theory and research. *Management Science*, 34, 5 (1988), 583–598.

Morris, M.H.; Brunyee, J.; and Page, M. Relationship marketing in practice. *Industrial Marketing Management*, 27 (1998), 359–371.

Munkvold, B.E. Perspectives on IT and organizational change: Some implications for ISD. In *Proceedings of the Tenth International Conference on Information Systems Development* (September 2001), London.

Orlikowski, W.J. Improvising organizational transformation over time: A situated change perspective. *Information Systems Research*, 7, 1 (March 1996) 63–92.

———. Evolving with notes: Organizational change around groupware technology. *MIT Center for Coordination Science*, Working Paper No. 186 (1995).

———. Learning from notes: Organizational issues in groupware implementation. In *CSCW92 Proceedings* (November 1992), pp. 362–369.

Peppard, J. Customer relationship management (CRM) in financial services. *European Management Journal*, 18, 3 (2000), 312–327.

Plakoyiannaki E. and Tzokas N. Customer relationship management: A capabilities portfolio perspective. *Journal of Database Marketing*, 9, 3 (March 2002), 228–237.

Rigby, D.K.; Reichheld, F.F.; and Schefter P. Avoid the four perils of CRM. *Harvard Business Review* (February 2002), 108–109.

Romano, N.C. Jr. and Fjermestad, J. Customer relationship management research: An assessment of research. *International Journal of Electronic Commerce*, 6, 2 (2001–2002), 59–111.

Starkey, M. and Woodcock, N. CRM systems: Necessary, but not sufficient. REAP the benefits of customer management. *The Journal of Database Marketing*, 9, 3 (March 2002), 267–275.

Sturdey, A. and Grey, C. Beneath and beyond organizational change management: Exploring alternatives. *Organization*, 10, 4 (2003), 651–662.

Tsoukas, H. and Chia, R. On organizational becoming: Rethinking organizational change. *Organization Science*, 13, 5 (September–October 2002), 567–582.

Van de Ven, A. and Poole M.S. Explaining development and change in organizations. *Academy of Management Review*, 20, 3 (1995), 510–540.

Wigand, R.T. Electronic commerce: Definition, theory and context. *The Information Society*, 13, 1 (1997), 1–16.

Yu, L. Successful customer relationship management. *MIT Sloan Management Review*, 42, 4 (2001), 18–19.

CHAPTER 5

SUCCESS FACTORS IN CRM IMPLEMENTATION

Results from a Consortial Benchmarking Study

RAINER ALT AND THOMAS PUSCHMANN

Abstract: Information systems that implement customer orientation strategies are currently discussed as most promising to achieve and sustain competitive advantage. Among the desired benefits are increased customer satisfaction and retention by providing personalized products and value-added services. The main technological enablers are customer relationship management (CRM) systems, which are introduced with substantial financial effort in many organizations. Despite the obvious potentials of CRM, several studies report a high failure rate, and little research is available on success factors for CRM solutions. This article describes the results of a cross-industry benchmarking project, which combines a questionnaire sample with more detailed case studies. The results show that there is no typical CRM project and that successful implementations are rarely based on technical excellence. This research proposes six critical success factors for CRM projects: stepwise evolution, straightforward implementation and long-term project scope, organizational redesign, integrated system architecture of standard components, change management, and top management support. The six successful practice companies show examples of how these critical success factors are applied.

Keywords: Customer Relationship Management, Customer Process, Benchmarking, Critical Success Factors

INTRODUCTION

Building and maintaining customer relationships is neither new nor necessarily tied to the use of information technology. Nonetheless, the use of customer relationship management (CRM) systems is becoming increasingly important to improve customer lifetime value, a metric which is believed to closely correlate with a company's competitive advantage (Winer 2001). By providing information on customer data, profiles and history, CRM systems support an important area of a company's core processes, especially in marketing, sales, and service (e.g., Fingar et al. 2000, Ling and Yen 2001, Nairn 2002). In fact, their adoption enables centralized and consolidated information, similar to the effect which enterprise resource planning (ERP) systems have had on production-oriented processes. In spite of the wide use of sales-force automation systems in sales (Rackham 1999), a Forrester study observes significant deficits in today's marketing, sales, and service processes (Chatham et al. 2000). Just 22 percent of the companies surveyed possess a uniform customer view, and only 37 percent know which customers are looked after by the individual business units.

69

A customer profiling concept for customer selection is used by just 19 percent of the companies surveyed, and only 20 percent know whether a customer has visited their Internet portal.

To eliminate weaknesses in customer contact, many companies are either planning or in the process of implementing CRM systems. According to a Gartner (2001) survey, 65 percent of US companies intended to initiate CRM projects in 2002 (see also Radcliffe 2001). In Europe, roughly 3 percent of the companies had fully implemented a CRM project in 2001, 17 percent had initiated more than one local project, and 35 percent were developing concepts for the introduction of CRM (Thompson 2001). Another 45 percent have not pursued any CRM activities to date. As Wayland/ Cole (1997) point out, CRM projects have new implementation qualities, which may also be connected with the high number of failed CRM projects (Ryals et al. 2000). For example, 55 percent of a CRM project sample analyzed by the Gartner Group did not deliver results, and a survey among 451 decision makers conducted by Bain reports that one out of five interviewees even experienced negative effects of CRM activities on existing customer relationships (Rigby et al. 2002).

This research aims to understand the scope of existing CRM activities and to identify factors which characterize successful CRM projects. Since measuring the degree of success is a difficult undertaking, a multicompany consortium of sales, marketing, and service executives was organized to determine the criteria and to guide the entire evaluation process. This benchmarking consisted of questionnaires, interviews, and site visits. The second section describes the research method and the six successful practice companies. The third section provides the results of the CRM benchmarking project based on five benchmarks. The last section describes six generic success factors and presents an outlook into future CRM developments.

LITERATURE AND RESEARCH METHODOLOGY

Literature on CRM and Success Factors

Obviously, the first requirement for the successful implementation of CRM is clarity regarding the underlying CRM terminology. There is a broad variety of heterogeneous CRM interpretations (Romano and Fjermestad 2002; Ling and Yen 2001) which range from strategic concepts such as relationship marketing (Kotler 2003) to technical approaches which conceive CRM as a set of information technology components (Xu et al. 2002). In the following, a process-oriented interpretation is adopted which follows established business (re)engineering thinking. Processes are regarded as links between strategy and information systems (Österle 1995). Three process areas have become generally accepted in the literature (Fayerman 2002):

- *Operational CRM* supports front office processes, for example, the staff in a call center (see Vervest and Dunn 2000; Myers 1998; Crego and Schiffrin 1995; and Greenberg 2001).
- *Analytical CRM* builds on operational CRM and establishes information on customer segments, behavior, and value using statistical methods (see Nykamp 2001; Peppers and Rogers 2001).
- *Collaborative CRM* concentrates on customer integration using a coordinated mix of interaction channels (multichannel management), for example, online shops, and call centers (see Keen et al. 2000).

CRM is therefore understood as a customer-oriented management approach where information systems support operational, analytical, and collaborative CRM processes and thus contribute to customer profitability and retention.

Research on success factors is an area that has already received some attention in the IS literature. An important early contribution (Boynton and Zmud 1984) defines critical success factors (CSF) as "those few things that must go well to ensure success for a manager of an organization" (p. 17). Based on the CSF methodology, Williams and Ramaprasad (1996) develop a general taxonomy of CSF and distinguish between causal, necessary and sufficient, necessary, and associated success factors. Whereas the former present a clearly empirically testable relationship between the CSF and a specific outcome (ROI, cash flow, etc.), the latter are most widespread and encompass only weak correlations. Even the well-known PIMS studies (see www.pimsonline.com) have not led to the preferred causal relationships. Therefore, the following will refer to success factors in their "weakest," but also more "down-to-earth" form. In this sense some studies on interorganizational success factors have emerged. For example, Saxena and Wagenaar (1994) define CSFs on a country, industry, and organization level in five areas: strategy, technological infrastructure, education, coordination, and culture.

Benchmarking Methodology

At the outset of the present study no specific studies on CRM success factors were available. Therefore a benchmarking methodology was chosen to (1) obtain first empirical insights in the nature of existing implementations, and (2) identify factors which were regarded as critical to the implementation. In the final section, these success factors will be linked to other studies on CRM success factors which have been published since 2001.

Benchmarking methodologies aim at the systematic comparison of key performance factors and enable learning from other organizations. The design of benchmarking studies may differ in many dimensions, such as internal/external and qualitative/quantitative design (Camp 1989). The external and qualitative consortium benchmarking approach adopted here has proved suitable for obtaining information on current practices and results (Morris and LoVerde 1993). Due to the chosen research methodology—a mix of questionnaire and case study approach—this research presents a broad and in-depth picture of CRM. Four phases were completed within the timeframe May through September 2001 (see Figure 5.1):

- *Preparation and first consortium meeting.* A research team consisting of four researchers outlined the benchmarking project and organized the consortium, which encompassed executives from twelve organizations.[1] The consortium members were required to have responsibility for customer relationship measures within their organizations. Based on a literature survey (see the second section) introduction project, CRM organization and processes, system architecture, efficiency, and culture have been proposed as general benchmarking areas. Table 5.1 shows the benchmarking criteria after the refinements and prioritizations made during the first consortium meeting. Successful practices were expected to meet these criteria.
- *Screening phase.* The research team identified 200 potential successful practice organizations, of which 120 received questionnaires structured according to the benchmarking criteria (see Table 5.1). Out of the 55 returned questionnaires, 13 structured telephone interviews and ten in-depth case studies were conducted.
- *Second consortium meeting.* At the second meeting the research team presented the questionnaire results and the case studies on an anonymous basis. These were analyzed and evaluated by the consortium, who finally selected six companies as successful practices.
- *Company visits and final consortium meeting.* The research team and the consortium mem-

Figure 5.1   **Steps in the CRM Consortium Benchmarking**

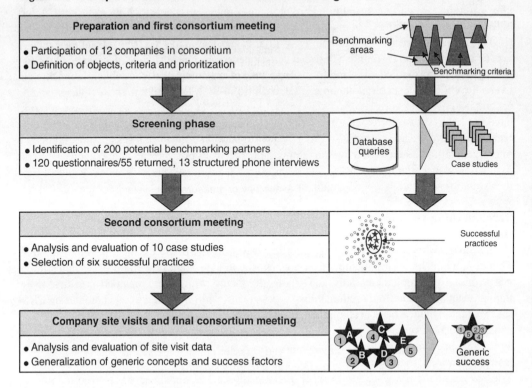

bers visited all six successful practice organizations, spending one day at each. Prior to each visit a detailed questionnaire was sent, which mainly determined the structure and the contents of the presentations made from members of the management and the project team. After the visits the results were generalized by the research team and presented to the consortium at the third and final meeting.

Following this methodology, two data sources for evaluation purposes were available: (1) the 55 questionnaires returned, which originated primarily from European companies (59 percent) with over 50,000 employees (48 percent), and (2) the six comprehensive case studies recorded onsite at the successful practice organizations. Both sources are described in detail in the following sections.

Successful Practice Organizations

The successful practice organizations selected during the review meeting consisted of the following:

- *Alta Resources Corp.* in Neenah (WI), United States, a service provider in the area of call centers and customer interaction (e.g., complaint management, lead generation). As early as 1995 Alta Resources implemented a Vantive system for managing customer contacts across existing channels such as telephone, e-mail, letter, and internet portals.
- *Bertelsmann AG* in Gütersloh, Germany, whose Direct Group is responsible for the rela-

Table 5.1

Benchmarking Criteria

Benchmarking Areas	Benchmarking Criteria (Requirements for Potential CRM Successful Practices)
Introduction project	• High level of implementation
	• Running CRM system (> 6 months)
Organization and customer process	• Customer process thinking
	• Analytical CRM (customer segmentation)
	• Customer-centered organization structures
System architecture	• Centralized customer database
	• Integration of CRM applications
	• Integration of Internet portals
Operational efficiency	• Quantification of CRM effects
	• Availability of measurement system
Culture	• CRM as corporate philosophy
	• Availability of change management

tionships to approximately 20 million book club and online customers worldwide. With its subsidiary Syskoplan the company set up a 'Market Intelligence Organization' in 1996 and implemented an integrated SAP system with the modules CRM, APO, BW, and PS.

• *Consors Discount-Broker AG* in Nuremberg, Germany, a financial services provider focusing on Internet-based securities transactions. Consors handles interactions to its 450,000 customers primarily via its call center and Internet portal. In October 2000 the company began with the introduction of an integrated Clarify system.

• *Heidelberger Druckmaschinen AG* in Heidelberg, Germany, an international supplier of printing solutions which aimed to improve the contact and direct sales to its 100,000 customers worldwide. Starting in 1996, Heidelberg designed a CRM strategy which also included the implementation of a Clarify system.

• *Swisscom AG* in Zurich, Switzerland, reorganized its customer contacts in 1998. With a direct marketing center (DMC) the company created two corporate areas which have been supported by a Vantive system for customer contact management since 1999. It handles 6 million telephone calls per annum, and 1.5 million incoming and 2 million outgoing letters.

• *Unisys (Schweiz) AG* in Thalwil, Switzerland, a subsidiary of the Unisys Corporation in Blue Bell, Pennsylvania, United States, supplies IT-services to about 220 big customers. Following a reorganization of its sales structure at the end of the 1990s, the company introduced a Siebel system, which provides uniform customer data for sales, reporting, and forecasting at a global level.

BENCHMARKING RESULTS

Introduction Project

Almost all of the 55 companies who returned the questionnaires mentioned a similar set of motivations for the initiation of their CRM activities. Among the examples are improved customer selection, the targeted use of channels for customer contact, enhanced customer value through cross- and up-selling opportunities, and increased transparency in CRM processes. Only 11 percent of the companies stated efficiency as a major motivator for CRM.

Figure 5.2   **Entities and Departments Involved in CRM Implementation Projects**

Number of Companies   (N = 55)

The strategic nature of CRM is also reflected in the implementation projects, which typically begin with coordination between the areas of marketing, sales/distribution, and IT, and the definition of common goals. In the majority of the organizations surveyed (80 percent), an overall concept formed the starting point for the introduction of CRM, which in 64 percent of cases was coordinated with an e-business strategy and the reorganization of business processes (44 percent). At Heidelberg CRM was part of a corporate e-business project called e-Forum, which defined transformation maps and standards for R&D, finance and production, administration and marketing, sales and after-sales. In the latter, CRM comprised ten customer-focused projects which were offered as preconfigured solutions to the country organizations.

An important part of the introduction projects was the implementation of the CRM-system. This phase was completed in an average of seven months and included the definition of evaluation criteria, the software selection, customizing, pilot, and rollout. Sixty-seven percent of all companies implemented a pilot application before rolling out the system. Similar evaluation criteria were used in each case: in addition to manufacturer-related criteria, such as manufacturer's vision, support, and globality, importance was attached above all to product-related characteristics such as functionality, product maturity, integration capability, and modularity of the solution.

In all organizations, project coordination was handled centrally, while less than one-third of CRM projects were the responsibility of the IT department. As shown in Figure 5.2, marketing, sales/distribution, and management were most frequently involved in the projects.

CRM Organization and Processes

CRM involves significant changes regarding the organization of marketing, sales, and service activities. Most companies reorganized internal processes and implemented them on a cross-functional and cross-organizational basis (see Figure 5.3). Remarkably, only 30 percent involved the customers themselves in the design process. More information on redesign efforts was provided by the six successful practice companies:

Figure 5.3 Process Design at the Benchmarked Companies

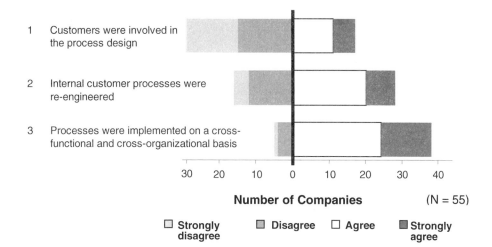

1   Customers were involved in the process design

2   Internal customer processes were re-engineered

3   Processes were implemented on a cross-functional and cross-organizational basis

30   20   10   0   10   20   30   40

Number of Companies   (N = 55)

☐ Strongly   ▨ Disagree   ☐ Agree   ■ Strongly
disagree   agree

- *Customer life-cycle models.* Customer relationships are divided into various phases, and individual services are offered to the customer in each phase. For example, customers in the service phase at Heidelberg may obtain information and spare parts through their online shop. Companies such as Consors and Swisscom link analytical CRM processes to the operational activities. The life cycle is used to predict customer behavior—for example, when a customer can be addressed via a campaign, when he or she is likely to cancel a relationship, and so on. Customers are assigned based on past purchases, volumes, and sociodemographic or geographical data.
- *Customer segmentation.* Responsibility for customers has been redesigned on the basis of customer and/or market segments. For example, a board member at Consors has responsibility for large-volume customers ('heavy traders') across the company's entire product portfolio. Unisys (Switzerland) is now organized according to 'financial industries' and Swisscom according to 'Fixnet' and 'Mobile' customers.
- *Centralized organization units.* Responsibility for CRM activities is usually organized in new organizational units which act as internal service providers. Heidelberg covers local markets with 85 sales and service units (SSU), which provide the business areas with marketing tools, know-how, and experience. A new department, Marketing Intelligence & CRM (MI-M), coordinates marketing activities and utilizes synergies on a corporate basis. Bertelsmann, Swisscom, and Consors have also established corporate centers which offer specialist skills and know-how in the area of analytical CRM (e.g., churn analyses, data mining).
- *Link to forecasting.* Information from operational CRM processes is used in predicting sales volumes and in supply chain planning. Unisys implemented a fortnightly evaluation of opportunities which led to a maximum sales forecasting variance of +/- 2 percent. Bertelsmann uses the planned campaign successes for requirements planning in the supply chain to their book stores; for example, a campaign success of 15 percent leads to an equivalent increase in the demand for books.
- *Centralization of CRM responsibility.* This proved important for achieving the necessary standardization of CRM activities. Unisys (Switzerland) had already adapted a global standardized sales process which ensures a uniform understanding of the terms "lead," "opportunity," "quo-

Figure 5.4   **CRM Systems Used by Benchmarking Participants**

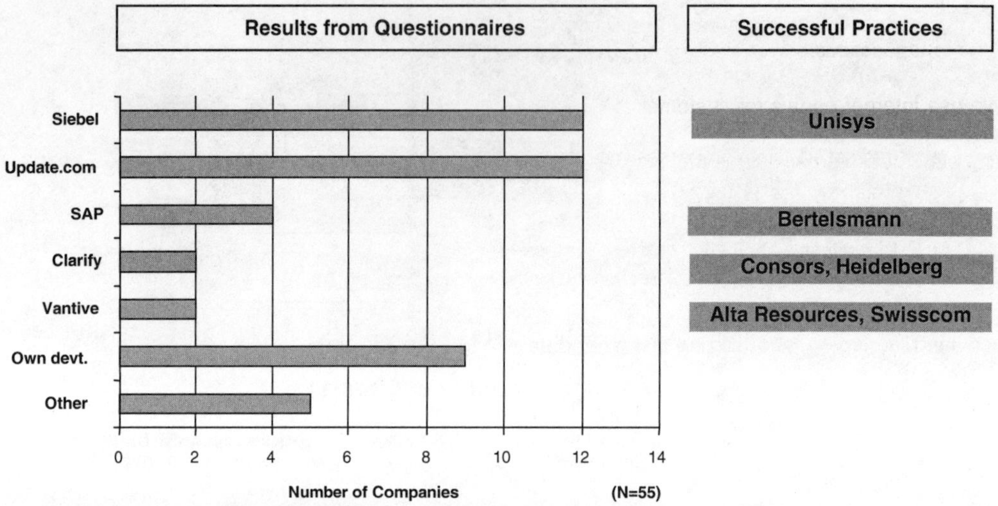

tation," and the like. Standardized interfaces between complaints and service management have enabled the integration of two formerly separate processes. Heidelberg's service engineers, for example, now know when a production manager is planning to buy a new machine.

System Architecture

CRM systems usually replace isolated solutions which support specific activities in marketing, sales, and service. A centralized database provides a uniform view of customers and support for standardized processes. Although 58 percent of all companies said they had a CRM system in operation, less than half of them used it on a cross-organizational basis. As Figure 5.4 shows, almost all companies pursue a best-of-breed approach; i.e., specialized systems from Siebel, Vantive, Update, or Clarify complement existing ERP systems. Four companies, including Bertelsmann, use SAP CRM linked with other SAP components. Although similar in their basic functionalities, the system decisions reflect each vendor's strengths: sales-force support at Siebel, service and call center support at Vantive and Clarify, and integrated processes at SAP. Most companies customized the selected systems to suit their individual requirements. At Heidelberg the MI-M department defined three reference models for a global standard functionality together with the local SSUs and customized roughly 20 percent at local level. This ratio was also observed at the other successful practice organizations (20 to 30 percent).

Many of the surveyed companies had centralized system architectures. Globally operating companies, such as Bertelsmann, Heidelberg, and Unisys, had local systems with periodically replicating customer databases. These architectures also provided integration across different CRM dimensions:

- *Operational CRM.* Operational integration points exist for human resource systems for user data and ERP systems for transferring order information that was captured, for example, from a call center representative. Integration to supply chain systems was illustrated by Bertelsmann: Campaign data from SAP CRM are sent to SAP SD for the calculation of sales

Figure 5.5 **Questionnaire Results on System Architecture**

CRM is optimally integrated into the existing
system landscape

We use internet portals for customer

The view of customer data is uniform

We use mobile devices in our personal
contacts with customers

We use a cross-organizational CRM system

We have a customer profiling concept for
acquiring, recording, and utilizing customer data

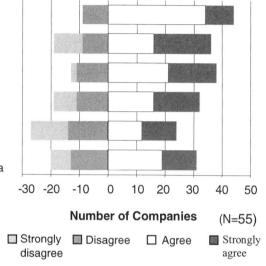

-30 -20 -10   0   10   20   30   40   50

Number of Companies   (N=55)

☐ Strongly   ■ Disagree   ☐ Agree   ■ Strongly
disagree   agree

plan data and then routed to SAP MRP for requirements and procurement planning. 'Anoma-
lies'—i.e., products where inventories remain significantly above or below demand—are
shown in the SAP APO alert monitor.

- *Analytical CRM.* For management and evaluation purposes, operational customer data are
integrated with a centralized data warehouse which has consolidated data (e.g., sales, profits) in a uniform data model. Consors, for example, has stored all its 30 million transactions
performed to date. A customer's transactions can be analyzed over time, for example, all
customers who opened a securities account in 1997/98 and since then have only carried out
1–5 transactions. The data mining tool analyzes defined dimensions, for example, compares
the characteristics of one building loan customer with another, leading to the determination
of a customer segment with an 'affinity' for building loans and thus providing the basis for a
targeted marketing campaign.
- *Collaborative CRM.* Approximately 60 percent of the companies surveyed use Internet portals in their customer communication (see Figure 5.5) for selected or suitable activities.
Heidelberg, for example, offers the sale of some consumer goods (e.g., printing cartridges)
and service management. At Alta Resources a green light in the Vantive system alerts the call
center representative that personal data have been entered in a customer's portal and that the
customer requires further information on a specific product. Consors also has a distinctive
collaborative CRM system which handles customer transactions both through the call center
and via the portal. The latter also features additional services such as insurance.

Operational Efficiency

Implementing a CRM system is not mainly driven by the possible savings. Fifty-five percent of
the benchmarked companies agreed that strategic or qualitative goals have been the main drivers
for introducing CRM. Among the effects are improved process and data transparency, better customer retention, higher consultancy quality, more targeted customer communication, or proactive

Figure 5.6   **Potentials of CRM Projects**

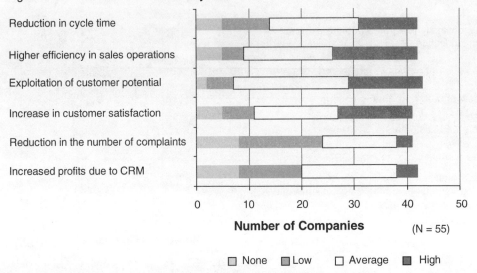

customer management. Only 38 percent have proved the operational efficiency, compared to 50 percent which reported difficulty in measuring CRM effects. Figure 5.6 summarizes the most frequently used benefit arguments.

Among the successful practices, Swisscom performed an operational efficiency analysis composed of direct effects (savings relating to operational processes in direct marketing and data maintenance), indirect effects (fewer misses, greater productivity in sales), increased sales volume and additional business, which led to a ROI of 2.9 years for the CRM project. At Consors, qualitative goals such as improved customer service were the clear priority, but have been supported by a thorough control of timeframe and budget, as well as by process savings of 30 percent and increased revenues of 40 percent. Both figures were detailed, for example, process savings with reduced postage costs due to more focused mailings (from 500,000 to 1,000 letters per mass mailing).

Heidelberg calculated a positive net present value which also included the corporate standardization of CRM systems (cost-effective rollout, release change, etc.). Bertelsmann expected improved customer care for its twenty million club customers and is trying to increase the success rate of campaigns through more targeted customer communication. Purely qualitative arguments were mentioned at Unisys, for example, the strategic necessity of systematic opportunity management with key accounts.

Culture

Involving as many potential system users as possible is vital to the adoption of CRM within an organization. This refers not only to establishing the necessary skills for operating the system but also to convincing staff that the system will be beneficial. In all benchmarked companies management played an active role in the decision-making process and the implementation of CRM (see Figure 5.7). Other departments involved included marketing, customer contact centers, finance and/or accounting, sales and technical service, and, infrequently, logistics and production.

Figure 5.7   **Organizational Units Responsible for CRM**

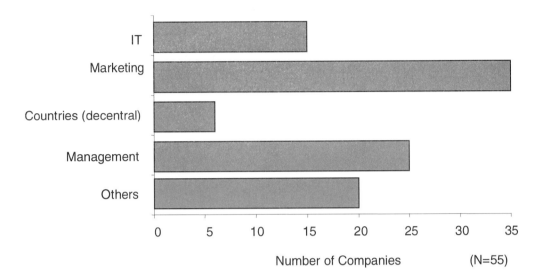

Although most CRM projects were within time and budget, the effort to obtain adoption varied. In call center implementations (Swisscom, Consors, Alta Resources, Bertelsmann) employee acceptance largely existed. At Bertelsmann, call center staff were involved in the CRM design and were able to relate to the goals of CRM (better call center support, no loss of jobs) from the outset. Heidelberg and Unisys used a similar strategy to convince field sales force who consider their knowledge of customers and markets to be personal advantages and therefore are reluctant to share it throughout the company. Heidelberg's goal was to shape an understanding that CRM is about 'a transparent customer, not about transparent salesmen.' At Unisys all staff were trained and obliged to use the system. Despite organizational rules (no budget without system entry) that motivated users, some users had to be 'motivated' with pressure, and some nonusers were observed after two years. Unisys and Heidelberg estimate a minimum of two years for filling the database with customer data. Use of the systems by board members themselves was considered as an important motivator as well.

SUCCESS FACTORS AND OUTLOOK

Identification of Success Factors

The benchmarking consortium detailed and prioritized measurements for each benchmark identified in the kickoff meeting (see Table 5.1) and guided the entire selection of successful practices. Our analysis yielded success factors in five areas. These CSFs were reported explicitly during the onsite visits at the six successful practice companies (see Table 5.2). Although the implementation of a CRM system often marks the start of a company's reorganization in marketing, sales, and service, the success is mainly determined on organizational and cultural turf.

Table 5.2

Success Factors in the Case Studies

Benchmarking Areas	Success Factor (SF)	Alta Resources	Bertelsmann	Consors	Heidelberg	Swisscom	Unisys
1. Introduction project	1.1 Introduction concept with manageable phases		•		•	•	•
	1.2 Centrally coordinated introduction	•					
	1.3 Support from top management	•	•	•	•	•	•
	1.4 Early involvement of users	•	•	•	•	•	•
	1.5 Interdisciplinary project team			•	•		•
	1.6 Appropriate selection of implementation partner		•	•	•	•	•
2. Organization	2.1 Centrally controlled marketing and sales area	•	•		•	•	•
	2.2 Organization according to customer segments					•	
3. Processes	3.1 Service definition along customer life cycle	•		•	•	•	•
	3.2 Customizing and standardization of CRM processes				•		•
	3.3 Channel integration		•			•	
4. System architecture	4.1 System selection among market leaders	•	•	•	•	•	•
	4.2 Minimal customizing of the CRM system	•					
	4.3 Comprehensive integration of the CRM system	•	•	•	•	•	•
5. Operational efficiency	5.1 Link with Balanced Scorecard	•	•	•	•	•	
	5.2 Measuring system for CRM effects	•		•	•	•	

In the *introduction project* the companies first developed a CRM concept which specified work packages and the timetable for their introduction. As with classic project management, a targeted approach calls for a clear focus in respect of operational, analytical, and collaborative CRM activities, particularly in view of the broad nature of CRM. In general, the CRM projects were coordinated with existing e-business strategies, began with a focus on operational CRM (call centers, sales), and were only successively extended to include analytical and finally collaborative functionalities. As part of a goal-oriented implementation, the subprojects comprised manageable timeframes of six months at the most. Since the first system modules were implemented in four to six months, initial results of the CRM project may become available after this period. However, the case studies showed that creating a filled and widely used customer database in the areas of marketing, sales, and service required a minimum of two years. Consequently, the expected benefits of the CRM system will emerge only in the medium term, which means that the support of top management was of great importance in all the case studies in order to overcome disappointments and setbacks. To achieve a high level of acceptance, CRM project teams were comprised of representatives from marketing and/or sales, IT, and top management. They involved subsequent users at an early stage in the requirements analysis as well as in the specification and pilot phases, since there were significant problems with adoption, particularly in the area of sales. Here again, for this change management the role of top management was of great importance (penalizing nonuse, use by management as motivator).

In order to secure a cross-functional view of customer data and processes, all companies implemented one central responsibility for their CRM activities. In all companies this resided with the marketing area, which possessed competencies in the creation of cross-organizational process, data, and system standards. The introduction of CRM had two major effects on the company's *organization.* First, a structure based on business functions or products was replaced by one oriented toward customer segments. These organization units were given a wide scope of action, so that they could cater to the requirements of the segment for which they were responsible and then provide the connection with the internal departments. The latter were located either at a subsidiary level or as a second dimension in a matrix organization. Alongside these, central organization units provided specific CRM tasks, for example, call center operation or customer segmentation. These areas act as service providers and bundle specific know-how, for example, on statistical methods in analytical CRM. Among the examples are Swisscom's direct marketing center and the customer care center at Consors.

In order to identify services, all the case examples used customer life-cycle models which differentiate the *processes* in four to seven steps. These corresponded to established approaches from Ives and Learmonth (1984) or Vandermerwe (2000) and led to customer segment-specific services through different customer contact channels. At Heidelberg, the 'service' phase no longer consisted only of the services of field sales but now also included information and spare parts procurement via the online shop. Assignment to a life-cycle phase was performed on the basis of customer history and profile as well as sociodemographic and geographical criteria (Swisscom) and was closely linked with analytical CRM. The company addressed customers with a high cancellation probability (and high sales potential) with win-back campaigns which had a 15 to 20 percent likelihood of success due to more focused target groups. In the case of companies with a high level of process integration, this value was immediately incorporated in sales planning to ensure product availability after campaigns (Bertelsmann). The prerequisite is a cross-functional standardization of processes so that, for example, all CRM users have the same understanding of the terms 'lead,' 'opportunity,' or 'quotation' (Unisys), or that information from service management is incorporated in the quotation process (Heidelberg). If, for example, a service engineer learns that a production manager is planning to buy a new machine, this information will be routed on to sales.

Consistent with our expectations, a central customer database for operational CRM, a data warehouse for analytical CRM, and the use of portal systems for collaborative CRM were the main elements of a CRM *system architecture*. Because no manufacturer covered all areas comprehensively, heterogeneous "best-of-breed" architectures predominated, which have been realized on both a centralized and a decentralized basis. When it came to selecting the system for operational CRM, a variety of strategies can be observed: from the strategic decision (Unisys) and a short selection from a small number of providers (Consors) to an in-depth and time-intensive evaluation process (Swisscom). Considering that in all of the case studies, the decision was made in favor of a leading product on the market, the success factor may well lie in a systematic selection limited to market leaders. With 20 to 30 percent user-specific customizing, the companies retained a large part of the standard functionality. Critical integration points existed to operational applications, for example, to the human resources system for user data or to the CRM system for order forwarding, but also to systems belonging to analytical and collaborative CRM. Although often implemented only in a second step, both areas were already taken into account in the CRM design phase.

All except one of the case study companies have performed a benefit analysis. While the Balanced Scorecard is widely used at the strategic, qualitative level, different criteria were observed for measuring *operational efficiency*. The metrics cited by (Winer 2001, 102) "customer acquisition costs," "conversion rates" (from lookers to buyers), "churn rates," or "same customer sales rates" were applied in some cases (e.g., Swisscom). In addition, the companies used metrics for process efficiency, for example, call center productivity (number of telephone calls/employee, etc.) or the costs of mass mailing campaigns.

Assignment of Success Factors to Literature

Since the beginning of this benchmarking, various articles on success factors and metrics have been published. This shows, on the one hand, that there is interest in the subject, and on the other that the search for success factors is in the early stages. A first category of CSF publications are general studies on the success of e-commerce or Web presences. For example, Straub et al. (2002) summarize metrics that aim at measuring performance at the user interface, such as navigability, shopping convenience, ease of use, and the like. Usually, these articles do not provide insights into how the activities are organized during the project and operation. The second category contains studies more specific to CRM. For example, using the induction method, Wilson et al. (2002) discovered the need for project approval procedures, the need to leverage best practices, the importance of prototyping new processes, and the need to manage for the delivery of the intended benefits. Based on the work of Wells et al. (1999), Bose (2002) describes more specific critical issues that need to be addressed during the CRM development life cycle. The recommendations include conducting a complete business analysis, since CRM implics changes along customer interaction points, to ensure long-term commitment of senior level management, to consider a stagewise implementation of the CRM modules, and to carefully address 'people problems' during the implementation process. In a study of 96 organizations, Yu (2001) reports that corporate culture and process and technology improvement were the "best predictors of CRM success." Table 5.3 summarizes the success factors stated in seven articles along with the respective research methods used and assigns them to the success factors identified in this article. This leads to the following comments:

- Most studies employ unstructured case study methodologies. In four articles, procedures and data sources are not specified. The remaining articles concentrate on case studies, and only the benchmarking study performed by Reinecke et al. (2002) from a marketing perspective deduces success factors from a larger total population.
- In the majority of cases, it was possible to assign the benchmarking success factors to factors taken from the literature. Where no clear assignment was possible, the success factors are given in brackets. The five success factors which could not be assigned, with the exception of the twice-named features of the system architecture (flexibility and scalability), involved specific success factors (e.g., a customer profile extended to include nontransaction data). Overall, however, the success factors taken from the literature provide an initial confirmation of the benchmarking results.
- The success factors are concentrated on the introduction project, in particular the existence of a concept and the performance of the introduction in manageable project phases. At the same time, the users should be involved, and top management should give their full backing. The second most frequent success factors are those for customer orientation, in particular the identification of services along entire customer processes and the creation of an organization structure based on customer segments. Success factors for system architecture and operational efficiency are found less frequently, which indicates a lower relevance of these aspects.

Outlook

None of the benchmarked companies had fully implemented its CRM plans. Although the initial modules existed in the form of a customer database, data warehouse, and portals, CRM continues to be of strategic importance and is being leveraged by technological potentials. The stated areas include:

- *Communities* give rise to horizontal communication among customers, businesses, and suppliers. With online chat rooms, online seminars, or FAQ forums, additional possibilities were mentioned for supporting the customer process and promoting customer retention.
- Following the Bertelsmann example, several companies are planning to *integrate CRM and supply chain systems.* Standard software vendors such as SAP are already positioning their CRM systems as a leading system for customer interaction and envisage various integration scenarios with other modules. The interfaces are provided by data warehouse and middleware systems.
- *Mobile technologies* create additional possibilities for customer contact (Sadeh 2002). While field sales staff already works with mobile terminals, companies are investigating which services can be offered to customers via smart devices (e.g., patient monitoring, off-board navigation).
- With *predictive customer care* companies try to identify customer requirements and behavior in advance. They expand their analytical CRM tools and try to analyze customers not only statically at a particular point in time but also cyclically over the entire life cycle.
- Strategies to *intensify the integration of business partners* (collaboration). This can mean extending internal systems to customers on the one hand and integrating the services of external providers on the other. Consors, for example, is opening up its internal transaction system for customers.

The aim of this exploratory study was to describe the use of CRM and to identify success factors for CRM projects based on a broader empirical basis. It shows that CRM is still at an early stage regarding the understanding of success factors on a detailed level. Obviously, the described

Table 5.3

CRM Success Factors in Literature

Paper	Method	Success Factors in Literature	SF
Behr (2001)	Not specified (consulting projects)	1. Orientation toward customer groups and segments	2.2
		2. Customer-oriented organization	2.2
		3. Selection of appropriate technology	4.1
		4. Definition of metrics for customer orientation	5.2
Reinecke et al. (2002)	Structured interviews (n = 77)	1. Integrated CRM approach	1.1
		2. Closed management loop	(4.3)
		3. Segmentation	2.2
		4. Coherence of customer acquisition and retention	(3.1)
		5. Resource orientation	1.4
Wilson et al. (2002)	Case studies (n = 5)	1. Gain champion/sponsor	1.3
		2. Define approval procedures which allow for uncertainty	–
		3. Gain board awareness of strategic potential of IT	1.3
		4. Organize around customer	2.2
		5. Involve users interactively in system design	1.4
		6. Design for flexibility	–
		7. Rapid strategy/action loops	1.1
Kim et al. (2002)	Case studies (n = 4)	1. Organizational factors (champion, management support, resource)	1.3
		2. Process factors (CRM strategy, CRM process)	3.1
		3. Technological factors (complexity, compatibility, source systems, channel integration)	4.3
		4. Project factors (user participation, project team skills)	(1.4)
Rigby et al. (2002)	Not specified (consulting projects)	1. Create customer strategy before CRM implementation	1.1
		2. Change your organization to match before rolling out CRM	3.2
		3. More CRM technology is not better	1.1
		4. Wooing, not stalking, customers	3.1
Ling and Yen (2001)	Not specified	1. Phased implementations	1.1
		2. Teaming/dealing with the systems integrator	1.6
		3. Managing the change	1.1
		4. No surprises (involving end users from the beginning)	1.4
		5. Team structure and executive sponsorship	1.3
		6. Identification of CRM 'infrastructure' projects	4.3
		7. Standards for customer data and customer processes	3.2
		8. Ability of the business areas and IT to collaborate	1.5
		9. Formalized ROI approach	5.2
Bose (2002)	Not specified	1. Commitment from senior level management	1.3
		2. Identification of customer interaction points and decision points	3.1
		3. Customer chooses the type of interaction	3.1
		4. Selecting experienced vendors or consulting firms	1.6
		5. Stagewise system implementation	1.1
		6. Data integrity and integration with legacy systems	3.2
		7. Expanding customer data profile to include non-transactional information	–
		8. Scalable system to meet changing (future) needs	–
		9. Precise selection of software packages	4.1
		10. Training of users	1.4
		11. Continual evaluation of system performance	–

critical success factors have limitations in several dimensions: (1) The critical success factors derived from the benchmarking provide only a spotlight and could be different in a future analysis. (2) The rough mapping of the success factors to similar studies in literature indicates a high accordance, but, of course, these are not empirically validated relations. (3) The presented study has no representative character.

Further research is needed to derive empirically testable hypotheses and to embed the success factors in a methodology which guides companies in their CRM projects. A more accurate examination will be necessary with broader empirical backing in order to make rigorous statements based on correlated success factors. The fact that research into the topic of CRM is still in its early stages would appear to be confirmed. According to Romano and Fjermestad (2002, 85), this is characterized by a lack of representative studies with validated tools and empirically testable theories. On the other hand, conceptual models, anecdotal case studies, and initial explorative studies are also suitable methods for young research fields.

ACKNOWLEDGMENTS

This research was conducted as part of the Competence Center Business Networking at the Institute of Information Management (IWI-HSG) in collaboration with the Transfer Center for Technology Management (TECTEM) at the Institute of Technology Management, University of St. Gallen. The authors would like to thank the staff from TECTEM, in particular Mrs. Ulrike Huetter, for their excellent cooperation.

NOTES

1. These twelve companies were: Alstom (Switzerland), Carl Zeiss IMT, CWS / HTS, Hapimag , Hawag, Leica Geosystems, SIG Pack International, SAP, Siemens, Telekurs Group, Unaxis Balzers, and VP-Bank.

REFERENCES

Behr, C. Erfolgreiche Einführung von CRM in Unternehmen, *HMD* 221, 38 (2001), 37–46.

Bose, R. Customer relationship management: Key components for IT success. *Industrial Management & Data Systems* 2, 102 (2002), 89–97.

Boynton, A.C. and Zmud, R.W. An assessment of critical success factors. *Sloan Management Review*, 4, 25 (1984), 17–27.

Camp, R. *Benchmarking: The Search for Industry Best Practices that Lead to Superior Performance*. Milwaukee, WI: Quality Resources, 1989.

Chatham, B.; Orlov, L.M.; Howard, E.; Worthen, B.; and Coutts, A. *The Customer Conversation*. Cambridge, MA: Forrester Research, 2000.

Crego, E.T. and Schiffrin, P.D. *Customer-centered Reengineering: Remapping for Total Customer Value*. Burr Ridge, NY: Irwin, 1995.

Ebner, M.; Hu, A.; Levitt, D.; and McCrory, J. How to rescue CRM. *The McKinsey Quarterly* (2002) 4, S. 49–57.

Fayerman, M. Customer relationship management. In A.M Serban and J. Luan, eds., *Knowledge Management: Building a Competitive Advantage in Higher Education*. New Directions for Institutional Research no. 113. San Francisco: Jossey-Bass, 2002, 57–67.

Fingar, P.; Kumar, H.; and Sharma, T. *Enterprise E-Commerce: The Software Component Breakthrough for Business-to-Business Commerce*. Tampa, FL: Meghan-Kiffer, 2000.

Gartner. *CRM in 2002: Redesign From the Customer Perspective*. San Jose, CA: Gartner Group, 2001.

Greenberg, P. *CRM at the Speed of Light: Capturing and Keeping Customers in Internet Real Time*. Berkeley, CA: McGraw-Hill, 2001.

Ives, B. and Learmonth, G. P. The information system as a competitive weapon. *Communications of the ACM*, 27, 12 (1984), 1193–1201.

Keen, P. W.; Ballance, C.; Chan, S.; and Schrump, S. *Electronic Commerce Relationships: Trust by Design*. Upper Saddle River, NJ: Prentice Hall, 2000.

Kim, H.-W.; Lee, G.-H.; and Pan, S.-L. Exploring the critical success factors for customer relationship management and electronic customer relationship management systems. In S. T. March, A. Massey, and J.I. DeGross, eds., *Proceedings 23rd International Conference on Information Systems*, Barcelona, 2002, 885–890.

Kotler, P. *Marketing Management*, 11th ed. Upper Saddle River, NJ: Pearson, 2001.

Ling, R. and Yen, D.C. Customer relationship management: An analysis framework and implementation strategies. *Journal of Computer Information Systems*, 41, 3 (2001), 82–97.

Morris, G.W. and LoVerde, M.A. Consortium surveys. *American Behavioral Scientist*, 36, 4 (1993), 531–550.

Myers, J. *Reconnecting with Customers: Building Brands and Profits in the Relationship Age*. Encino, CA: Knowledge Exchange, 1998.

Nairn, A. CRM: Helpful or full of hype? *Journal of Database Marketing*, 4 (2002), 376–382.

Nykamp, M. *The Customer Differential: The Complete Guide to Implementing Customer Relationship Management*. New York: American Management Association, 2001.

Österle, H. (1995): *Business in the Information Age: Heading for New Processes*. Berlin: Springer, 1995.

Peppers, D. and Rogers, M. *One to One B2B: Customer Development Strategies for the Business-to-Business World*. New York: Currency, 2001.

Rackham, N. *Rethinking the Sales Force: Redefining Selling to Create and Capture Customer Value*. New York: McGraw-Hill, 1998.

Radcliffe, J. *Eight Building Blocks of CRM: A Framework for Success*. San Jose, CA: Gartner Group, 2001.

Reinecke, S.; Mühlmeier, S.; and Köhler, S. Customer relationship management and European service providers: Empirical investigation into the fundamental links associated with customer relationship management, as well as differences across nations and industries. In F. Bliemel, A. Eggert, and G. Fassott, eds., *Proceedings 10th International Colloquium in Relationship Management*, Kaiserslautern (2002), 649–672.

Rigby, D.K.; Reichheld, F.F.; and Schefter, P. Avoid the four perils of CRM. *Harvard Business Review*, 80, 2 (2002), 101–109.

Romano, N.C. Customer relationship management research: An assessment of subfield development and maturity. In R. H. Sprague, ed., *Proceedings 34th Hawaii International Conference on Systems Sciences*. Los Alamitos, CA: IEEE, 2001.

Romano, N.C. and Fjermestad, J. Electronic commerce customer relationship management: An assessment of research. *International Journal of Electronic Commerce*, 6, 2 (2001–2002), 59–111.

Ryals, L.; Knox, S.; and Maklan, S. *Customer Relationship Management (CRM): Building the Business Case*. London: Xlibris, 2000.

Sadeh, N.M. *M-Commerce: Technologies, Services, and Business Models*. Chichester: John Wiley & Sons, 2002.

Saxena, K.B.C. and Wagenaar, R.W. *Critical Success Factors of EDI Technology Transfer: A Conceptual Framework*. Rotterdam: Erasmus University, 1994.

Straub, D.W.; Hoffman, D.L.; Weber, B.W.; and Steinfield, C. Measuring e-commerce in net-enabled organizations: An introduction to the special issue. *Information Systems Research*, 13, 2 (2002), 115–124.

Thompson, E. *CRM Is in Its Infancy in Europe*. San Jose, CA: Gartner Group, 2001.

Vandermerwe, S. How increasing value to customers improves business results. *MIT Sloan Management Review*, 42, 1 (2000), 27–37.

Vervest, P. and Dunn, A. *How to Win Customers in the Digital World*. 1st ed., Berlin: Springer, 2000.

Wayland, R. E. and Cole, P. M. *Customer Connections: New Strategies for Growth*, Boston, MA: Harvard Business School Press, 1997.

Wells, J. D., Fuerst, W. L. and Choobineh, J. Managing information technology for one-to-one customer interaction. *Information & Management*, 35, 1 (1999), 54–62.

Williams, J. J. and Ramaprasad, A. A taxonomy of critical success factors. *European Journal of Information Systems*, 5, 4 (1996), 250–260.

Wilson, H., Daniel, E. and McDonald, M. Factors for success in customer relationship management (CRM) Systems. *Journal of Marketing Management*, 18, 1/2 (2002), 193–219.

Winer, R. S. A framework for customer relationship management. *California Management Review*, 43, 4 (2001), 89–105.

Xu, Y., Yen, D. C., Lin, B. and Chou, D. C. Adopting customer relationship management technology. *Industrial Management & Data Systems*, 102, 8 (2002), 442–452.

Yu, L. Successful customer-relationship management. *Sloan Management Review*, 42, 4 (2001), 18–20.

CHAPTER 6

COLLABORATIVE CUSTOMER RELATIONSHIP MANAGEMENT IN FINANCIAL SERVICES ALLIANCES

MALTE GEIB, LUTZ M. KOLBE, AND WALTER BRENNER

Abstract: *The integration of the financial services industry and the focus of many financial services companies on core competencies have led to the emergence of financial services alliances. These alliances face a variety of challenges regarding an integrated approach to customer relationship management (CRM) by the partner companies. In this paper we describe the challenges derived from an analysis of five financial services companies that formed different financial services alliances. The main inhibitors of a consistent approach toward customers are found in business processes and information systems that are not sufficiently integrated. Some partner companies' customer-oriented business processes have only an incomplete knowledge of their customers, which is especially conspicuous in after-sales service management and complaint management processes. The limitations of the information systems infrastructure are the source of most challenges in collaborative CRM processes. The partial standardization of CRM systems in financial services alliances inhibits the exploitation of economies of scale as well as the integration of systems. Consequently, obtaining a comprehensive view of a customer relationship becomes complicated if the integration of systems containing knowledge of customers, such as operational and analytical CRM systems as well as transaction systems, is limited. An increased integration of these systems has the potential not only to improve the quality of customer consultancy, but also to foster the exploitation of a customer's potential. To illustrate how a state-of-the-art IT infrastructure for CRM can be designed in financial services alliances, we present a case study of a leading financial services alliance in Germany.*

Keywords: *Customer Relationship Management, Knowledge Management, Business Networks, Financial Services*

INTRODUCTION

During the last few years we have witnessed a continuing trend toward integration of the financial services industry. To offer customers a complete range of financial services, many banks and insurance companies merge, or launch collaborations for the joint distribution of their products. Examples of this development in German-speaking countries are the mergers of Dresdner Bank and Allianz insurance as well as that of Credit Suisse and Winterthur insurance.

On the other hand, the financial services industry is in the middle of a structural change, a "deconstruction" of the value chain. Increasing competition and customer demands require companies to focus on core competencies in order to deliver better value for their customers.

Moreover, many companies are embarking on the concept of customer relationship management (CRM) that has the potential for a positive impact on the cost–revenue ratio by aligning the company with its customers and focusing resources on high-value customers.[1] Although many companies have successfully implemented certain aspects of CRM, an integrated approach to CRM in financial services alliances remains to be developed. Most alliances confine themselves to the joint distribution of products without an intensive exchange of knowledge about customers or the performance of sales, service, and marketing activities. According to *The Economist*, "Many CRM systems used by financial conglomerates cannot even tell whether a banking customer also has, say, a mortgage or a stock broking account with its various subsidiaries" (*The Economist* 2003).

The research questions we want to answer with this paper are: What are the current challenges faced by CRM in financial services alliances and what are the reasons for these challenges? Having discovered that the challenges largely stem from the supporting information systems infrastructure, we want to answer the question, How can these challenges be addressed by focusing on the support of information systems?

Using case study research, we analyze five financial services companies that are part of different financial services alliances and present the discovered challenges and recommendations on how to address them.[2] To further detail the recommendations and to illustrate how they can be set into action, we present a best-practice case study of MLP, a leading financial services alliance in Europe. This case study can serve as best-practice example for the design of CRM systems in such alliances.

The next section introduces the theoretical background to financial services alliances and customer relationship management. We also introduce the concept of business engineering as the analytical framework of our research. The third section delineates our research methodology, with the fourth section presenting the results and recommendations for the improvement of CRM in financial services alliances. In the fifth section we show how these recommendations can be realized by means of the MLP best-practice case study. Finally, we summarize our findings and present further research opportunities.

THEORETICAL BACKGROUND

The Emergence of Financial Services Alliances

Three major trends have led to the emergence of financial services alliances. First, customers increasingly demand a comprehensive coverage of their financial requirements. This forces financial services companies to offer customer support for every financial requirement, ranging from account management to life insurance and the granting of a home loan, realizing the idea of "one-stop finance," which is also termed "bancassurance." The integration of different financial services is often realized by specialized companies (*relationship managers*) that have direct contact to customers as distribution intermediaries (Figure 6.1) (Lehmann 2000).

Second, threats from new and aggressive market entrants (Knights et al. 1993) as well as constantly growing customer requirements force financial services companies to focus on core competencies (Prahalad and Hamel 1990) to remain competitive. This development has given rise to a deconstruction of the industry, with specialized companies or business divisions (*product providers*) focusing on the delivery of specific products and services.

Figure 6.1   **Trends in the Development of Value Chains in the Financial Services Industry**

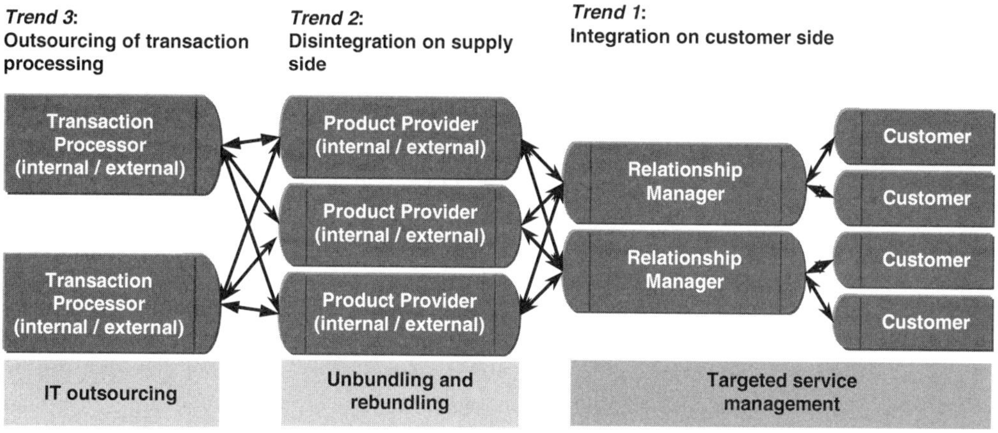

Trend 3:
Outsourcing of transaction processing

Trend 2:
Disintegration on supply side

Trend 1:
Integration on customer side

Source: Based on Lehmann, (2000). Adapted with permission.

Third, financial services companies increasingly outsource transaction processing to external *transaction processors* in order to focus on their core competencies (*The Economist*, 2003).

To overcome the contrariness of these trends—especially of service integration and focusing on core competencies—networks consisting of relationship managers, product providers and transaction processors have emerged (Hagel and Singer 1999; Heinrich and Leist 2002; Lehmann 2000). While each network company can focus on the delivery of a specific product or service, the objective of the entire network is to support customers in their specific *customer processes* (Österle 2001), for example, building a house, receiving an inheritance, or moving. These customer processes often require several financial services as well as additional nonfinancial services. For example, moving may require finding an appropriate house, a home loan to buy the house, and household insurance. The ultimate objective is to support customers in every single step of a customer process to ensure a true "one-stop" experience.

In this paper, we focus on the coordination challenges faced by relationship managers and product providers.

An Analytical Framework Based on Business Engineering

To structure our analysis of existing challenges in these networks, we use concepts from business engineering (BE) as our analytical framework. Business engineering is the transformation of enterprises from the Industrial Age into the Information Age by means of procedure models, methods, and tools (Österle 1995). To control the transformation complexity, a division into several levels is often suggested (Ferstl and Sinz 1998; Scheer, 1995). Österle and Blessing (2002) propose three levels of business engineering: *strategy, process,* and *system,* each dealing with different business questions:

- On the *strategy* level, decisions regarding the long-term development of an enterprise have to be made. This comprises decisions on strategic alliances, company structure, market services offered, customer segments addressed, and distribution channels.
- Within *processes,* strategic decisions are implemented. A process produces a company's services through the execution of a number of tasks with defined inputs and outputs. Ques-

tions to be answered in process development concern the planned process outputs, the optimal sequence and distribution of tasks, and process management.

- The execution of processes is supported by information *systems* (IS) in the form of application software. The foundation for information systems is information technology (IT), consisting of hardware, networks, and operating systems software.

In this chapter, we describe the challenges facing CRM in financial services alliances on each business engineering level.

Customer Relationship Management in the Financial Services Industry

Customer relationship management emerged as a response to decreasing customer loyalty in different industries. The reasons for decreasing customer loyalty in the financial services industry are manifold and closely interconnected. Three fundamental factors can be identified (Körner and Zimmermann 2000; Krishnan et al. 1999; Walter 2000):

- *New technological opportunities:* The conceptual nature of financial services makes them ideal for distribution through electronic channels, for example, the Internet, which then makes it easier for competitors to enter a market.
- *Increasing competition by new market entrants:* Supported by new technological opportunities and deregulation, the market for financial services is being transformed into a globally connected emporium. Non- and near-banks, for example, telecommunication providers and financial consultancies, especially constitute a growing threat to established banks.
- *Customers' changing behavior:* Financial services customers are increasingly self-confident, better informed about products and services, and demanding of services, also as a result of technological possibilities.

These factors have led to the emergence of concepts that focus on the nurturing of customer relationships (Payne and Ryals 2001; Peppard 2000). Customer relationship management emerged as an amalgamation of different management and information system approaches, in particular relationship marketing (Sheth and Parvatiyar, 2000), and technology-oriented approaches such as computer-aided selling (CAS) and sales-force automation (SFA) (Gebert et al. 2003). Following Shaw and Reed (1999), we define CRM as an interactive approach that achieves an optimum balance between corporate investments and the satisfaction of customer needs in order to generate maximum profits. It entails:

- acquiring and continuously updating knowledge on customer needs, motivations, and behavior over the lifetime of the relationship.
- applying customer knowledge to continuously improve performance through a process of learning from successes and failures.
- integrating marketing, sales, and service activities to achieve a common goal.
- implementing appropriate systems to support customer knowledge acquisition, sharing, and the measurement of CRM effectiveness.

To integrate marketing, sales, and service activities, CRM requires business processes that involve customers to be fully integrated. These customer-oriented CRM processes are mostly semistructured, and their performance is predominantly influenced by the underlying supply of

Figure 6.2   **CRM Processes in a Business Engineering Context**

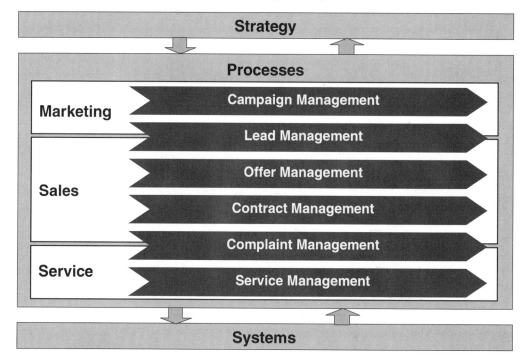

Source: Based on Gebert et al. (2003). Adapted with permission.

knowledge on products, markets, and customers (Day 2000; Garcia-Murillo and Annabi 2002; Schulze et al. 2001). Gebert et al. (2003) identified six CRM macroprocesses: campaign management, lead management, offer management, contract management, complaint management, and service management (Figure 6.2).

Campaign management is the planning, realization, control, and monitoring of marketing activities aimed at known recipients who are either current or prospective customers. The objective of campaign management is to generate valuable opportunities or "leads," which can be further qualified by *lead management.*

Lead management is the consolidation, qualification, and prioritization of contacts with prospective or current customers. Contacts may be received from *campaign management* or other sources, for example, the *service management* process. The objective is to provide sales staff with a qualified and prioritized list of presumably valuable customers to make the offer management process more precise and effective.

The objective of *offer management* is the consistent creation and delivery of individualized offers. An offer management process may be triggered by a customer inquiry, a qualified lead, or an otherwise discovered opportunity.

Contract management is the creation and maintenance of contracts for the supply of a product or service.

Within the scope of *complaint management,* customers' complaints are received, processed, and communicated within the enterprise. The objectives are to improve customer satisfaction in the short run by directly addressing problems that led to complaints, and to feed a continuous improvement process to avoid complaints in the long run.

Service management is the planning, realization, and control of measures for the provision of services in the after-sales phase.

We used the three levels of business engineering and the six CRM processes as a priori specifications to shape the design of our case study research. Our objective was to obtain a more accurate deconstruction of the problem domain (Eisenhardt 1989).

RESEARCH METHODOLOGY

Since the objective of our research was to analyze CRM challenges and opportunities in current financial services alliances, we adopted an exploratory case study approach, which is described in this section. Our approach is based on a case study method by Senger and Österle (2002), which is an adaptation of Yin's methodology (2002) for business engineering transformation projects.

Case Sites

The research data were collected in a study of five Swiss and German financial services companies (Table 6.1) from April to September 2003. These sites were chosen for theoretical rather than statistical reasons. Selection was based on two criteria: purposeful sampling (different roles in the value chain, see Figure 6.1) and a willingness to cooperate (Yin 2002). Two of the companies are product providers, one is a relationship manager, and two are universal banks that assume both roles. Analyzing the different roles, we discerned different viewpoints and consequently gained a more complete picture of the possible challenges (Eisenhardt 1989). Table 6.1 provides a brief overview of the case sites.

Data Collection

In all five cases, data were collected through semistructured interviews with key informants and a document analysis of annual reports, organizational charts, and system charts. The structure for the central semistructured interviews was provided by Senger and Österle's case study method (2002). The interview questions were based on the classification of the business engineering levels *strategy, process*, and *system* and may be summarized as follows:

- *Strategy:* Why and how do you cooperate with partner companies in a financial alliance?
- *Process:* How do you cooperate in the CRM processes of marketing, sales, and service, as well as in product development?
- *System:* How is this cooperation supported by information systems?
- *CRM challenges:* What are the challenges and opportunities in the area of CRM collaboration (on the strategy, process, and system levels)? How do you address them?

To clarify and elaborate on the case descriptions, they were reconciled with the interview partners, and sometimes required further interviews.

Data Analysis

We used a two-stage strategy for data analysis (Yin, 2002). During the first stage, the *within-case* analysis of the data from each case study site was undertaken. The objective was to build an

Table 6.1

Overview of Case Sites

	UBS Global Asset Management (UBS GAM)	HomeLoanBank (HLB)	InvestmentBank (IB)	Lucerne Cantonal Bank (LCB)	UniversalBank (UB)
Description	Business unit of UBS, a Swiss universal bank	German home loan bank in a cooperative financial alliance with other product providers and banks (as distributors)	German fund managing company in a cooperative financial alliance with other product providers and banks (as distributors)	Independent Swiss cantonal bank cooperating with other cantonal banks and product providers	Swiss universal bank with legally independent business units (banking & insurance)
Value chain position	Product provider and relationship manager	Product provider	Product provider	Relationship manager	Product provider and relationship manager
Business segments	Asset management	Home loan funding	Investment funds, asset management	Retail and private banking, asset management	Corporate/retail/private banking, insurance
Total assets	€340 billion	€30 billion	€100 billion	€11 billion	€640 billion
Employees (approx.)	3,000	3,000	2,000	1,000	75,000
Customers (approx.)	1,000 institutional investors	6 million private investors	4 million private and institutional investors	590,000 private and institutional customers	3 million private and institutional customers
Analyzed relationships	Cooperation with other UBS business units focusing on institutional investors	Cooperation with other product providers and banks within the alliance	Cooperation with other product providers and banks within the alliance	Cooperation with other cantonal banks and product providers	Cooperation between banking & insurance business units

Note: The names of some companies were changed due to nondisclosure agreements.

explanation of the case, using a cycle of deduction and induction. The validity of the data was ensured through multiple sources of evidence, reviews of case interpretations by interviewees, and a chain of evidence provided by the case data.

The second stage involved the *cross-case* analysis of the data, locating and examining similarities and differences across the five cases. In the process, the companies' different roles in the financial services value chain had to be taken into account. The objective was to generalize beyond the data and thereby discover the challenges that play an important role in financial services alliances. These challenges are described in the next section.

ANALYSIS AND DISCUSSION OF CRM IN FINANCIAL SERVICES ALLIANCES

Strategy Level

On the strategy level, we observed that all of the companies cooperate *horizontally* with other financial services companies or divisions offering complementary products. Except for the two universal banks, the companies are part of financial services alliances with *vertical* cooperation, i.e., between product providers and relationship managers (mainly banks). In contrast, the universal banks have their own product-oriented divisions and distribution organizations.

The companies mentioned four strategic objectives of cooperation with partner companies. The two most prevalent ones were 'comprehensive coverage of financial demands of customers' and 'new distribution channels and customers.' The fact that these objectives were mentioned for horizontal as well as vertical collaboration illustrates that they can be achieved by either collaboration. They also emphasize the importance of trend 1 (integration on customer side, see Figure 6.1). In addition, LCB mentioned 'economies of scale' as a major objective of collaboration with other cantonal banks. The reason is that, as a small relationship manager, LCB can achieve improvements in productivity by using the same CRM systems as other cantonal banks to support standardized CRM processes. Moreover, LCB sees the standardization of products and processes as a prerequisite to the standardization of systems, which itself is a prerequisite for IT outsourcing (trend 3).

Finally, UBS GAM sees the merging of customer knowledge owned by different divisions of UBS as its major goal, the aim being to create a more complete view of customers to better address their needs and to identify prospects.

Regarding challenges on the strategy level, three companies mentioned overlapping competencies in different partner companies (or business units in the case of UBS GAM) as a major challenge. This can lead to redundantly executed processes (see next section) with inconsistent results. Moreover, in alliances between legally independent companies, data privacy protection can inhibit the exchange of customer knowledge.

Process Level

On the process level, we analyzed collaboration in the CRM processes (see Figure 6.2) as well as in product development.

Although all companies cooperate with partners in *product development,* cooperation is often not strategic, but reactive to market demands. For example, HLB and IB offer a composite product in reaction to changing market demands as a result of changing regulations. UBS GAM jointly develops complex products with other business units to address institutional investors' demands. In contrast, LCB jointly standardizes commodity products with other cantonal banks in order to achieve economies of scale by using the same CRM processes and supporting information systems.

Strong collaboration can also be found in marketing. Most partner companies conduct joint market research activities. Some *campaign management* activities are also performed jointly, especially with respect to composite products.

Cooperation focuses mainly on sales processes, particularly *lead management* and *offer management,* where cooperation can lead to direct results in the form of additional turnover. Regarding lead management, three companies exchanged customer information—identified only by customer numbers—with partner companies to tap the potential of the partner's customers. As far as offer management is concerned, most companies also offer their partner companies' products. There is usually a "preferred provider" status between partner companies; i.e., the partners' products are preferably sold to their own customers.

The least intensive cooperation was observed in *service management* and *complaint management* processes. These processes are mostly handled by each partner company individually for its respective products, because collaboration would require the exchange of extensive customer and product knowledge, which the underlying CRM systems do not support. Consequently, a customer of a financial alliance often has multiple contact persons in the various companies of the alliance. The most prevalent challenges on the process level were:

- *Insufficient transparency regarding customer knowledge:* Due to legal constraints and bank-focused CRM technology (see next section), product providers have customer knowledge related only to their specific product and do not, therefore, have a complete overview of their own customers, let alone customers of their partner companies. Only banks with direct contact with customers can obtain a complete overview of a customer's characteristics and product use. Strict data privacy protection laws often prevent banks from sharing customer knowledge with their product providers.
- *Redundant tasks:* To obtain or update specific knowledge about customers, product providers and distributors sometimes undertake redundant tasks, for example, changing a customer's address or determining a customer's estimated credit rating, financial circumstances, and external exposure.
- *Different contact persons for a financial alliance customer* (no 'single point of entry'): Customers often have different contact persons—sometimes one for every product they own—in a financial alliance. This is especially prevalent in complaint and service management processes.

In conclusion, we observed that all companies cooperated in CRM processes and product development, with a focus on sales processes. Nevertheless, most cooperation is reactive to market demands or confined to the development and distribution of composite products. More comprehensive cooperation, especially in service management and complaint management processes, is hindered by insufficient transparency regarding customer knowledge and redundant task distribution between partner companies.

System Level

On the system level, we observed that in most financial services alliances there is a wide variety of separate analytical and operational CRM systems as well as of different transaction systems that are not standardized or seamlessly integrated.

Figure 6.3   CRM Application Architecture of the Financial Services Alliance of One Case Site

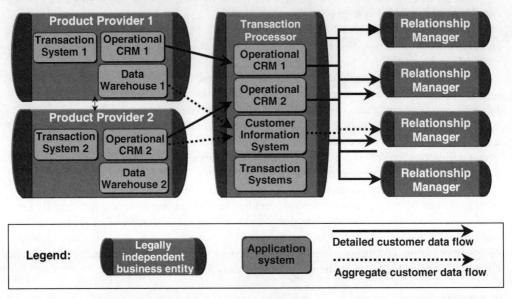

An exemplary CRM application architecture of one financial alliance we studied is shown in Figure 6.3. Each product provider operates its own application systems—*transaction systems* and *operational CRM* (oCRM) *systems* (Gebert et al. 2003)—containing all relevant knowledge about customers (e.g., the contacts and characteristics of a customer's products). Moreover, many product providers have an infrastructure for analytical CRM, including a *data warehouse.* Various relationship managers (banks), which jointly own a transaction processor (Figure 6.1) in order to achieve economies of scale, are the product providers' main distributors. The transaction processor operates the *transaction systems* for all banks. Moreover, it hosts copies of the product providers' *operational CRM systems* to give the banks' customer consultants insight into the customer information owned by the product providers. In one of the financial alliances we studied, a bank's customer consultants have to cope with its product providers' approximately 30 different operational CRM systems. In addition, to provide customer consultants with an overview of the products owned by a customer, each product provider regularly transmits the most important, aggregated customer information to the transaction processor. This information is then integrated into a *customer information system,* comprising aggregated customer information from all product providers.

In addition to data exchange with the transaction processor, some product providers also exchange anonymous customer data to support the decentralized lead management processes of each product provider (see previous section). Usually the exchange is informal and achieved via flat files.

The main challenge on the system level is that the wide variety of separate CRM systems and transactional systems inhibits an integrated view of customers. We noted the following shortcomings in particular:

- *Insufficient integration of operational CRM systems:* Relationship managers' customer consultants frequently have to cope with a large number of different operational CRM systems that are used by different product providers. This complicates the achievement of high-quality sales and service management, because customer consultants are often unable to find and integrate required customer information.

- *Insufficient integration of customer data sources:* Each product provider often has his own separate customer database and data warehouse, complicating an analysis of a customer's overall relationship with a financial alliance.
- *Insufficient integration of qualitative (CRM systems) and quantitative (transaction systems) customer data:* The lack of integration between operational CRM systems and transaction systems leads to a separation of qualitative and quantitative customer data in these systems, which impedes an integrated customer view.

In conclusion, we observed that CRM application infrastructures in financial services alliances are largely dispersed as well as lacking integration. This leads to challenges in the collaborative processes, especially in sales and service processes.

Table 6.2 summarizes the findings on the strategy, process, and system levels of the case study sites.

Recommendations

As we have shown, the emergence of financial services alliances has led to challenges on the strategy, process, and system levels. In addition, we have shown that challenges on the process level can largely be traced to shortcomings on the system level in the form of nonintegrated CRM systems.

Based on our analysis, we derived the following recommendations for the improvement of CRM in financial services alliances:

1. *Distribute disjoint CRM competencies among partners of an alliance.* Overlapping competencies lead to task redundancy in the different companies, as well as to redundant systems, and may result in inconsistent results. To increase efficiency, each partner should focus on core competencies through which the advantages of disintegration (trend 2, Figure 6.1) can be exploited.
2. *Establish single point of entry for customers.* To realize service integration on the customer side (trend 1, Figure 6.1) and to promote the concept of a relationship manager, multiple contact persons for a financial services alliance's customers have to be abandoned in favor of a single point of entry. Nevertheless, relationship managers and product providers can jointly perform the execution of business processes, for example, service management.
3. *Establish transparency regarding customer knowledge among partner companies.* To prevent task redundancy and to support collaborative CRM processes, customer knowledge has to be shared among the companies of a financial services alliance while taking data privacy protection laws into account.
4. *Integrate CRM systems of different partner companies.* To reach the abovementioned goals, it is imperative to integrate customer data (derived from transaction systems and data warehouses) and to integrate operational CRM systems to create an integrated view on customers.

For the integration of CRM systems, there are two alternatives: the standardization of systems (*ex ante* integration) and the integration of systems using an integration infrastructure (*ex post*

Table 6.2

Characteristics and Challenges of Collaboration in Customer Relationship Management

Level	Characteristic	UBS Global Asset Management	HomeLoanBank	InvestmentBank	Lucerne Cantonal Bank	UniversalBank
Strategy	Business network relationships	Horizontal (to other UBS business units)	Horizontal (to other financial product providers), vertical (to distributing banks)	Horizontal (to other product providers), vertical (to distributing banks)	Horizontal (to other cantonal banks), vertical (to product providers)	Horizontal (between banking and insurance business units)
	Objective of collaboration	Comprehensive coverage of financial demands, combination of customer knowledge to utilize customer potential	New distribution channels and new customers, comprehensive coverage of financial demands	New distribution channels and new customers	Comprehensive coverage of financial demands, economies of scale	New distribution channels and new customers, comprehensive coverage of financial demands
	Challenges	Overlapping competencies in different business units	Overlapping competencies in different partner companies, protection of data privacy hinders exchange of knowledge	Overlapping competencies in different partner companies, protection of data privacy hinders exchange of knowledge	—	Protection of data privacy hinders exchange of knowledge
Process	Product development	Joint development of complex products with other business units	Development of combined products with other product providers	Development of combined products with other product providers	Standardized commodity products for cantonal banks of an IT cooperation	Joint product development in contractual relationship
	Marketing	Joint marketing activities with other business units	Joint marketing activities with other product providers and distributing banks	Joint marketing activities with other product providers and distributing banks	Joint marketing initiatives with other cantonal banks	Joint marketing activities of banking and insurance units
	Sales	Collaborative lead management with other business units	Collaborative lead management with other product providers and distributing banks, mutual distribution of	Collaborative lead management with distributing banks, sales support for distributing banks	Distribution of partner products (of product providers)	Mutual distribution of products between banking and insurance units, collaborative lead management

99

Service	—	partner products (of product providers) First-level service by banks, second-level service by product providers	First-level service by banks, second-level service by product providers	—	—
Challenges	Insufficient customer knowledge exchange between business units	Product providers have insufficient knowledge about customers, redundant tasks in different partner companies	Unsystematic gathering of customer knowledge	Unsystematic gathering of customer knowledge, standardization opportunities in commodity products and processes	Loose sales collaboration between banking and insurance units
System CRM applications	7 separate operational CRM systems (in different business units)	Wide variety of separate analytical and operational CRM systems for each product provider and banks (more than 30)	Wide variety of separate analytical and operational CRM systems for each product provider and banks	Standardized CRM solution for cantonal banks of an IT cooperation	Separate CRM systems of banking and insurance units
Customer data exchange	—	Systematic data exchange with banks via processing centers, ad hoc flat file exchange with product providers	Systematic data exchange with banks via processing centers	Systematic data exchange with product providers (not with other cantonal banks)	Anonymous customer data exchange via flat files between banking and insurance units
Challenges	Distributed CRM and transaction systems inhibit an integrated customer view	Standardization and integration of CRM systems, integration of customer data	Standardization and integration of CRM systems, integration of customer data	Further standardization of CRM systems	—

Figure 6.4 **MLP AG Organizational Structure**

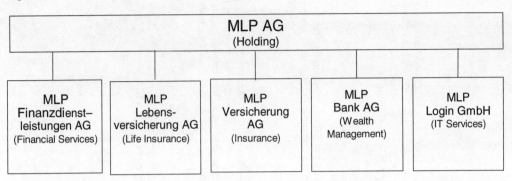

integration) (Linthicum 2000; Ruh et al. 2001). The first alternative may be practical for the business units of a universal bank, where standards can be established more easily than in an alliance with legally independent companies. *Ex post* integration using an EAI (enterprise application integration) infrastructure may be especially useful in such loosely coupled networks. In practice we expect to observe a mixture of both *ex ante* and *ex post* integration of CRM systems.[4]

To further detail the recommendations and to illustrate how they can be set into action, in the following section we present a best-practice case study of MLP, a financial services provider that uses state-of-the-art technology and application architecture to realize the recommendations described in this section. In contrast to the five case studies of the previous analysis, MLP has already integrated its processes and systems. Therefore, it can serve as a best-practice example.

CASE STUDY: COLLABORATIVE CUSTOMER RELATIONSHIP MANAGEMENT AT MLP

MLP is an independent financial services provider that focuses on the *relationship manager* role. Since its founding in 1971, it has focused on advising university graduates and clients with sophisticated requirements on pension provision, asset management, and risk management. With around 2,800 financial consultants and an extensive service offering, MLP is able to guide its 560,000 clients in six European countries through every aspect of personal financial management (MLP 2004).

Strategy Level

MLP uses the best products available in the marketplace from external product providers to develop innovative financial solutions that are tailored to its clients' individual requirements. The MLP group comprises a brokerage business, a bank with an asset management department, a life insurance company and a non–life insurance provider, which offer tailored solutions using external product providers' products and complementing them with own products. Figure 6.4 shows the organizational structure of the MLP group.

As a strategic listed holding company, *MLP AG* defines the goals and coordinates business strategies within the group. *MLP Finanzdienstleistungen AG* is the core company in the MLP group. It is responsible for customer consulting and the development of tailored solutions using the best products and components (modules) in the financial market. *MLP Bank AG* performs the role of a 'general contractor' for the MLP group's investment and financing products. It coordinates the combination of product modules from different banks and investment companies and

Figure 6.5   **MLP Business Model**

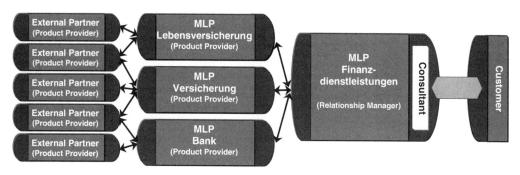

serves as custodian. *MLP Lebensversicherung AG* produces endowment policies, life insurance policies, occupational disability policies, and annuities. It also coordinates the MLP operations in this field, acting as a 'general contractor' to the life insurance companies involved. *MLP Versicherung AG* is the central service center for non–life insurance. *MLP Login GmbH* is the IT service provider for the MLP group. It is responsible for the technical development and operation of the Internet platform and customer consulting systems.

Process Level

The goal of MLP is to offer its customers integrated solutions for their financial needs using the best products on the market. Therefore, MLP Finanzdienstleistungen AG integrates product modules of partner companies and complements them with products of MLP product providers (MLP Bank, MLP Lebensversicherung, and MLP Versicherung). Figure 6.5 shows the business model of MLP (Stockmann 2003).

In the *product development* process, the MLP product providers develop products that complement products of external product providers. The resulting banking, life insurance, and non–life insurance products can then be bundled with external partner products by MLP Finanzdienstleistungen AG to receive integrated solutions (MLP best-partner concept) that can be tailored to a customer's needs.

In the *offer management* process, clients are advised by an MLP consultant according to their overall financial needs. Depending on the client's needs, a customer consultant can offer products of external partner companies, MLP products, or integrated solutions comprising modules of external partner companies as well as MLP products. After the conclusion of a contract, *contract management* is carried through decentrally by the respective MLP product provider.

Each customer has one customer consultant as his single point of entry. *Complaint management* and *service management* are handled centrally by the respective customer consultant. Also, each customer consultant is responsible for acquiring additional customers in the *lead management* process. Moreover, customer consultants are supported by central *campaign management* activities carried through by MLP Finanzdienstleistungen AG.

System Level

The business model of MLP is enabled by a modular, but highly integrated IT landscape (Figure 6.6). IT's strategic objective is to enable the distributed management and processing of products

Figure 6.6 **MLP Application Architecture**

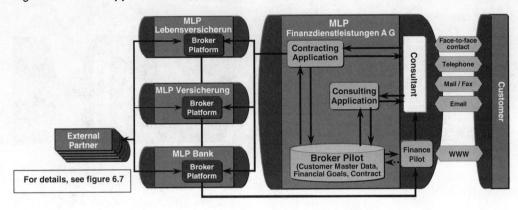

For details, see figure 6.7

and contracts by the MLP product providers while allowing customer consultants (and the customer himself) to obtain an integrated view of information on a customer (needs, products, activities) (Mehlau 2001; Stockmann 2004).

Consulting and Contracting Applications. The beginning of the consulting process is the so-
called 'fact finding.' The consultant uses different consulting applications to enter customer master data and to find out the customer's financial goals. Typical consulting applications are modules
for liquidity planning, asset management, risk management, and loan management. All customer
data gathered in the consulting process are transferred into a central customer database (broker
pilot). Therefore, customer consultants can always use the customer data gathered so far.

At the end of the consulting process, about 80 percent of customer data is available to fill out
a contract. Depending on the product that a customer wants to buy, some additional data may be
needed. These data are entered into a contracting application by a customer consultant. The contracting application can get already-gathered customer data from the broker pilot database. For
some commodity products (e.g., car insurance) the respective contracting applications can also
be accessed by customers directly via the Internet.

After entering all needed customer data, the contracting application sends it to the broker
platform of the MLP product provider that offers the respective product.

Broker Platforms. The broker platforms are used to create and manage contracts. In contrast to
classical brokers that have no influence on data processing after the initial transfer of a contract to
an external product provider, the MLP product providers process accounts, deposits, and contracts on their own broker platforms. Therefore, they have all customer data in their own systems.
This is a prerequisite to realize the integrated view of customers in order to consult them comprehensively. The broker platforms have interfaces to transaction systems of external product providers. Figure 6.7 shows the application architecture of the broker platform of MLP Bank.

Broker Pilot. The broker pilot is the central database for customer master data. It stores all customer data gathered in the consulting and contracting process. Moreover, it stores the relations
between customers, customer consultants, and products (contract IDs). Detailed contract and
product data are not stored in the broker pilot because they are available in the broker platforms.
The connection to a customer's products on the broker platforms is realized via contract IDs.

Figure 6.7 **Broker Platform of MLP Bank**

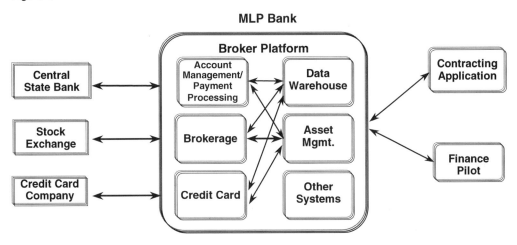

The broker pilot serves as data source for consulting and contracting applications, as well as for the finance pilot. It is also the source for analytical CRM systems which analyze unusual customer activities and customer potential for new consulting outlets.

Finance Pilot. The finance pilot is a Web-based system which integrates all customer data from different systems (broker pilot and broker platforms) to realize an integrated view of a customer. It can be used both by customer consultants and by customers themselves. In addition, it offers functions for electronic banking and brokerage. The finance pilot can be realized because MLP has all customer data and contract data available on its own systems and can integrate this information using a unique customer ID in all systems.

How MLP Realized the Four Recommendations

With its business model and supporting IT architecture, MLP has realized the four recommendations mentioned in the previous section:

1. *Distribute disjoint CRM competencies among partners of an alliance:* Each subsidiary company of MLP AG focuses on specific tasks as its core competencies. In particular, each subsidiary focuses on one role in the value chain: product provider or relationship manager. For example, MLP Bank is responsible for the provision of banking products, whereas MLP Finanzdienstleistungen is responsible for the integration of products for customers.
2. *Establish single point of entry for customers:* Each MLP customer has one customer consultant responsible for every aspect of the customer's personal financial management. Consultants and customers are supported by the finance pilot, which realizes an integrated view of a customer.
3. *Establish transparency regarding customer knowledge among partner companies:* Customer data that are important to different MLP subsidiary companies are consolidated and stored in a central database (broker pilot). Contract- and product-related data are stored at the respective MLP product provider but can be merged with customer master data—by the finance pilot—using a unique customer ID and contract IDs.

4. *Integrate CRM systems of different partner companies:* Operational CRM systems (consulting and contracting applications), analytical CRM systems (data warehouses), and transaction systems (broker platforms) are tightly integrated to support CRM processes in an integrated way.

To realize the recommendations, MLP uses a supportive application infrastructure with the following characteristics:

- *Highly modular application systems:* CRM systems and transaction systems are not monolithic, but highly modular and distributed to ensure flexibility and short time-to-market for new products.
- *Central database for customer master data:* Customer master data are stored centrally in the broker pilot database to ensure consistency.
- *Joint data model with unique customer ID:* To integrate customer master data, contract data, and transaction data related to a specific customer, MLP uses a joint data model and a unique customer ID with which each customer can be identified in any application system.
- *Integrated processes across applications:* Contracting and transaction processing are carried through via integrated processes over several different application systems.
- *Customer data integration via views:* Customer master data from the central database, contract data, and transaction data from the broker platforms are integrated in the finance pilot using an integrated view of these different data sources.

With this state-of-the-art architecture, MLP can serve as 'best-practice' example for financial services alliances that face the abovementioned challenges regarding collaborative customer management.

CONCLUSIONS AND FURTHER RESEARCH

The emergence of financial services alliances has led to challenges related to an integrated approach to CRM among partner companies. Whereas, on the strategy level, the elimination of redundant competencies among partner companies has the potential to provide opportunities for improvement, the main inhibitors of integrated CRM can be found on the process and systems level.

Both product providers and relationship managers often have customer-oriented business processes with incomplete customer knowledge. Moreover, redundant tasks are undertaken by more than one company in an alliance, for example, the detection of a customer's external exposure. Having different contact persons for each product, some alliances have still not implemented the idea of one-stop finance for customers. This is especially evident in after-sales service management and complaint management processes.

Most challenges in interorganizational CRM processes can be traced to the limitations of the information systems infrastructure. An incomplete standardization of the CRM processes and systems inhibits the exploitation of economies of scale as well as inhibiting systems integration. Consequently, a limited integration of systems containing customer knowledge, such as operational and analytical CRM systems as well as transaction systems, complicates the process of obtaining a comprehensive view of a customer relationship. An increased integration of these systems suggests an opportunity not only to improve the quality of customer consultancy, but also to improve the exploitation of a customer's potential. We derived the following recommendations from our analysis of financial services alliances:

- Distribute disjoint CRM competencies among partners of an alliance.
- Establish a single point of entry for customers.
- Establish transparency regarding customer knowledge among partner companies.
- Integrate the CRM systems of different partner companies.

Finally, we presented a best-practice case study of MLP to show how these recommendations can be realized using state-of-the-art technology. The MLP application architecture has the following characteristics: It has highly modular application systems, a central database for customer master data, a joint data model with unique customer ID, integrated processes across applications, and integration of customer data via views. MLP can serve as "best-practice" example for financial services alliances that face challenges regarding collaborative customer management.

Our study provides the initial basis from which CRM application architecture should be designed in financial services alliances. However, to develop detailed guidelines for such an architecture, it is necessary to conduct further research. Our objective is to analyze financial services alliances' CRM application architectures to derive guidelines in the form of a reference application architecture that can overcome the shortcomings observed. Using additional case studies and quantitative empirical research, we shall try to develop and validate such an architecture.

NOTES

An earlier version of this article was presented at the 2004 Americas Conference on Information Systems (AMCIS 2004). (Geib et al. 2004)

1. For an assessment of current research on CRM, see Romano and Fjermestad (2003).

2. We are aware that, especially in Europe, data privacy protection laws play an important role in the exchange of customer data between different partner companies. Nevertheless, in this paper we do not contribute to this discussion, as this topic has been extensively covered. For a detailed discussion see Bennett (1997), Fjetland (2002), Klosek (2000), Smith (2001).

3. In certain instances, confidentiality rules do not allow us to specify the financial network and the details of the architecture to which we refer.

4. For a detailed discussion of the effects of EAI technology, see Linthicum (2000), Ruh et al. (2001).

REFERENCES

Banking on the technology cycle. *The Economist* (September 4, 2003). Available at www.economist.com/displaystory.cfm?story_id=2019991. Accessed December 2005.

Day, G.S. *Capabilities for Forging Customer Relationships.* Cambridge, MA: Marketing Science Institute, 2000.

Bennett, C.J.A.R. The adequacy of privacy: The European Union data protection directive and the North American response. *Information Society,* 13, 3 (July–September 1997), 245–263.

Eisenhardt, K.M. Building theories from case study research. *Academy of Management Review,* 14, 4 (1989), 532–550.

Ferstl, O.K. and Sinz, E.J. SOM: Modeling of business systems. In P. Bernus, K. Mertins, and G. Schmidt, eds., *Handbook on Architectures of Information Systems.* Berlin: Springer, 1998, 339–358.

Fjetland, M. Global commerce and the privacy clash: There are critical gaps in the privacy rights laws of Europe and the United States that pose a major challenge to companies embracing global commerce. *Information Management Journal,* 36, 1 (January/February 2002), 54–57.

Garcia-Murillo, M. and Annabi, H. Customer knowledge management. *Journal of the Operational Research Society,* 53, 8 (2002), 875–884.

Gebert, H.; Geib, M.; Kolbe, L.M.; and Brenner, W. Knowledge-enabled customer relationship management. *Journal of Knowledge Management,* 7, 5 (2003), 107–123.

Geib, M.; Kolbe, L.M.; and Brenner, W. Collaborative customer management in financial services alliances. In *2004 Americas Conference on Information Systems (AMCIS 2004),* New York, NY, 2004, 3805–3817.

Hagel, J., III and Singer, M. Unbundling the corporation. *Harvard Business Review,* 77, 2 (1999), 133–141.

Heinrich, B. and Leist, S. Nutzung und Entwicklung von Geschäftsmodellen—Ergebnisse des Kompetenzzentrums Bankenarchitekturen im Informationszeitalter [Development and use of business models in the financial services industry]. In H. Österle and R. Winter, eds., *Business Engineering*, 2d ed. Berlin: Springer, 2002, pp. 329–352.

Klosek, J. *Data Privacy in the Information Age*. Westport, CT: Quorum Books, 2000.

Knights, D.; Murray, F.; and Willmott, H. Networking as knowledge work: A study of strategic interorganizational development in the financial services industry. *Journal of Management Studies*, 30, 6 (1993), 975–995.

Körner, V. and Zimmermann, H.-D. Management of customer relationship in business media—The case of the financial industry. In *33rd Hawaii International Conference On System Sciences*, Maui, Hawaii. Los Alamitos, CA: IEEE Computer Society Press, 2000.

Krishnan, M.S.; Ramaswamy, V.; Meyer, M.C.; and Damien, P. Customer satisfaction for financial services: The role of products, services, and information technology. *Management Science*, 45, 9 (1999), 1194–1209.

Lehmann, A.P. Financial services—Veränderungen von Märkten, Leistungen und Unternehmen [Change of Markets, Services, and Enterprises]. In C. Belz and T. Bieger, eds., *Dienstleistungskompetenz und innovative Geschäftsmodelle* [Service Competency and Innovative Business Models]. St. Gallen: Thexis, 2000, 22–35.

Linthicum, D.S. *Enterprise Application Integration*. Upper Saddle River, NJ: Addison-Wesley, 2000.

Mehlau, J.I. State-of-the-art report: IT-Architekturen für Finanzdienstleister [IT architectures for financial services providers]. *Banking and Information Technology*, 3, 2 (2001), 41–58.

MLP. The MLP group. 2004 (available at www.mlp-ag.com, accessed on 21.07.2004).

Österle, H. *Business in the Information Age: Heading for New Processes*. Berlin et al.: Springer, 1995.

Österle, H. Enterprise in the information age. In H. Österle, E. Fleisch, and R. Alt, eds., *Business Networking: Shaping Collaboration Between Enterprises*. Berlin: Springer, 2001, pp. 17–54.

Österle, H. and Blessing, D. Business engineering model. In H. Österle and R. Winter, eds., *Business Engineering*, 2d ed. Berlin: Springer, 2002, pp. 65–86.

Payne, A. and Ryals, L. Customer relationship management in financial services: Towards information-enabled relationship marketing. *Journal of Strategic Marketing*, 9, 1 (2001), 3–27.

Peppard, J. Customer relationship management (CRM) in financial services. *European Management Journal*, 18, 3 (2000), 312–327.

Prahalad, C.K. and Hamel, G. The core competence of the corporation. *Harvard Business Review*, 68, 3 (May–June) (1990), 79–91.

Romano, N.C. and Fjermestad, J. Electronic commerce customer relationship management: A research agenda. *Information Technology and Management*, 4, (2003), 233–258.

Ruh, W.A.; Maginnis, F.X.; and Brown, W.J. *Enterprise Application Integration at Work; How to Successfully Plan for EAI*. New York: John Wiley & Sons, 2001.

Scheer, A.-W. *ARIS—Business Process Frameworks*. Berlin: Springer, 1995.

Schulze, J.; Thiesse, F.; Bach, V.; and Österle, H. Knowledge enabled customer relationship management. In H. Österle, E. Fleisch, and R. Alt, eds., *Business Networking: Shaping Collaboration Between Enterprises*. Berlin: Springer, 2001, pp. 135–152.

Senger, E. and Österle, H. *ProMet BECS—A Project Method for Business Engineering Case Studies*, Research Report, Institute of Information Management, University of St. Gallen, St. Gallen, 2002.

Shaw, R. and Reed, D. *Measuring and Valuing Customer Relationships: How to Develop the Measures That Drive Profitable CRM Strategies*. London: Business Intelligence Ltd., 1999.

Sheth, J.N. and Parvatiyar, A. *Handbook of Relationship Marketing*. Thousand Oaks: Sage Publications, 2000.

Smith, H.J. Information privacy and marketing: What the US should (and shouldn't) learn from Europe. *California Management Review*, 43, 2 (2001), 8–32.

Stockmann, C. Private Financial Engineering: Vorraussetzung integrierter Finanzdienstleistungen [Private financial engineering: Prerequisite of integrated financial services]. *Banking and Information Technology*, 4 (2003), 37–43.

Stockmann, C. Die IT-Strukturen bei MLP [The IT structures at MLP]. In J. Moormann and T. Fischer, eds., *Handbuch Informationstechnologie in Banken* [Handbook of Information Technology in Banks]. Wiesbaden: Gabler Verlag, 2004.

Walter, G. Customer Relationship Management bei Banken—Von reiner Transaktionsorientierung zu einem umfassenden Beziehungsansatz [Customer relationship management in banks—from pure transaction orientation to a comprehensive relationship approach]. *Banking and Information Technology*, 4 (2000), 9–22.

Yin, R.K. *Case Study Research. Design and Methods*, 3d ed. London: Sage Publications, 2002.

PART III

ENHANCING
PERFORMANCE OF CRM

CHAPTER 7

IMPROVING CUSTOMER INTERACTION WITH CUSTOMER KNOWLEDGE MANAGEMENT

ADRIAN BUEREN, RAGNAR SCHIERHOLZ,
LUTZ M. KOLBE, AND WALTER BRENNER

Abstract: *In this paper, we will illustrate the use of modern information technology to provide knowledge support to CRM processes. This knowledge support allows for performance enhancements in customer-oriented business processes. We will base our reasoning on a "customer knowledge management" process model, which identifies six CRM subprocesses and four aspects of knowledge management and which integrates epistemological and ontological knowledge models with process-oriented knowledge models. It aims at achieving knowledge transparency, knowledge dissemination, knowledge development, and knowledge efficiency. The application of the different aspects in the model will be demonstrated in several action research cases. These cases were implemented in European companies in the financial services sector and concern the support of customer-facing processes across all channels. They validate the proposed architecture while indicating critical success factors for a successful implementation of customer knowledge management.*

Keywords: *Knowledge Management, Customer Relationship Management, Process Management, Customer Knowledge Management, Process Performance*

INTRODUCTION

Challenges for Businesses in the Information Age

Ever-increasing demands of customers concerning quality and innovativeness of products and services put companies under pressure. In combination with global competition, they change the rules of the market and force companies to adapt swiftly (Österle and Winter 2000). This challenge, together with rising pressure to reduce costs, requires enterprises to redesign their business model. One possible solution is to focus the value chain on the processes of the customers. For example, a company could support the customer process "car ownership," which extends from the purchase, financing, and usage of the vehicle all the way to maintenance, sale, or scrapping. A single provider could cover this process entirely with an innovative combination of products and services. Efficiently collaborating within dynamic networks based on modern information technologies, companies can provide these process-oriented offerings (Fleisch 2001). The growing importance of customer-oriented business models is emphasized by numerous publications within the area of customer relationship management (CRM)—for example,

Greenberg (2001), Shaw and Reed (1999), Schulze (2000). A comprehensive overview over the literature in the field of CRM with a focus on e-commerce can be found in Romano and Fjermestad (2002). CRM aims at leveraging investments in customer relations to strengthen the competitive position and maximize returns.

Focusing on customer processes requires considerable knowledge. Customer-focused companies have to provide knowledge that customers demand, process the knowledge that customers pass to the company, and possess knowledge about customers. As a consequence, knowledge is considered a critical resource in the competition of the twenty-first century (Drucke 1999; Davenport and Prusak 1998)). The cultivation of knowledge to support business processes is the task of knowledge management (KM). Thus the application of KM concepts and technologies in the context of CRM is a relevant field of research (Romano and Fjermestad 2003).

Research Goals and Structure

Our research focuses on how concepts of KM can be applied within the area of CRM. This approach enables companies to improve knowledge support of their customer-oriented business processes, which in turn aims at improving the overall performance of the enterprise.

The resulting customer knowledge management (CKM) process model, as introduced by Gebert et al. (2003), aims at integrating the two concepts of CRM and KM. We consider KM to be a toolset which cannot be applied independently of business processes. Thus we focus on the application within the area of CRM. The contribution of this chapter is to describe cases in which the performance of CRM was improved by applying the CKM process model.

Therefore, we will proceed as follows: Section two will provide an overview of related research within the areas of CRM and KM which form the foundation of the CKM process model. Subsequently, we will introduce the CKM process model based on a framework of six CRM subprocesses. In section three, four action-research cases with companies in the financial services sector will illustrate the application of the CKM process model. Our cross-case analysis in section four will specifically focus on how the illustrated cases managed to improve company performance through the application of KM instruments within CRM. In section five we will conclude this chapter with an outlook on further research opportunities.

Research Methodology

To achieve our research goals and derive the CKM process model, we employed the research approach "action research" as defined by Gummesson: "On the basis of their paradigms and pre-understanding and given access to empirical, real-world data through their role as change agent, . . . action scientists . . . generate a specific (local) theory, which is then tested and modified through action. The interaction between the role of academic researcher and the role of management consultant, within a single project as well as between projects, can also help the scientist to generate a more general theory, which in turn becomes an instrument for increased theoretical sensitivity . . ." (Gummesson 2000). Apart from this foundation, we also used in-depth case study analysis to complement our experiences and validate the conclusions derived from the CKM process model. The CKM process model is based on nearly six years of research in a special corporate–academic partnership. Research partners were major European players in sectors such as financial services and insurance, telecommunications, and chemicals.

To structure our analysis of existing challenges in these cases, we employ the concept of business engineering (BE) as our analytical framework. Business engineering is the transformation of enterprises from the industrial age into the information age by means of procedure models, methods, and tools (Österle 1995). To control the transformation complexity, a division into several levels is often suggested ((Ferstl and Sinz 1998; Scheer 1995)). Österle and Blessing (2003) propose three levels of business engineering: strategy, process, and system, each dealing with different business questions:

- On the *strategy level*, decisions are made regarding the long-term development of an enterprise. This comprises decisions on strategic alliances, company structure, market services offered, customer segments addressed, and distribution channels.
- Within *processes*, strategic decisions are implemented. A process produces a company's services through the execution of a number of tasks with defined inputs and outputs. Process development includes the planned process outputs, the optimal sequence and distribution of tasks, and process management.
- The execution of processes is supported by *information systems* (IS) in the form of application software. The foundation for information systems is information technology (IT), consisting of hardware, networks, and operating systems software.

The research described in this chapter concentrates on the process and information systems level of CRM and CKM.

A MODEL FOR CUSTOMER KNOWLEDGE MANAGEMENT

Customer Relationship Management

The origins of CRM can be traced back to the management concept of *relationship marketing* (RM) (Levitt 1983). Relationship marketing is an integrated effort to identify, build up, and maintain a network with individual customers for the mutual benefit of both sides (Shani and Chalasani 1992). RM is largely of strategic character and lacks a holistic view of business processes, although they are regarded as important (Parvatiyar and Sheth 2000).

Advances in information technology (IT) had a significant influence on CRM, focusing mainly on the information systems layer in the past. The goal was to support the existing isolated approach of dealing with customer relationships. With the CRM philosophy aiming at creating an integrated view of the customer across the enterprise, these systems were connected, and today they form the building blocks of comprehensive integrated CRM systems.

We consider CRM to view the customer relationship as an investment, which is to contribute to the bottom line of the enterprise. The design and management of customer relationships is to strengthen the competitive position of an enterprise by increasing the loyalty of customers. While this extends beyond the use of information technology, IT is an important enabler of modern CRM.

Apart from the strategy-oriented concept of RM and systems-oriented concepts, there are several CRM approaches with special focus on business processes (Schulze et al. 2000). However, these approaches are based on the separation of the functional areas of marketing, sales, and service, which by itself does not provide a cross-functional process view.

A very common approach to describe CRM is to define different types of information systems which form a life cycle for data in CRM, as shown in Figure 7.1 (Greenberg 2001). *Analytical CRM* is used to gather, store, and analyze data from different sources to gain more insight into the preferences of customers and their value to the company. *Operative CRM* directly supports em-

Figure 7.1 **Closed Loop Approach to CRM**

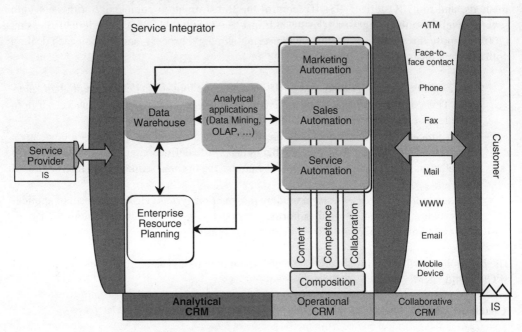

Source: Hettich, et al. (2000). Used with permission.

ployees in executing CRM processes, such as designing a campaign or processing a complaint, and provides means to access the information gained by the analytical applications and also store new information, so that it is available to other processes and can be used for other customer contacts as well as further analyses. *Collaborative CRM* includes the integration and synchronization of different communication channels (Schwede and Spies 2001) and is often referred to as multichannel management. Together, the three types of CRM systems form a closed loop, which primarily focuses on the flow of data and therefore is mainly intended to deal with technical issues. However, it does not consider the systems or processes relevant to manage explicit or tacit knowledge in CRM processes.

CRM processes typically require not only transactional data, which can be automatically collected and stored in relational databases, but also a significant amount of knowledge. Also, CRM processes typically are complex and are structured only to a certain extent. Hence, they can be considered knowledge-intensive processes (Eppler et al. 1999). Besides developing an integrated view of CRM processes, it is therefore critical for our framework to address the management of knowledge flows from and to the customer across all communication channels as well as the use of knowledge about the customers. This is why we will focus on KM in the next section.

Knowledge Management

Up to now, there has been an abundance of publications concerning KM, which fall into two broad categories, epistemologically and ontologically oriented KM models. Within epistemology, mainly the cognitivistic and the autopoietic approaches have been of significance to the area of KM (von Krogh et al. 1994). The cognitivistic approach describes knowledge as stored in distinct knowledge structures which are created through rule-based manipulation and can exist independently of an individual. In contrast, the autopoietic approach, according to von Krogh et al. (1994), states that knowledge is context sensitive and embodied in the individual.

According to the autopoietic epistemology, individuals acquire knowledge by observing and interpreting their environment (von Foerster 1984). They can actively transfer knowledge between themselves through articulation and different types of interaction (Watzlawick et al. 1967). The main differentiating characteristic of knowledge is the difficulty of its articulation. Knowledge that can be easily articulated is labeled *"explicit knowledge."* Knowledge that is difficult to articulate and therefore difficult to transfer is labeled *"tacit knowledge"* (Polanyi 1966), a term that has been superseded by *"implicit knowledge."* With their SECI KM model, Nonaka and Takeuchi have formulated an encompassing epistemological autopoietic KM model (Nonaka and Konno 1998). Boisot (1987) and McLoughlin and Thorpe (1993) also provide examples of this approach.

Ontological KM models, on the other hand, view knowledge as a "black box." The characteristics of knowledge are defined through its relationships with a constructed universe of discourse. Modeling dimensions frequently used by ontological KM models include a process dimension and an agent dimension (individual vs. group).

Process-oriented KM models focus on the characteristics of knowledge during its life cycle. They analyze the relationships and environmental variables that influence the processes of knowledge development, dissemination, modification, and use. Examples for process-oriented KM models include Probst et al. (1999) and Wiig (1995). Agent-oriented KM models focus on the characteristics of knowledge during the flow between individuals. They analyze the variables that expedite or hinder the flow of knowledge in social networks. Examples for agent-oriented KM models include Wenger (1997) and Enkel et al. (2000).

Most KM models developed within the last decade include characteristics of both views. Nonaka has integrated an agent ontology dimension in 1993 (Hedlund and Nonaka 1993) and he tries to fully bond both views in his concept of "ba" (Nonaka and Konno 1998). The process oriented KM models of (Demarest 1997) or (Blessing 2001) focus on the processing of explicated knowledge. As a consequence, however, a fully balanced model is yet to be created (McAdam and McCreedy 1999).

In the next section we introduce a CKM process model which, based on the findings in this section, connects the concepts of CRM and KM. It also integrates the different aspects of knowledge by combining elements of the epistemological and the ontological view of knowledge management.

Deriving an Integrated Customer Knowledge Management Process Model

CRM Process Model. Marketing, sales, and service are primary business functions (Porter and Millar 1985) characterized by a high degree of direct customer interaction and knowledge intensity. We derive our process model by detailing these functions into relevant business processes, which may be cross-functional. A CRM business process involves the processing of customer knowledge to pursue the goals of relationship marketing. Usually, it also involves direct customer contact and the exchange of information or services between enterprise and customer. Such processes are triggered either by the customer with the aim of receiving information or services or by the enterprise with the aim of delivering information or services to customers. Each process handles a specific business object which distinguishes it from other processes. Schmid (2001) established marketing, sales, and service as core CRM processes and specified process activities in further detail. Based on Schmid (2001) and our own action research experience, we identified *campaign management, lead management, offer management, contract management, service management,* and *complaint management* as the six relevant CRM business processes. *Campaign management, complaint management,* and *service management* are already included in the work of Schmid (2001). In our action research cases, however, we identified an insufficient linkage between marketing and sales activities, which we resolved by the introduction of *lead management.* We also regrouped process activities within sales to *offer management* and *contract management* to further reduce the complexity of the model.

Campaign management is the core marketing process which fulfills the idea of interactive, individualized contacts in contrast to traditional transaction marketing (Grönroos 1994). It deals with the planning, realization, control, and monitoring of marketing activities toward known recipients. Marketing campaigns are individualized (one-to-one marketing) (Peppers and Rogers 1993) or segment specific and offer communication channels for feedback. The objective of campaign management is to generate valuable opportunities or *"leads"* as the basis for lead management.

Lead management is the consolidation, qualification, and prioritization of contacts with prospective customers. The objective is to provide sales staff with a qualified and prioritized list of presumably valuable prospects to be precisely addressed within the offer management process.

Offer management is the core sales process. Its objective is the corporationwide consistent creation and delivery of individualized, binding offers. An offer management process may be triggered by a customer inquiry, a qualified lead, or a discovered opportunity.

Contract management is the creation and maintenance of contracts for the supply of products and services. As such, it supports *offer management* or *service management* processes. Contract management also comprises the maintenance and adjustment of long-term contracts, for example, for outsourcing agreements or insurances.

Service management is the planning, realization, and control of measures for the provision of services. A service is an intangible output of an enterprise generated with direct involvement of customers. Examples include maintenance, repair, and support activities in the after-sales phase as well as the provision of financial or telecommunication services after the conclusion of contracts.

Within the scope of *complaint management,* articulated dissatisfaction of customers is received, processed, and communicated into the enterprise (Stauss and Seidel 2002). The objectives are to improve customer satisfaction in the short run by directly addressing problems that led to complaints and to design a continuous improvement process in the long run.

Operative CRM system components directly support the six CRM subprocesses described above. Analytical components primarily emphasize the processes of campaign management, lead management, and offer management, evaluating different data sources and deriving conclusions about what customers are likely to need and buy. To cover the collaborative aspects on the process level, CRM requires activities to design interfaces to customers at customer interaction points. *Interaction management* is the design and selection of media-based communication channels like interactive voice response (IVR), the World Wide Web (WWW), or mobile communication channels (m-commerce) to achieve an optimal channel mix (Senger et al. 2002). The objective is to increase the quality and value of interactions while decreasing the cost of interactions by shifting customers to less costly channels, for example, Web self-service.

Closely connected to interaction management is *channel management,* which addresses the challenge of configuration and synchronization of different communication channels (Gronover 2003). Key objectives are to define organizational responsibilities for each channel, to avoid conflicts between channels, and to ensure consistent knowledge flows across different channels.

Integrating Customer Relationship Management and Knowledge Management. To achieve their goal of providing a solution for the process of the customers, enterprises need to focus on three

Figure 7.2   **Knowledge Management Pyramid**

Source: Gebert et al. (2003). Used with permission.

sorts of knowledge in CRM processes (Österle 2001), which make up what we consider to be customer knowledge.

- They need to understand the requirements of customers in order to address them. This is referred to as *"knowledge about customers."*
- Customers have information needs in their interaction with the enterprise. This is *"knowledge for customers."*
- Finally, customers have knowledge about the products and services they use as well as about how they perceive the offerings they purchased. This *"knowledge from customers"* is valuable, as it feeds into measures to improve products and services. Efforts need to be made to channel this knowledge back into the enterprise.

We therefore consider CKM to include more than just knowledge from customers [in contrast to Gibbert et al. (2002)] and perceive it as a comprehensive approach for customer knowledge. The CKM process model as introduced by Gebert et al. (2003) was the result of a collaborative research process in which the authors were involved as well. It offers two perspectives to address the challenge of managing customer knowledge. The KM goal perspective offers a hierarchy of four interdependent goals to best support business processes (see Figure 7.2). The process perspective illustrates which knowledge management tools need to be applied to the CR subprocesses to achieve effective customer knowledge management (see Figure 7.3).

- The goal of *knowledge transparency* applies to existing knowledge within an organization that needs to be readily available and retrievable so it can be used in CRM processes.
- The goal of *knowledge dissemination* employs measures to better distribute the use and development of knowledge throughout an organization. It is based on knowledge transparency and fo-

Figure 7.3 **Customer Knowledge Management Process Model**

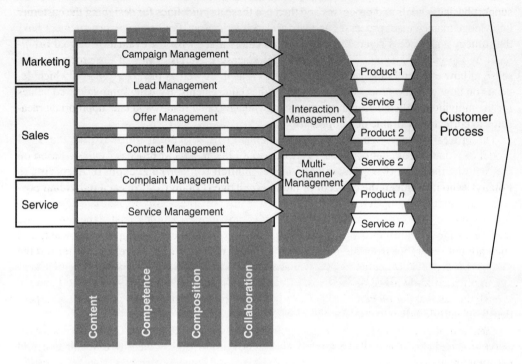

Source: Gebert et al. (2003). Used with permission.

cuses particularly on aspects of collaboration and knowledge sharing when individuals interact.
- The goal of *knowledge development* supports the business process in defining current gaps that require the future creation or acquisition of knowledge. To assess knowledge gaps on a process level, knowledge dissemination and transparency are required, because when combined they offer an overview of present customer knowledge.
- The goal of *knowledge efficiency* supports the business process in limiting the available knowledge to the knowledge crucial for CRM. Knowledge efficiency facilitates the successful application of knowledge in CRM processes. However, it is not worthwhile until the other goals have been reached, as a lack of knowledge will always have a greater effect than an overload, although in some cases it might lead to the same result.

While allowing process owners the direct articulation of their knowledge needs, the four KM goals do not provide guidelines for managing customer knowledge based on its relevant characteristics and additional relations. The CKM model therefore is enhanced through the integration of the four aspects *content, competence, collaboration,* and *composition* which are introduced in the process perspective. These aspects were derived by analyzing existing KM models [for details, see Gebert et al. (2003) and Riempp (2003)]. They will be further reinforced by the action research examples we introduce in the next section.

To comprehensively cover the customer knowledge management approach, the model would also have to encompass the layers of strategy and information systems. We chose to omit these layers in the graphical representation to avoid excessive complexity but will explain them in this section.

On a strategy level, companies need to determine how customer knowledge management can support business goals and processes and then use these as guidelines for designing the customer knowledge management processes and performance indicators. Performance measurement links the strategy and process layers by providing indicators that enable the evaluation of goal fulfillment by the process. Typically, these indicators measure the efficiency of the process, in the sense of how efficiently the necessary output is created, as well as the effectiveness, which depends on how well the process output matches the requirements. By determining desired values for the individual indicators, management can evaluate actual results and take appropriate measures to correct undesirable developments.

The process level, our main focus in this chapter, is derived as follows: Like the SECI model of Nonaka/Takeuchi (Nonaka and Konno 1998), the CKM process model is based on the fact that there are two types of knowledge, implicit (or tacit) and explicit. According to Polanyi, who introduced the concept of tacit knowledge (Polanyi 1966), each individual possesses an amount of implicit knowledge which influences the ability to articulate and therefore explicate and create knowledge. Implicit knowledge includes past experiences and influences the perception of the environment. However, explicit and implicit knowledge as such are not separable from the particular individual possessing it. Therefore, we term it the knowledge aspect "competence." As a consequence, the organization can only directly manage explicated knowledge in the form of media such as text or images, which we term the knowledge aspect "content." Content is part of the business processes and exists independently of individuals.

Similar to the revised SECI model of Hedlund and Nonaka (1993), the CKM process model also introduces two aspects that take into account how knowledge is created, disseminated, and used within an organization. As a consequence, the model contains elements of both the epistemological view and the ontological view with an agent dimension. The ontological view is represented by the two aspects of "*collaboration*" and "*composition*." Collaboration deals with the creation and dissemination of knowledge among few individuals, for example, in project teams. The knowledge aspect composition, on the other hand, deals with the dissemination and usage of knowledge among a large number of individuals. An important issue for composition is helping people find explicated knowledge—for example, in enterprise portals.

The four knowledge aspects deliver services that support the CRM subprocesses. This sometimes requires support processes, such as managing content or competency information from creation to application in a life cycle. The aspects of collaboration and composition serves as an infrastructure that supports the provision of knowledge to business processes while not being a process itself. Furthermore, as proposed by the business engineering approach (see Österle and Blessing 2003), all knowledge aspects need to be supported by information systems that deliver specific functions for each aspect. The aspect *content* typically requires the use of content management or document management systems. The aspect *competence* makes use of expertise directories as well as skill management or e-learning systems. E-mail, group information tools, and instant messaging systems are typical functions that support the aspect of *collaboration*. Finally, the aspect of *composition*, which primarily deals with search and navigation uses systems such as knowledge mining systems, personalization, taxonomy management systems, and knowledge maps. While it is beyond the scope of this chapter to illustrate the use of all these systems to support CRM subprocesses, we will focus on three cases which are part of our action research work and provide insights on how to improve performance by employing the four aspects of knowledge and supporting information systems.

ACTION RESEARCH CASES OF CUSTOMER KNOWLEDGE MANAGEMENT

Case 1. Knowledge Support for the Customer Communication Center of Union Investment

The following action research case of Union Investment, a large mutual fund company in Germany, shows the importance of explicated knowledge for the CRM subprocess service management. The case focuses on a major element within modern *service management*, the customer communication center (CCC), which usually integrates the communication channels phone, fax, and e-mail to serve customers via multiple channels.

In this case, the CCC serves bank employees and retail customers alike. It consists of 120 employees who offer support on two levels, depending on the expertise and knowledge required to resolve inquiries about a wide array of topics connected to complex financial products.

CKM Challenges. In order to address the needs of their customers, CCC agents utilized different information channels provided by an internal unit named Information Support. Initially, the content was disseminated via e-mail. While this was possible without further investments in the technical infrastructure, each CCC employee had to organize his or her content individually, and new employees did not have access to older information. Therefore, using basic Web technology, a knowledge platform was created that offered the same information as e-mail with a certain time delay. As the amount of content increased, the navigational structure eventually became more and more cluttered. Since no search function was available, the CCC agents tended to primarily use their personal e-mail folders rather than the central knowledge platform for information retrieval.

The existing solution also caused significant costs for creating, formatting, and publishing content. The complicated process, with only very basic support by information systems in converting documents to a Web-based format, also delayed timely publication, which is critical to supporting the CCC agents.

Relevant Knowledge Aspects. The relevant knowledge aspects in this case were *content* as well as *composition*. The focus of the project was to provide the CCC employee with knowledge for the customer. However, there was a major shortcoming in the current design of knowledge composition. The navigational structure was unwieldy; searching for content was not possible. This also applied to information support, since the editors had no adequate tool to help them structure the knowledge and get an overview of existing documents.

The major *content* challenge, requiring up to 50 percent of the time to supply information to the CCC, was the conversion of documents from office application format delivered by other departments into content displayable in a Web browser. Up to the project, editors had to convert content manually with specialized HTML editors.

To overcome the challenges, a new content management system was selected. It included a conversion tool which was based on newly created templates in office applications and could create HTML content automatically. The application for the editors enabled them to publish new content directly from the office application and provided an overview of existing documents. They could be directly accessed and edited from within the tool. On the part of the CCC agents, the content management system offered a search function in addition to a redesigned consistent navigational structure.

Results. Based on a detailed analysis of the processes of CCC agents and editors, knowledge dissemination was significantly improved. The new structure and improved timeliness of information available on the knowledge platform is an important factor in supporting CCC agents. It enables them to provide faster answers with higher quality. By saving time, customers are served faster. An individual agent can serve more customers, thereby increasing service levels and reducing waiting time.

For the information support department, the cost and time needed to maintain the new platform were greatly reduced by eliminating most efforts to convert existing content. The structure could now be maintained much more easily. The focus on just one information source made it easier for agents to find what they needed and reduced operational costs of publication for editors as well as strain on the network infrastructure caused by large e-mail attachments.

Case 2. Skill Management as a Customer-Oriented Human Resource Management Instrument at Helsana Health Insurance

The following action research case of the Swiss health insurance provider Helsana shows the business impact of the knowledge aspect of *competence* for all CRM subprocesses. The case focuses on strategic skill management as a means to support complex customer processes, to improve the corporate ability to react quickly to changing market requirements, and to manage and improve the corporate skill set.

CKM Challenges. Customers demand individual, affordable insurance services. This requires employees in the customer-oriented units that are organized along marketing, sales, and services to have complex, comprehensive and flexible knowledge for and about the customers. Without a management tool for managing and making visible the required knowledge and skills on a corporate level, the organization could suffer competency shortages with a negative impact on business performance.

Relevant Knowledge Aspects. This case focuses on the knowledge aspect of *competency* and therefore concentrates on the management of implicit knowledge. The project aimed at establishing an IT solution to support corporate skill management. The main services to be delivered by the new system were derived from the requirements by the business units. They required competency profiles of employees combined with a search functionality to locate employees with certain skills. Also, the system was to create competency maps of the organization based on individual competency profiles. In addition, human resources (HR) demanded that the competency profiles be usable for goal definition, human resource planning, and to derive training measures.

To develop the competency profile, a "skill tree" was used which included professional competencies as well as information about education, language skills, and experience. The identification of competencies critical for the success of the company was based on criteria such as relevance to strategic goals, relative steadiness (i.e., how much effort it takes to acquire a skill that lasts), and relative scarceness.

The project team used these criteria to develop a hierarchical ordering, with relative steadiness being the top hierarchy level. This ensured that the skill tree could be aggregated into a skill map reflecting the skill development costs in an appropriate manner. For each qualification in the skill tree, the competency profile stated whether it was present or not. A multilevel grading scheme measured professional competency and soft skills.

Results. The prototype for the skill management system was developed based on standard software. The skill profiles and the skill history enabled managers and HR personnel to efficiently plan training measures for each individual employee. On a corporate level, the aggregation of data within the skill profiles allowed for the analysis of the existing skill set and for the deduction of required strategically relevant skills. With this information, a gap between the required skill set and the existing skill set could be identified and addressed via corporate training measures or new hiring policies.

Also, the skill profiles allowed for quick and easy location of required expertise within the company during any step of any process. Thus the resource allocation could be optimized, since long searches for experts were avoided. Additionally, project team members with the required skills could be recruited more easily.

The prototype was field tested and the results were very good. All participants assessed the system as essential to their daily work and ranked its benefit as "good" or "very good." Therefore, it will be rolled out to further parts of the organization in the near future.

Case 3. Global Collaboration at Winterthur Life & Pensions

The third case concerns Winterthur Life & Pensions, a Swiss insurance company which is one of the major players in Europe and worldwide. The company had experienced strong growth, especially with acquisitions. As a result, in the area of life insurance products, abundant information systems were in use to manage contracts. To enable a more efficient *contract management*, especially for closed blocks (contracts that were still running but no longer offered to new customers), the company decided to standardize processes and systems in this area on a global scale as far as possible.

CKM Challenges. In order to standardize the management of closed blocks, projects were initiated worldwide on a country-level. The teams consisted of members of the global core team as well as of local experts who reengineered the processes, calculation models, and information systems involved in the management of closed blocks. As a consequence, a number of globally dispersed teams were working on similar problems. To communicate within and between the teams and with headquarters, e-mail was the primary medium. In some countries, access was also available to a file server which stored relevant content. However, communication and knowledge exchange, based primarily on documents, were not entirely satisfactory. As a result of the use of e-mail, team members could never be sure of having the most up-to-date version of a document. As in the first case, new members had to start from scratch, since they had missed past communication. The file server was not globally accessible. E-mail communication within projects also made it virtually impossible for the core team to get an overview of the progress of the different projects and the lessons learned. Finally, knowledge transfer was hampered by a lack of consistent documentation of projects.

Relevant Knowledge Aspects. To improve knowledge dissemination across the different projects, the insurance company implemented a new knowledge portal based on a standard software product. The portal was to be globally available and enhance the dissemination of knowledge across all projects within the management of closed blocks.

The portal included elements of three aspects, with *composition* being the most prominent. It provided a standardized process-oriented navigational structure to be used by all projects. This went hand in hand with the introduction of a common taxonomy which defined the most relevant terms needed for categorization. Besides the navigational structure, a comprehensive search function also allowed the retrieval of relevant documents. With the new access-rights management, individual team members saw only content relevant to them.

Concerning *content*, documents were now available on a Web-based platform. The system included version control, making sure that documents were available only in their newest version. It also provided templates to standardize content creation processes and therefore facilitated a review of relevant documentation across multiple projects. The templates also provided means to record feedback and lessons learned from the project teams.

The aspect of *collaboration* was based on the features already described and primarily concerned the organizational setting in which the portal was used. It enabled the dispersed project teams to store and retrieve documents from virtually anywhere and to work together on common documents. By linking to other projects, it was possible to work on common problems across projects more easily. On the other hand, version control helped team members recognize whether they were using the most current version in their work.

Results. The new portal improved the efficiency of the projects in a variety of ways, thus enabling the standardization of contract management for closed blocks.

The primary goal was to facilitate knowledge dissemination for *collaboration*. Since all projects would place their documentation into the portal, the status of the different projects could now easily be analyzed and compared. A special reporting function further extended this aspect. When a certain step in a project was concluded, lessons learned were reviewed and could now immediately be incorporated into the process-oriented structure and the templates. This made them available to every project that had not yet reached the relevant step. As a result, many potential problems were eliminated before they actually came up.

On the individual project level, documents were now kept centrally. In contrast to e-mail, all project members had access to all documents. It was no longer possible to encounter outdated versions, and the structured navigation reduced information overload. For the infrastructure, the portal brought significant relief. as not every document needed to be sent to every project member anymore. After one year of use, the portal included over 10,000 documents and was employed in 21 projects in nine countries worldwide.

Case 4. Enhancing the Performance of the Call Center of Signal Iduna Bausparen AG

The fourth case focuses on how the improved knowledge provision is provided to employees in the CRM business processes. The case is based on the service and call center process of Signal Iduna Bausparen AG, a leading provider of financial products to support the development of funds for private persons intending to finance their own home. Signal Iduna Bausparen aimed especially to integrate all necessary information in one application for the call center agents and to integrate a performance measurement system to evaluate how it performed in the light of current business goals. Therefore, this case focuses on the aspect of *composition*, which it extends further than in the other cases with the integration of structured and unstructured information. It also highlights the link between the process level and business goals, which is established by performance measurement.

CKM Challenges. Although supporting CRM processes with knowledge about products and processes is of crucial importance, the CRM philosophy also requires the provision of information that pertains directly to the customer. This relatively dynamic type of information describes the interaction of the customer with the company and should reveal a particular customer's preferences, which he might have articulated directly or which can be inferred from certain characteristics which the customer displays.

Originally, call center staff did not have specialized applications. This had two consequences. First, the employees had to use existing user interfaces to legacy applications, which required extensive practice to use efficiently, since information was spread over many screens and masks. Therefore, retrieval of knowledge could prove quite challenging during phone calls, when answers needed to be quickly available. Second, a lot of information about customers was simply not available. For example, past interactions had not been recorded, so when a customer called more than once about the same problem, he had to tell the story once again. Also, the data about customers was very limited, precluding the analysis of personal characteristics which might point out special preferences and ultimately be used for cross- and up-selling purposes.

On the other hand, the implementation of improved customer relationship management was crucial with regard to the competitive situation of Signal Iduna Bausparen, which sold highly standardized products via a network of independent salespersons and needed to differentiate itself from the competition mainly via services.

Relevant Knowledge Aspects. Like Union Investment in the first case, Signal Iduna Bausparen was determined to address the issue of information about products and processes as well as about customers. However, they decided to emphasize the provision of customer-related information typically administered in a CRM system. To integrate all relevant information in a process-oriented manner into one application interface, the project mainly had to focus on the aspect of *composition*.

The design of the new application was centered on the service process in the call center. Basically, two stages can be identified in the process of a customer interaction. When a customer contacts Signal Iduna, especially via phone, he first needs to be identified, so that the system can provide a complete picture of his preferences, his product portfolio, and past interactions with the company. In a second stage, the system needs to support the employee in dealing with the reason for the customer call. This could be providing information on a specific topic, changing existing customer data or preferences, executing a transaction, or filing a complaint. The document-based content was directly connected to a specific activity (e.g., change of address, consulting about specific products, or cancellation of a contract) and provided a step-by-step guide for employees as well as additional explanatory information if necessary. The information, therefore, was available only in the context of the particular processes and could not be accessed with a search or navigation functionality from elsewhere.

In contrast to all other cases presented in this chapter, Signal Iduna Bausparen decided to develop a custom CRM application and not use standard software. The developer team created the application based on the programming language Java and designed appropriate interfaces for the computer telephone integration (CTI) and the information contained in legacy applications.

The integration of explicit knowledge contained in documents to support processes and the transactional data about customers and their products enabled a high degree of process support. It offered means of dealing with the customers to the level of providing scripts for a variety of issues and showing all relevant preferences and past interactions that might help the agent improve his work. It also allowed agents to record the result of their interaction with customers, making it clear what had been communicated and ensuring that critical information contained in complaints, for example, could reach the parties who needed to deal with them in the organization.

Results. The introduction of the new CRM system was part of a reengineering of the entire service area. The new solution facilitated the hiring of new, younger employees who were well suited to sustain a service-oriented culture. This target group was especially well acquainted with the modern graphical and mouse-based user interfaces that the new CRM system provided.

The service process could be drastically accelerated for different channels, such as phone, e-mail, or letter. Major customer requirements, such as not having to state problems or personal data over and over, could be fulfilled only with the new application.

These changes were also reflected in the results of the service process. With the new system, more employees could be employed to deal with more customer enquiries at 20 percent less than the previous total costs. The reason was that the new system allowed for employment of younger agents, who were less costly and more flexible than those employed previously—for example, when it came to working part time in order to cover peaks. By automating tasks such as filling out forms with customer data by hand, employees could spend more time speaking to the customers. With service agents being better informed, members of other corporate departments had significantly less work to do in helping out on difficult cases. The "one face to the customer" vision could be better fulfilled through the use of scripts, so that different agents would give the same answer to a particular problem.

Typical performance indicators that the project team introduced with the new CRM system are the statistical analysis of the different process steps (which step takes how long, how are different cases recorded in the system), the average time for solving a customer enquiry in different channels, and the first-call resolution rate. Although these indicators were not recorded before the project, they helped management to analyze the current performance of the service process and to develop appropriate measures for improving process flow and knowledge provision.

CONCLUSIONS

The aforementioned case studies show successful applications of parts of the CKM model introduced by Gebert et al. (2003). In each case critical customer processes were identified, KM instruments suitable for those processes selected according to the CKM model and then implemented. This produced significant performance improvements in those processes, eventually enabling higher revenues and/or lower costs.

Case 1 identified content creation and knowledge navigation as crucial elements within the CCC and service management. The CKM model suggests content management systems with an easily maintainable content structure and a search functionality as appropriate KM instruments for these elements.

With the implemented system the duration of service calls and the quality of the service provided could be improved, enhancing knowledge transfer to the customer and resulting in higher customer satisfaction, higher loyalty, and, thus, higher revenue. Also, more efficient content creation was facilitated, resulting in lower costs.

Case 2 identified skill management and staffing and planning as crucial elements. The CKM model suggests skill management systems and expertise directories to be suitable KM instruments for these elements.

Case 2 demonstrates how a skill management system allows the recording of employee skills according to a corporate skill tree. This led to increased transparency of existing and required skills and competencies. Hence location of expertise was accelerated, resulting in better and faster service to customers and more efficient project staffing and planning of individual and corporate training measures. This produced higher customer satisfaction as well as more efficient resource allocation, eventually raising revenue and lowering internal costs.

Case 3 focused on communication support, community management, knowledge navigation, and knowledge discovery as elements of CKM. The CKM model suggests portals, personalization, and discussion boards as suitable KM instruments for these elements.

The company implemented a portal facilitating global collaboration across members of multiple project teams. This made project management more efficient and lowered the costs of implementation for standardized contract management. Standardization made contract management more efficient, enabling the insurance company to reduce costs significantly in managing customers and their contracts.

Case 4 emphasizes the aspect of composition in a process-oriented structure and the importance of performance management in CKM. The CKM model contains the navigational structure as one of the primary means of retrieval and suggests the use of process-oriented navigation. The CKM model also stresses the vertical integration between strategy, processes, and information systems which this example illustrates. The integration of different types of information can be achieved only with a strong link between the process and the systems layer, while performance measurement links the process layer to strategic goals.

The project mainly improved the CRM processes of service management and complaint management, where significant reduction in cycle times and process costs could be achieved. This also enhanced the provision of service to the customers. However, it was not possible to draw a direct link from better service and higher customer satisfaction to improved financial results, although this can be assumed in a market where service is the key to differentiation. The other CRM processes also profited from the new solution, as there is less need to involve them to help solve customer inquiries.

This chapter illustrates how, in each case, the CKM process model was used to identify the potential for knowledge management tools to support customer-oriented business processes in the field of CRM. Thus the cases show that the proposed CKM model is a valid framework for designing efficient CRM process by providing knowledge support.

SUGGESTIONS FOR FURTHER RESEARCH

Even though the application of KM instruments in customer processes can lead to increased process performance, as experienced in the cases we have described, there still is no comprehensive, proven system of measuring process performance in knowledge-intensive processes. No generally applicable metrics along with key performance indicators (KPI) have been defined. Common tools for performance measurement such as the balanced scorecard (BSC) (Kaplan and Norton 1996) need to be adapted to provide the aggregated data necessary for measuring CKM-specific KPI or to allow for automatic measuring of CKM performance.

The definition of such metrics and KPIs for the different processes mentioned in the CKM architecture is a goal currently targeted by our research.

Furthermore, although the projects described could have been extended to include all knowledge aspects, this hasn't been done yet in our practice. Further research is required to determine how all knowledge aspects together affect the performance of enterprises and what challenges come up with the integration of all four knowledge aspects. The combination of transactional data, such as the customer purchase history, and knowledge content, such as product information about items purchased, as well as the presentation of the combined information to employees working in customer-facing functions is a field that seems promising for further research. Tools such as data warehouses and data mining and their performance effects are not yet incorporated into the CKM architecture. Thus an extension of this architecture toward analytical CRM is a next step on our research agenda. Finally, we will address the scientific development of methods to leverage innovative technologies such as mobile commerce in CRM.

REFERENCES

Blessing, D. Content Management für das Business Engineering—Fallbeispiele, Modelle und Anwendungen für das Wissensmanagement bei Beratungsunternehmen, Dissertation, University of St. Gallen, St. Gallen, 2001.

Boisot, M. H. *Information and Organisations: The Manager as Anthropologist.* London: Fontana/Collins, 1987.

Davenport, T. H. and Prusak, L. *Working Knowledge: How Organizations Manage What They Know.* Boston: Harvard Business School Press, 1998.

Demarest, M. Knowledge management: An introduction. *Long Range Planning,* 30, 3 (1997), 374–385.

Drucker, P. F. Knowledge worker productivity—The biggest challenge. *California Management Review,* 41, 2 (1999), 79–94.

Enkel, E.; Raimann, J.; Seufert, A.; Vassiliadis, S.; Wicki, Y.; Back, A.; and von Krogh, G. *MERLIN—Materializing, Experience, Refining and Learning in Knowledge Networks.* Institute of Information Management, University of St. Gallen: St. Gallen, 2000.

Eppler, M.; Seifried, P.; and Röpnack, A. Improving knowledge intensive processes through an enterprise knowledge medium. In *ACM SIGCPR Conference on Computer Personnel Research.* New York: ACM Press, 1999, 222–230.

Ferstl, O. K. and Sinz, E. J. SOM: Modeling of business systems. In P. Bernus, K. Mertins, and G. Schmidt, eds., *Handbook on Architectures of Information Systems.* Berlin: Springer, 1998, 339–358.

Fleisch, E. *Das Netzwerkunternehmen. Strategien und Prozesse zur Steigerung der Wettbewerbsfähigkeit in der "Networked Economy."* Berlin: Springer, 2001.

Gebert, H.; Geib, M.; Kolbe, L. M.; and Brenner, W. Knowledge-enabled customer relationship management. *Journal of Knowledge Management,* 7, 5 (2003), 107–123.

Gibbert, M.; Leibold, M.; and Probst, G. Five styles of customer knowledge management, and how smart companies use them to create value. *European Management Journal,* 20, 5 (2002), 459–469.

Greenberg, P. *CRM at the speed of light.* Berkeley: Osborne/McGraw-Hill, 2001.

Gronover, S. Multi-Channel-Management—Konzepte, Techniken und Fallbeispiele aus dem Retailbereich der Finanzdienstleistungsbranche, Dissertation, University of St. Gallen, University of St. Gallen, 2003.

Grönroos, C. From marketing mix to relationship marketing: Towards a paradigm shift in marketing. *Management Decision,* 32, 2 (1994), 4–20.

Gummesson, E. *Qualitative Methods in Management Research,* 2d ed. London: Sage Publications, 2000.

Hedlund, G. and Nonaka, I. Models of knowledge management in the West and Japan. In B. Lorange, B. Chakravarthy, J. Roos, and H. Van de Ven, eds., *Implementing Strategic Processes, Change, Learning and Cooperation.* London: Macmillan, 1993, 117–144.

Hettich, S.; Hippner, H.; and Wilde, K. Customer relationship management (CRM). 2000 (available at http://www.ku-eichstaett.de/Fakultaeten/WWF/Lehrstuehle/WI/Forschung/schwerpunkte.de, accessed on February 21, 2005).

Kaplan, R. S. and Norton, D. P. Using the balanced scorecard as a strategic management system. *Harvard Business Review,* 92, January–February (1996), 75–85.

Levitt, T. After the sale is over. *Harvard Business Review,* 63, 5 (September–October 1983), 87–93.

McAdam, R. and McCreedy, S. A critical review of knowledge management models. *The Learning Organization,* 6, 3 (1999), 91–100.

McLoughlin, H. and Thorpe, R. Action learning—a paradigm in emergence: The problems facing a challenge to traditional management education and development. *British Journal of Management,* 4 (1993), 19–27.

Nonaka, I. and Konno, N. The concept of "Ba": Building a foundation for knowledge creation. *California Management Review,* 40, 3 (1998), 40–54.

Österle, H. *Business in the Information Age: Heading for New Processes.* Berlin: Springer, 1995.

Österle, H. Enterprise in the information age. In H. Österle, E. Fleisch, and R. Alt, eds., *Business Networking: Shaping Collaboration Between Enterprises,* 2d revised and extended ed. Berlin: Springer, 2001, 7–54.

Österle, H. and Blessing, D. Business engineering model. In H. Österle and R. Winter, eds., *Business Engineering*, 2. Aufl. ed. Berlin: Springer, 2003, pp. 65–85.

Österle, H. and Winter, R. *Business Engineering: Auf dem Weg zum Unternehmen des Informationszeitalters.* Berlin: Springer, 2000.

Parvatiyar, A. and Sheth, J. N. The domain and conceptual foundations of relationship marketing. In J.N. Sheth and A. Parvatiyar, eds., *Handbook of Relationship Marketing.* Thousand Oaks: Sage Publications, 2000, pp. 3–38.

Peppers, D. and Rogers, M. *The One to One Future—Building Relationships One Customer at One Time* New York: Currency, 1993.

Polanyi, M. *The Tacit Dimension.* Gloucester: Routledge & Kegan Paul, 1966.

Porter, M. E. and Millar, V. E. How information gives you competitive advantage. *Harvard Business Review*, 63, 4 (1985), 149–160.

Probst, G. J. B.; Raub, S.; Romhardt, K.; and Doughty, H. A. *Managing Knowledge: Building Blocks for Success.* London: John Wiley & Sons, 1999.

Riempp, G. Von den Grundlagen zu einer Architektur für Customer Knowledge Management. In L. Kolbe, H. Österle, and W. Brenner, eds., *Customer Knowledge Management.* Berlin: Springer, 2003, pp. 23–55.

Romano, N. C. and Fjermestad, J. Electronic commerce customer relationship management: An assessment of research. *International Journal of Electronic Commerce*, 6, 2 (2001–2002), 61–113.

———. Electronic commerce customer relationship management: A research agenda. *Information Technology and Management*, 4, 2–3 (2003), 233–258.

Scheer, A.-W. *ARIS—Business Process Frameworks.* Berlin: Springer, 1995.

Schmid, R. E. Eine Architektur für Customer Relationship Management und Prozessportale bei Banken, Dissertation, University of St. Gallen, St. Gallen, 2001.

Schulze, J. Prozessorientierte Einführungsmethode für das Customer Relationship Management, Dissertation, University of St. Gallen, St. Gallen, 2000.

Schulze, J.; Thiesse, F.; Bach, V.; and Österle, H. Knowledge enabled customer relationship management. In H. Österle, E. Fleisch, and R. Alt, eds., *Business Networking: Shaping Enterprise Relationships on the Internet.* Berlin: Springer, 2000, pp. 143–160.

Schwede, S. Spies, R. customer relationship management: Rettende Oase oder Fata Morgana in der Servicewüste?—Eine internationale Betrachtung durch die META Group. In J. Moormann and P. Roßbach, eds., *Customer Relationship Management in Banken,* Frankfurt/Main: Bankakademie Verlag, 2001, pp. 21–42.

Senger, E.; Gronover, S.; and Riempp, G. Customer Web interaction: Fundamentals and decision tree. In *Proceedings of the Eighth Americas Conference on Information Systems (AMCIS).* Dallas: AmCIS, 2002, 1966–76.

Shani, D. and Chalasani, S. Exploiting niches using relationship marketing. *The Journal of Consumer Marketing*, 9, 3 (1992), 33–42.

Shaw, R. and Reed, D. *Measuring and Valuing Customer Relationships: How to Develop the Measures That Drive Profitable CRM Strategies.* London: Business Intelligence, 1999.

Stauss, B. and Seidel, W. *Beschwerdemanagement: Fehler vermeiden—Leistung verbessern—Kunden binden*, 3. ed. Munich: Hanser, 2002.

von Foerster, H. Principles of self-organization in socio-managerial context. In H. Ulrich and G.J.B. Probst, eds., *Self-organization and Management of Social Systems.* Berlin: Springer-Verlag, 1984, 2–24.

von Krogh, G.; Roos, J.; and Slocum, K. An essay on corporate epistemology. *Strategic Management Journal*, 15, Special Issue: Strategy: Search for New Paradigms (Summer 1994), 53–71.

Watzlawick, P.; Beavin, J. H.; and Jackson, D. D. *Pragmatics of Human Communication: A Study of Interactional Patterns, Pathologies, and Paradoxes.* New York: W. W. Norton & Company, 1967.

Wenger, E. *Communities of Practice: Learning, Meaning, and Identity.* Cambridge: Cambridge University Press, 1997.

Wiig, K. M. *Knowledge Management: A Trilogy.* Volume 3. *Knowledge Management Methods: Practical Approaches to Managing Knowledge.* Arlington: Schema Press, 1995.

AN EXAMINATION OF THE EFFECTS OF INFORMATION AND COMMUNICATION TECHNOLOGY ON CUSTOMER RELATIONSHIP MANAGEMENT AND CUSTOMER LOCK-IN

JA-SHEN CHEN AND RUSSELL K.H. CHING

Abstract: *Continual advances in information technology (IT) have led to increased use of information and communication technologies (ICT) throughout business organizations. In seeking new opportunities, many businesses have turned to customer relationship management (CRM) to strategically compete in global electronic marketplaces. With greater emphasis being placed on the application of technology, does the infusion of ICT influence a business' ability to retain its customers? A survey of the 1,000 largest companies in Taiwan was conducted to examine the relationships among three CRM elements (market orientation, IT investment, and mass customization) benefiting from ICT, on CRM performance, partnership quality, and customer lock-in, as measured by customer network effect and information sharing. The results suggest that the three elements have positive relationships with CRM performance and partnership quality. However, only positive relationships exist between CRM performance and customer lock-in. None exists between partnership quality and customer lock-in. The findings further suggest that CRM performance mediates the effects of marketing orientation, IT investment, and mass customization on customer network effect. Partnership quality does not appear to influence either customer network effect or information sharing.*

Keywords: *Customer Relationship Management, Information and Communication Technology, Customer Lock-in, Partnership Quality, Market Orientation, Information Technology, Mass Customization*

INTRODUCTION

Continual advances in information technology (IT) have led to increased use of information and communication technologies (ICT) throughout business organizations. In seeking new opportunities, many businesses have turned to advanced ICT to strategically position themselves to compete in global electronic marketplaces. With its maturity, ICT has begun playing key roles in the implementation of many modern management concepts, such as business process reengineering (BPR), electronic business (e-business) and commerce (e-commerce), supply chain management (SCM), knowledge management (KM), and customer relationship management (CRM), and consequently has defined a new set of rules for competing. However, ICT provides only a short-term advantage. As it becomes readily available, ICT tends to equalize the presence of all competitors.

Hence, businesses must look beyond the mere implementation of ICT and seek competitive ICT-enabled means to maintain their customer base.

In marketing, ICT has enabled businesses to understand and leverage their marketing knowledge, and become more customer-centric in their marketing and servicing practices (Roberts 2000). An emerging technology that has assisted them is customer relationship management (CRM) systems. Businesses have adopted CRM as a means to build customer-centric strategies and create greater customer value by providing the right products and services to the right customer at the right place and time through the right channel to help gain a competitive advantage. The adoption directs the marketing emphasis on retaining existing customers through microsegmented, tailored products. A recent U.S. survey suggests that businesses need to maintain good customer relationships (with their existing customers) to sustain profitability (Li et al. 2001). The Mercer Market Survey (2000) has shown that acquiring a new customer can cost five times more than retaining an existing customer, and a 5 percent increase to the customer retention effort can generate a 60 percent boost in profits. Thus, the shift to customer-centric markets has forced these businesses to establish and build closer learning relationships and interactions with their customers to gain greater insights into their needs. As a result, many businesses have turned to CRM to manage their relationships (Ryals and Knox 2001).

CRM seeks to understand and influence customer behavior through meaningful two-way communication to improve customer acquisition, retention, loyalty, and profitability over time (Berry and Parasuraman 1991; Day 2000; Kohli et al. 2001; Peppers et al. 1999; Swift 2001). A common definition describes CRM as a process that utilizes technology as an enabler to capture, analyze, and disseminate current and prospective customer data to develop deeper and insightful relationships, and identify and more precisely target customer needs. Conceptually, CRM embodies the concepts of relationship marketing (RM). Hence, a CRM system can be seen as an information system to assist the customer retention process or as a methodology that extensively relies on IT, such as Internet applications, to enhance the effectiveness of relationship marketing practices.

However, as in the case of many major applications of ICT, implementing a CRM system looms as a formidable task, and CRM's benefits, such as improvements to customer service and increases to market share, are not reaped quickly. Underlying issues that bear heavily on its implementation include adopting a compatible marketing strategy and establishing the scope of ICT-enabled systems. Finding a compatible marketing strategy involves strategically leveraging ICT to enhance business growth and focuses on examining ICT leverages from different perspectives, including forming barriers to entry, dedicating organizational resources and firm capabilities, and engaging in time-based competition. Additionally, a number of empirical studies on ICT and business organizations reveal that greater investments in ICT, also referred to as ICT-intensiveness (ICT-ness), create positive perceived impacts on organizational productivity and customer service quality. Advances in the conceptualization of key elements exhibited by ICT-ness businesses and various CRM conceptual frameworks and key issues have been addressed in the literature. Few studies, however, have empirically tested the impact of ICT on CRM performance and customer lock-in—the willingness of a customer to engage in further transactions.

This chapter examines the effects of ICT on CRM and its impact on customer lock-in effect, and proposes a model of CRM success. It identifies three CRM elements—market orientation, mass customization, and IT investments—and examines their effect on CRM performance, partnership quality, and customer lock-in. In essence, with greater emphasis being placed on the application of technology, *does the infusion of ICT influence a business's ability to retain its customers?*

BACKGROUND

CRM and ICT

CRM can be viewed as an extension of relationship marketing (RM), a marketing paradigm that focuses on satisfying customers' needs through the development of close personal relationships, interactions, and social exchanges between the business and its customers, with ICT. Enhancing the business's competitive response to continually changing markets lies at the core of RM (Zineldin 2000). CRM expands upon this concept with its emphasis on information management (Peppard 2000) and draws upon ICT to further enhance its strength and capabilities. By taking advantage of advanced computing power and high-speed communication networks over the Internet, CRM allows businesses to quickly learn about and consequently better respond to their customers' needs and expectations with innovative customized products and services (Peppers and Rogers 1999). Also, advances in ICT have pushed database and data storage capabilities into the terabytes, facilitating the collection and retention of customer information. Thus, ICT is pivotal to CRM performance.

ICT covers the technological means for handling information and aiding communications. It involves information and communication channels as well as hardware and software used to generate, prepare, transmit, and store data (NORAD 2002). Generally, marketing applications of ICT in CRM fall into two general categories: (1) marketing process automation and (2) marketing intelligence. Marketing process automation concentrates on building information distribution efficiencies through the use of ICT. It often involves the use of database systems to collect and store customer and sales data, and the subsequent generation of reports for marketing analysis and planning. The use of ICT in electronic data interchange (EDI) and Internet technologies has helped improve fundamental channel management and communication efficiencies between organizations in sharing information to coordinate their activities.

In contrast, marketing intelligence entails knowledge discovery techniques, such as online analytical processing (OLAP), data mining, and intelligent agents, programs that search for information over a broad range of data sources, and focuses on gaining greater insights into customer behavior and market opportunities. Consequently, ICT has gained greater attention in marketing intelligence. Continual advances in technology will lead to further enhancements of CRM.

CRM Elements and ICT

The three CRM elements identified in this study include market orientation, mass customization, and IT investment (profile). ICT plays key roles in the functions of these elements. The sections that follow discuss each element.

Market Orientation. Market orientation is defined as the organizationwide generation, dissemination, and response to market intelligence and is characterized by multiple departments sharing information about customers and engaging in activities designed to meet their needs (Kohli and Jaworski 1990). These activities focus on creating and satisfying customers through a continuous needs assessment (Deshpande and Farley 1998). In contrast to product-driven marketing, which concentrates on pushing end-products into the market through the promotion of quality at low prices, market orientation focuses on detecting and quickly fulfilling customer needs. Prior studies suggest that market orientation practices have positive impacts on business performance and new products and are critical to achieving customer-centric value creation and profitability.

Market-sensing and customer-linking activities are two key cross-functional processes linked to market-driven organizations (Day 1994) that underlie the customer- and competitor-focus motivation of a business (Deshpande et al. 1993; Day 1994; Han et al. 2001). Customer focus seeks to provide the right product to the right customer at the right time and place through the right channel in the right amount and at the best price. Appearing distant and unattainable in the past, it has become more readily achievable with current ICT. For example, retailers such as Wal-Mart are capable of collecting sales and inventory data in real time through point-of-sale (POS) systems and barcodes imprinted on all merchandise, and immediately enacting decisions that may affect the entire organization (i.e., price changes, reordering, store operations, etc.). Thus, customer data can be continuously collected and immediately examined to identify customer preferences, and used to quickly predict changes in market trends. Using insights gained into their preferences, habits, and behavior, a business can further enhance its relationships with its customers.

Using ICT-enabled intelligence gathering methods, a competitor-focus maintains vigilance on developments in the market and impending threats, such as new product offerings, horizontal strategic alliances between competitors, or vertical alliances within distribution channels. Using this information, a business can launch a preemptive strike to counteract or dampen the effects of a threat or its competitors' actions. It could also use the information to reevaluate its market segmenting and targeting tactics to better position itself. For both market- and competitor-focus orientations, ICT enables quicker and more efficient intelligence gathering and responses, and consequently leads to better focused marketing strategies.

Mass Customization. The objective of mass customization is to provide every customer with products and services specifically tailored to fit his/her needs. Customization creates a business's greatest competitive advantages, as competitors cannot easily duplicate, imitate, or provide substitutes for its offerings. This involves having easy access to customer information to more precisely target market segments and identify customer buying behaviors within the segments. However, an organization's success with customization hinges on its ability to integrate its customers' feedback into its production processes (Pitta 1998). Customization entails a cost in flexibility and speed (Dewan 2000), especially since the goal is to reach a one-to-one marketing level with products and services that take into account personal differences and *perfectly* meet a customer's needs. With today's ICT, mass customization is more achievable and feasible. Individual customer preferences and behavior can be retained in massive data warehouses and analyzed with a variety of data mining techniques to create customer-centric solutions (Kalakota and Robinson, 2001).

IT Investments. Continual advances in IT have spurred changes in the way business is conducted, opened new opportunities, and offered new means for gaining competitive advantages (Venkatraman 1994; Scott Morton 1991). A business's IT investment reflects its commitment to IT and incorporates a vision of its expectations from IT. It typically involves developing an IT architecture that defines the organization's capabilities, and supporting it (IT architecture) with an IT infrastructure that covers hardware, software, applications, and people. Together, they represent a master plan and draw a profile of the types of ICT the business chooses to support its business activities. Two important goals of IT investments are to facilitate information sharing through IT integration and to empower people with information and knowledge (i.e., improved decision making). As it applies to CRM, IT investment focuses on integrating and coordinating business activities, opening dialogs with customers to share information, enabling CRM practices, and developing employee skills to benefit the business from CRM. Overall, greater IT investments favorably influence the business performance of an organization.

Partnership Quality

Partnerships enable a business to open channels of communication to its customers. Therefore, partnership quality involves building customer satisfaction, trust, and commitment between a business and its customers. It results through two-way communication and a willingness to learn from customers. The satisfaction [i.e., the differences among expectations, conformation, and performance (Oliver and DeSarbo, 1988)] and added value that customers receive through transactions and interactions often characterize partnership quality. Oliver and DeSarbo (1988) examined several potential determinants of satisfaction and found five significant satisfaction-process theories: (1) expectancy disconfirmation, (2) assimilation theory, (3) equity theory, (4) attribution theory and (5) performance. A study conducted by Jones and Suh (2000) empirically tested transaction-specific satisfaction, overall satisfaction, and repurchase intentions. Their findings suggest that overall satisfaction directly influences repurchase intentions and moderates the relationship between transaction-specific satisfaction and repurchase intentions. Thus, partnerships between a business and its partners and customers are critical for fostering satisfaction, as they facilitate interactions and the exchange of information and knowledge.

CRM Performance and Lock-in Effect

CRM performance focuses on derived relationship benefits concerned with revenue and profitability, the acquisition and retention of customers resulting from more appealing product and service offerings, and the ability to customize product and service offerings to better fit customers' individuality (Swift 2001; Winer 2001). As the customer-business relationship flourishes (i.e., the business learns of and more precisely satisfies its customers' needs), both sides reap greater benefits. Customer loyalty develops and leads to repeated purchases of products and services (Reichheld and Teal 1996). In contrast to the costs of acquiring or winning new customers, businesses usually incur fewer expenses servicing their existing customers and can expect higher profit margins from their sales (Storey and Easingwood, 1999). Thus, building customer loyalty not only benefits the business with repeated sales, it also holds a key to retaining or locking in customers.

A lock-in effect refers to the extent to which customers are motivated to engage in repeat transactions (Amit and Zott 2001). A customer's preference to minimize immediate (short-term) costs while deemphasizing future costs drives lock-in (Zauberman 2003). Customer costs include explicit, implicit, and switching costs. Explicit costs fall into one of three categories (Klemperer 1987): transaction (i.e., costs incurred to start and sometimes to terminate a relationship), learning (i.e., the effort to reach the same level of comfort or facility with a new product), and artificial (i.e., earned rewards and discounts). Implicit costs involve risk aversion and decision biases (Chen and Hitt 2002). Often, switching costs carry an information economics implication, such that a search continues while the marginal cost of a search (i.e., acquiring new information) remains lower than its expected marginal benefit (Zauberman 2003). Thus, lock-in occurs when a perceived economic cost, such as one linked to acquiring new information about or learning to use another product or service, exceeds the expected benefit of switching. Also, Vandermerwe's (2000) description of customer *lock-on* suggests that customers will select a business that provides a superior value at a low delivered cost.

The two components of customer lock-in examined in this study are information sharing and customer network effect. Information sharing occurs after customers have established their trust in a business and sense a benefit from their relationship. It is a voluntary act that

Figure 8.1 **Research Model**

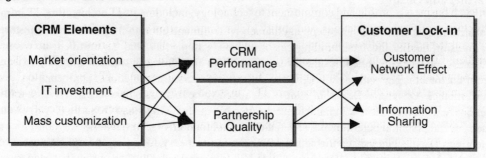

relies on an individual's attitude, often involves the exchange of personal information, and incorporates interpersonal relationships (Kolekofski and Heminger 2003). This also implies a willingness of the business to grant information and service privileges to its partners. Hence, the greater the trust and benefit, the more willing a customer is to share his/her information with the business. Lock-in occurs when the benefits from sharing cannot be obtained elsewhere, particularly when they are intangible and their value is derived only through continued patronage.

Customers communicating their perceived values and benefits of products and services to others of the segment (group) can also initiate lock-in. A customer network effect builds on the trust of members within the segment that allows them to rely upon each other for *assurance*. Lock-in occurs when the cost of acquiring a new source of information exceeds the perceived value or benefit of a product or service. CRM assists lock-in by identifying and targeting certain customers among the existing ones to build specific relationships.

If a business is highly successful in understanding and satisfying its customers' needs through its CRM, the effect of lock-in will be greater. Therefore, lock-in can be seen as the product of CRM performance.

RESEARCH MODEL AND TEST OF HYPOTHESIS

Figure 8.1 illustrates the research model of this study. The three CRM elements, CRM performance, and partnership quality will indirectly and directly affect customer lock-in (network effect, information sharing). As intervening variables, CRM performance and partnership quality will influence the relationship between the CRM elements and customer lock-in. Six major test hypotheses have been developed to test the relationships (i.e., associations) between the variables. The paragraphs that follow present and discuss each hypothesis.

Each of the three CRM elements—market orientation, IT investments, and mass customization—will positively affect CRM performance. Market orientation represents the business's orchestrated and coordinated efforts toward understanding and satisfying its customers' needs, most of which are enabled or enhanced through ICT. Businesses that are less inclined toward market orientation will not benefit from CRM, since they will be less sensitive to marketing intelligence. In customer-driven and ICT-enabled markets, market orientation is a critical element to CRM performance, as it provides direction, particularly through the discovery and dissemination of knowledge. The resources that a business dedicates to its market orientation should positively influence its use of CRM. Thus, increased market orientation should improve CRM performance, particularly in profits and revenues.

An emerging critical element to competing in customer-driven markets is IT. IT investments reflect a business's profile and commitment to technology, including its IT architecture, IT infrastructure, (software) applications, and ability to share information and knowledge across organizational boundaries both within the business and across to its partners. Various ICT are chosen for their different effects on the business (i.e., advantages, benefits), thus creating an IT profile of the organization. Because CRM requires the integration of business units, IT is essential to CRM performance. Organizations that recognize IT's strategic advantages and have committed themselves to its adoption (acceptance) will use it to boost their CRM performance. Often cost advantages (i.e., reduced operating and marketing costs) characterize IT investments.

Mass customization seeks to achieve a one-to-one marketing level through products and services specifically tailored to meet the needs of an individual customer. ICT has been pivotal in enabling this. When products and services are successfully presented in such a way, customer retention will be high. Although the cost of customizing products and services will be higher than that of a mass marketing approach (i.e., a product or service to fit a broad range of customers), the long-term benefits, revenues, and profitability will be greater. The more successful a business is with mass customization, the greater its ability to retain and satisfy its customers. Less successful efforts will be detrimental to CRM performance.

H1: *CRM elements have a positive relationship with CRM performance*
    H1a: *Market orientation has a positive relationship with CRM performance*
    H1b: *IT investments have a positive relationship with CRM performance*
    H1c: *Mass customization has a positive relationship with CRM performance*

Market orientation will also have a positive effect on partnership quality. Businesses that are dedicated to sensing the needs of their customers will engage in meaningful two-way dialogs with them. Opening channels of communication helps build customer satisfaction through feedback and education, and instills trust. As a business projects a single image to its customers, partnership quality will flourish.

Partnership quality also requires that the organization recognize its customers' individuality. Greater investments in IT to collect, retain, analyze, and organizationally share and integrate its customers' information into its production processes will improve the business's ability to reach each customer on a one-to-one basis. In the past, this was less achievable. However, continual advances in IT have opened new opportunities and lowered the cost of intelligence (i.e., scanning repositories for information and knowledge). IT now enables a business to personably manage its customer relationships. Thus, greater investments to boost IT capabilities will improve partnership quality.

Partnership quality reflects customer satisfaction built over time. A business's ability to meet its customers' needs and expectations and recognize their individuality contributes heavily toward forging closer relationships with them. Mass customization is based upon open two-way communication to create products and services specifically tailored to suit individuals. As the differences among expectations, conformation, and performance of these products and services approach zero, customers will be more willing to engage in further transactions. Thus, mass customization contributes to satisfaction and trust and improves partnership quality.

H2: *CRM elements have a positive relationship with partnership quality*
    H2a: *Market orientation has a positive relationship with partnership quality*
    H2b: *IT investments have a positive relationship with partnership quality*
    H2c: *Mass customization has a positive relationship with partnership quality*

Two major objectives of CRM are to retain customers through loyalty and to increase their switching costs. If a business succeeds with CRM, customer needs and expectations are more precisely met, leading to greater customer loyalty. Thus, the lock-in effect will result when the business uses its resources to instill confidence in its customers and give them incentives to maintain their relationships. The actual and perceived benefits they receive from the relationship add to the burden of opting out of the relationship. Thus, the more successful a business is in establishing close relationships with its customers through CRM, the greater the lock-in effect.

H3: *CRM performance has a positive relationship with customer lock-in*
    H3a: *CRM performance has a positive relationship with customer network effect*
    H3b: *CRM performance has a positive relationship with information sharing*

Partnership quality will also affect customer lock-in. Because lock-in is built on trust and loyalty, partnership quality is essential to achieving and sustaining the lock-in effect. When partnership quality is high, customers will be more motivated to engage in future transactions through means such as meaningful incentives and added value. Therefore, while the business maintains its partnership, switching costs remain high.

H4: *Partnership quality has a positive relationship with customer lock-in*
    H4a: *Partnership quality has a positive relationship with customer network effect*
    H4b: *Partnership quality has a positive relationship with information sharing*

Reaping the benefits of customer lock-in requires the business to commitment itself to market orientation, IT investments, and mass customization. These alone, however, cannot directly affect the lock-in, as it is derived through CRM performance. The infusion of ICT in the CRM elements will have a positive effect on CRM performance, which in turn will have a positive effect on customer lock-in. This suggests that CRM performance mediates the relationship between the CRM elements and customer lock-in.

H5: *CRM performance has a mediating effect on the relationship between CRM elements and customer lock-in*
    H5a: *CRM performance has a mediating effect on the relationship between CRM elements and customer network effect*
    H5b: *CRM performance has a mediating effect on the relationship between CRM elements and information sharing*

Partnership quality may also have a similar effect on customer lock-in. It builds a trusting relationship that enhances the customer network effect and information sharing. As in the case of CRM performance, partnership quality improves with ICT investments to the CRM elements. Thus, partnership quality mediates the effect of the CRM elements on customer lock-in; greater investments in ICT to the CRM elements increase partnership quality and assure the achievement of customer lock-in.

H6: *Partnership quality has a mediating effect on the relationship between CRM elements and customer lock-in*
    H6a: *Partnership quality has a mediating effect on the relationship between CRM elements and customer network effect*

H6b: *Partnership quality has a mediating effect on the relationship between CRM elements and information sharing*

The six preceding hypotheses were developed to test the relationships among the variables identified in this chapter's research model (Figure 8.1). CRM elements represent the fundamental components and reflect organizational factors. CRM performance and partnership quality reflect the organization's dedicated efforts in pursuing and retaining its customers.

METHODOLOGY

Data Collection

A survey was conducted of Taiwan's 1,000 largest companies, as published by the Ministry of Economic Affairs for the year 2000. Letters were sent that briefly explained the purpose of this research project, funded by the National Science Council (NSC) of Taiwan, and provided general instructions on completing the enclosed questionnaire. Sales and marketing managers and customer service department heads were specifically targeted.

Initially, only 85 responses were received. Follow-up telephone calls urging recipients to complete the questionnaire brought the total to 120—a 12 percent response rate. Of these, 17 were incomplete and had to be discarded, reducing the sample to 103. Nonresponse may be attributed to companies' either not practicing or not having sufficient experience with CRM. The sample covers various industries, including commerce and trade (4.5 percent), manufacturing (48.1), construction (6.4), financial services (18.2), transportation and logistics (2.7), real estate and general services (11.8), and others (8.2).

Measures

The standard psychometric scale development procedure of Gerbing and Anderson (1998) was followed to generate a series of multi-item scales. Items for each variable were either taken or patterned from previous studies (Table 8.1) and placed in the context of their abilities attributed to CRM (e.g., "with CRM, your company is able to . . ."). Others were based on interviews with IT and marketing professionals. Measures were formulated with single- and multiple-item formats; conceptualized multiple-item scales were developed as formative or reflective in nature. All items were operationalized on five-point Likert-type scales from strongly disagree (1) to strongly agree (5). The survey instrument was pretested on IT and marketing manager and later refined to improve clarity.

A factor analysis with a varimax rotation (using SAS 8.2) confirmed the existence of the seven hypothesized constructs: market orientation, IT investments, mass customization, CRM performance, partnership quality, customer network effect and information sharing. The factors, loadings, and variables appear in Table 8.2. A Kaiser's measure of sampling adequacy (MSA) of .798 supports the appropriateness of the factor analysis, given the 103 observations. Two variables, "valuable information shared with customers" and "customer satisfaction measured," cross-loaded on the IT investment and information sharing, and CRM performance and partnership quality constructs, respectively. The higher loadings, though, properly place them on their constructs. Other items that describe the acquisition and retention of customers, customization of products and services, and other derived benefits from CRM performance did not load.

The Cronbach's alphas for each of the constructs indicate an acceptable reliability of the mea-

Table 8.1

Operational Definitions

Variables	Variables	Operational Definition and Items	References
CRM Elements	Market Orientation	Customer focus, Competitor focus, Cross-functional integration	Narver & Stanley(1990), Jworski and Kohli (1993), Day (1994), Moorman and Rust (1999), Han et al. (2001)
	IT Investments	IT intensity, Process integration	Chou et al. (1998), Doms et al. (1997), Porter and Millar (1985), Weber and Pliskin (1996)
	Mass Customization	Customized services, Customized capability	Pitta (1998), Silveira et al. (2001), Gilmore and Pine (1997), Kotha, (1995), Pine (1993)
CRM Performance		Profit increases, Cost decreases, New opportunities	Storey and Easingwood (1999), Swift (2001), Winer (2001), Reichheld and Teal (1996)
Partnership Quality		Relationship commitment, Trust, Customer satisfaction	Babin and Griffin (1998), Cannon and Perreault (1999), Oliver and DeSarbo (1988)
Lock-In Effect	Network Effect	Influence value of purchase on products/services	Amit and Zott (2001), Granovetter and Soong (1986), Katz and Shapiro (1985)
	Information Sharing	Information sharing between the company and customers; Retrieving desired information	Nowak and Phelps (1992), Bitner et al. (1996), Davenport and Prusak (1998)

sures. Since the items loading onto a construct form a linear combination, they were added to produce aggregate scores (for each construct). The scores were then used in multiple regression models to test the hypotheses. Measures reflecting business capital and the number of employees provide a means to observe their influence on the dependent variables. As control variables, they help ensure that neither biases the results and allow for greater generalizability of the findings (Pedhazur and Pedhazur, 1991).

ANALYSIS AND DISCUSSION

Generally, the results indicate that CRM performance plays a mediating role in the relationship between the CRM elements (marketing orientation, IT investment, mass customization) and customer lock-in (customer network effect, information sharing). However, the same does not hold true for partnership quality (as a mediator). Models I and II (Table 8.3) summarize the positive relationships between the CRM elements and CRM performance (H1), and between CRM elements and partnership quality (H2), respectively. The nonsignificance of the control variables suggests neither has an effect on the relationships. This is consistent with the results of Luneborg and Nielsen's (2003) study. Also, the low variance inflation factors (VIF) reveal no collinearity problems.

The standardized coefficients in models I and II suggest that, of the three elements, market orientation has the greatest impact on CRM performance and partnership quality. Market orientation represents the analytical aspect of CRM. Customer-centric strategies, developed and based on marketing intelligence involving the systematic collection of customer information deposited

137

Table 8.2

Factor Loadings

Variable	Factor 1 IT Investment	Factor 2 CRM Performance	Factor 3 Market Orientation	Factor 4 Partnership Quality	Factor 5 Mass Customization	Factor 6 Information Sharing	Factor 7 Customer Network Effect
Kaiser's measure of sampling adequacy (MSA) = .798							
Cronbach alpha	0.861	0.855	0.821	0.825	0.745	0.804	0.817
Eigenvalue	7.712	3.265	2.017	1.726	1.625	1.232	1.141
Variable:							
Large IT budget	0.806	.	.	.	.	.	.
Advanced IT used in CRM practices	0.753	.	.	.	.	.	.
Large CRM training budget for IT staff	0.722	.	.	.	.	.	.
IT implementation in CRM practices	0.709	.	.	.	.	.	.
Information integration among business units	0.616	.	.	.	.	.	.
Organizational response and coordination	0.570	.	.	.	.	.	.
Valuable information shared with customers	0.544	.	.	.	.	0.446	.
Reduced marketing cost	.	0.869	.	.	.	.	.
Reduced operations cost	.	0.758	.	.	.	.	.
Increased profits	.	0.741	.	.	.	.	.
Increased revenues	.	0.589	.	.	.	.	.
Customer data analyzed to gain market information	.	.	0.825	.	.	.	.
Customer-centric marketing strategy	.	.	0.789	.	.	.	.

(continued)

Table 8.2 (continued)

	Factor 1 IT Investment	Factor 2 CRM Performance	Factor 3 Market Orientation	Factor 4 Partnership Quality	Factor 5 Mass Customization	Factor 6 Information Sharing	Factor 7 Customer Network Effect
Marketing strategies based on customer information	·	·	0.722	·	·	·	·
Systematic collection of customer information	·	·	0.704	·	·	·	·
Perceived extra value in product and service	·	·	·	0.819	·	·	·
Friendly and interactive customer service	·	·	·	0.768	·	·	·
After-sale service support	·	·	·	0.759	·	·	·
Customer satisfaction measured	·	0.443	·	0.593	·	·	·
Customer needs satisfied in products and services	·	·	·	·	0.829	·	·
Easy access to customer information	·	·	·	·	0.693	·	·
Market segmentation and positioning	·	·	·	·	0.692	·	·
Customer buying behavior identified to customize services	·	·	·	·	0.614	·	·
Information sharing between customers and company	·	·	·	·	·	0.839	·
Customers can retrieve desirable information or service	·	·	·	·	·	0.821	·
Other customers influence value placed on product or service	·	·	·	·	·	·	0.884
Other customers influence purchase of product or service	·	·	·	·	·	·	0.878

Note: Values less than .4 not shown.

Table 8.3

Effects of CRM Elements on CRM Performance and Partnership Quality

		Dependent Variables					
		Model I CRM Performance			Model II Partnership Quality		
		Standardized Coefficient	t value	VIF	Standardized Coefficient	t value	VIF
Predictors	Market orientation	.360	4.24***	1.11	.485	6.28***	1.11
	IT investment	.233	2.60*	1.24	.170	2.09*	1.24
	Mass customization	.208	2.20*	1.38	.266	3.10**	1.38
Control Variables	Business capital	.202	1.87	1.81	.084	0.85	1.81
	Number of employees	.042	0.38	1.83	.021	0.22	1.83
	R-Square	.373			.482		
	F value	11.55***			18.02***		
	n	103			103		

*Significant at $p < .05$.
**Significant at $p < .01$.
***Significant at $p < .001$.

in effective and responsive databases and data warehouses, and analyzed with sophisticated analytical software, such as data mining and OLAP, characterize market orientation. Consequently, the availability of quality information not only helps reduce risks and uncertainties in decision making, but also opens many opportunities for gaining competitive advantage. Leveraging such information leads to more precise and efficient ways of correctly identifying, accurately segmenting, and properly targeting customers, and eventually achieving higher customer satisfaction, loyalty, and trust. Thus, CRM performance reflects how well the organization has applied its information and knowledge in its CRM toward achieving one-to-one relationships with its customers. Increases to market orientation will contribute to increases in CRM performance.

IT investments have a smaller but significant impact on CRM performance and partnership quality. In CRM, IT assumes the roles of enterprise integrator and enabler. IT investments enable an enterprisewide technology infrastructure that facilitates the quick dissemination and exchange of information and knowledge throughout the organization. Those investments that promote quick response times in identifying and satisfying customer needs lend a competitive advantage to CRM. Furthermore, because they are instrumental in maintaining the satisfaction of existing customers, interesting them in future purchases, and in expanding the customer base with new customers, IT investments are vital to supporting CRM's processes and facilitating the interactions between the business and its customers to build trust and ensure continual satisfaction. Performance often reflects the effectiveness of the investments; sound investments in IT and ICT will positively contribute to CRM performance.

ICT and mass customization represent the execution of knowledge and the operational aspect of CRM. To succeed with mass customization, the business must be aware of what the customers need and expect, and the value they seek. These must be first elicited from the customers and then translated

Table 8.4

Effects of CRM Performance and Partnership Quality on Customer Lock-In

		Dependent Variables					
		Model III Customer Network Effect			Model VI Information Sharing		
		Standardized Coefficient	t value	VIF	Standardized Coefficient	t value	VIF
Predictors	CRM performance	.328	3.07**	1.27	.292	2.75**	1.27
	Partnership quality	.008	0.08	1.23	.127	1.21	1.23
Control Variables	Business capital	.053	0.41	1.85	−.035	−0.27	1.85
	Number of employees	−.133	−1.04	1.81	.011	0.09	1.81
	R-square		.127			.138	
	F value		3.52*			3.88**	
	n		102			102	

*Significant at $p < .05$.
**Significant at $p < .01$.
***Significant at $p < .001$.

onto a standard product or service in such a way so as not to lose the advantage of mass production or the attraction and appeal of *tailor-made*. The dissemination of information—to and from the customer and within the processes, at the right time, to the right place—must evoke a balance between production economics and potential long-term revenue. Mass customization's contribution to CRM weighs significantly, as it requires the organization to assess the customer's needs, innovate a product or service around those needs, and evaluate the extent to which the product or service meets the needs. The business's success with mass customization reflects its ability to use CRM effectively, thereby boosting CRM performance and solidifying customer partnership. Improvements to mass customization will impact CRM performance and customer partnership quality.

Models III and IV (Table 8.4) examined the effects of CRM performance and partnership quality on customer network effect and information sharing, respectively. The data partially support H3 and H4 and suggest that CRM performance positively affects both customer network effect (H3a) and information sharing (H4a). However, the data support no relationship between partnership quality and customer network effect (H3b) or information sharing (H4b). Lock-in focuses on motivating customers to engage in repeated transactions through products and services that precisely meet their needs and add value. While CRM involves processes that result in an end-product or service for the customer, partnership quality reflects satisfaction, trust, and commitment between the business and customer. It appears that a customer's assessment of a product or service's value plays largely in determining whether he/she will continue patronizing the business. Although we may assume that partnership quality is a basic quality that transcends all transactional relationships, and that when it is not present no relationship will exist, it appears insufficient to distinguish variations in lock-in.

Hypotheses H5 and H6 examined the mediating effects of CRM performance and partnership quality on the relationships between the CRM elements and customer lock-in. A mediating effect occurs when variations in the independent variables account for variations in the mediator (i.e.,

Table 8.5

Mediating Effect of CRM Performance

		Dependent Variables					
		Model V Customer Network Effect			Model VI Information Sharing		
		Standardized Coefficient	t value	VIF	Standardized Coefficient	t value	VIF
Predictors	Market orientation	−.040	−0.36	1.35	.051	0.52	1.35
	IT investment	.013	0.12	1.31	.442	4.59***	1.31
	Mass customization	.093	0.81	1.44	.109	1.08	1.44
	CRM† Performance	.306	2.53*	1.60	.108	1.02	1.60
Control Variables	Business capital	.050	0.38	1.90	−.044	−0.38	1.90
	Number of employees	−.123	−0.95	1.84	.020	0.18	1.84
	R-square		.135			.329	
	F value		2.46*			7.78***	
	n		102			102	

*Significant at $p < .05$
**Significant at $p < .01$
***Significant at $p < .001$
†Mediator

intervening variable), variations in the mediator account for variations in the dependent variable, and controlled the independent variables have no effect on the dependent variable. Model V (Table 8.5) lends support to H5a and suggests that CRM performance mediates the relationship between the three CRM elements and customer network effect. However, the same support cannot be found in model VI (Table 8.5); CRM performance does not mediate the relationship between the CRM elements and information sharing (H5b). The mediating effect suggests that increases to CRM performance, such as improving the CRM processes, will enhance the effects of the CRM elements on customer network effect. Customer network effect will benefit from improvements to the CRM elements, including ICT directed toward IT investments that better integrate the organization's processes (e.g., ERP), market orientation intelligence gathering (i.e., data mining tools, interactive customer Web software), and mass customization product design and manufacturing processes (i.e., modular design, delayed differentiation, expedition of delivery), through CRM performance, provided the elements improve or enhance the organization's use of CRM. As a mechanism that reassures customers of their choices, customer network effect builds upon the business's offering the right choices and provides the business an opportunity to assess these choices. Thus, a business stands a greater chance of achieving customer lock-in with CRM when it promotes customer networking.

The results of models VII and VIII (Table 8.6) indicate that partnership quality has no mediating effect, and the data do not support H6. Because there are no relationship between partnership quality and customer lock-in (models III and IV), this is expected. Interestingly, models VI and VIII reveal a positive direct effect of IT investments on information sharing. This may signify that achieving customer lock-in through information sharing depends largely on the IT invest-

Table 8.6

Mediating Effect of Partnership Quality

		Dependent Variables					
		Model VII Customer Network Effect			Model VIII Information Sharing		
		Standardized Coefficient	t value	VIF	Standardized Coefficient	t value	VIF
Predictors	Market orientation	.076	0.61	1.59	.122	1.15	1.59
	IT investment	.083	0.75	1.29	.478	5.00***	1.29
	Mass customization	.155	1.28	1.51	.147	1.42	1.51
	Partnership quality[†]	−.007	0.05	1.93	-.064	-0.55	1.93
Control Variables	Business capital	−.014	−0.11	1.84	−.072	−0.63	1.84
	Number of employees	−.109	−0.81	1.84	.027	0.23	1.84
	R-square	.076			.324		
	F value	1.30			7.60***		
	n	102			102		

*Significant at $p < .05$
**Significant at $p < .01$
***Significant at $p < .001$
[†]Mediator

ments the business pursues. The standardized coefficients of the paths provide an insight into the association between the variables in the research model (Figure 8.2).

The results suggest that of the three CRM elements, market orientation plays a major role in ensuring good CRM performance and customer partnership quality. Marketing intelligence provides the backbone for establishing customer relationships, and the infusion of ICT may open new opportunities for the business. The discovery of knowledge through intelligence can be leveraged to better meet (or to exceed) the needs and expectations of customers and consequently secure a competitive edge. Marketing orientation greatly benefits from ICT, as more reliable and accurate information can be extracted in real time and shorter time spans. In turn, this helps improve CRM performance. IT investments contribute to CRM performance to a lesser extent. This affirms and reemphasizes CRM as an RM solution and not one strictly of IT. Good RM practices need to be in place before CRM can be adopted; IT is not a substitute for them. Mass customization benefits from ICT, as it serves to open and maintain a crucial *learning* link between the customer and business. Effective two-way dialogs communicate valuable information to the business, which can later be used to improve CRM performance.

Partnership quality does not appear to influence either element of customer lock-in or mediate the relationship between the CRM elements and customer lock-in. This suggests that satisfaction, trust, and commitment are not significant antecedents to the customer network effect and information sharing. While customer lock-in orients itself toward short-term economic benefits (Zauberman 2003), partnership quality develops over time (i.e., long-term), particularly trust. Thus, the measures appear inconsistent to one another.

Figure 8.2 **Standardized Coefficients of the Associations**

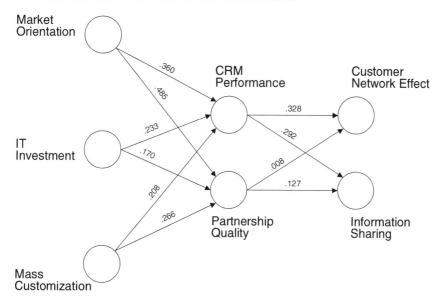

The low R-squares of the models indicate that other factors not included in the model account for a greater portion of the variations. However, the size of the survey instrument limits the number of variables to accurately measure the constructs and also limits the number of constructs to measure. Future studies might focus on improving the measures to capture these variations without necessarily increasing the number items on the survey instrument. Although the results of this study do not overwhelming support the research model, they can be viewed as exploratory and suggestive of a feasible research area to investigate further, particularly with establishing causality, in contrast to the associations demonstrated in this study. This study's results reflect business and CRM practices in Taiwan. However, it can be assumed to apply to all businesses.

FUTURE RESEARCH

As demonstrated in this study, achieving CRM success entails the integration of various organizational, human and technological aspects. Although technology has been the focus of many studies, other areas abound with opportunities, particularly in the context of electronic marketplaces and electronic commerce (e-commerce). The five-area research framework of Romano and Fjermestad (2003) indicates that, in addition to technology, the study of e-CRM (electronic commerce CRM) should include markets (behavior), business models, knowledge management, and human factors. The positive relationships between the CRM elements and CRM performance and partnership quality, CRM performance and customer lock-in, and CRM elements and customer network effect as moderated by CRM performance revealed in this study are consistent with their integrative framework and suggest areas for study in greater depth.

The effects of CRM elements and CRM performance involve a mixture of technology, market, business models, and knowledge management issues. For example, organizational absorptive capacity—the result of cumulative learning of individuals in the organization, the assimilation of information, and the application of the ensuing knowledge (Cohen and Levinthal 1990)—has been recognized as an underlying factor leading to successful innovation. The accelerated effects of advanced technology on absorptive capacity and knowledge management, and subsequently on CRM performance, may impact the interactions the business develops with its customers over time (i.e., how the business leverages its information resources).

Although human behavior in marketing has been studied in consumer behavior, the introduction of technology and the characteristics of electronic marketplaces and e-commerce may change the customer's perceptions of normative behavior. A factor revealed in this study as having benefited from CRM performance is customer network effect. IT enables and enhances communication among customers and enriches the information available to them, thereby increasing the value of their relationship to the business. Yet, much of the success the business reaps from the customer network effect depends on the presence of various organizational factors. Thus, customer lock-in may be closely intertwined with the business's adoption of technology, strategies to capturing markets, and development of its business model.

The research opportunities suggested in the integrative framework of Romano and Fjermestad (2003) follow similar avenues proposed in the MIT90 framework (Scott Morton 1991). Essentially, a change to any one of the five factors (i.e., research areas) will require "retaliatory" changes to the others for the organization to return to equilibrium. Future studies might take this enterprise approach to CRM research.

CONCLUSION

As technology continually advances, a greater portion of business functions will rely on the successful application of ICT. In particular, those businesses seeking to build closer relationships with their customers and distinguish themselves from others in the global marketplaces will turn to CRM. The three CRM elements identified in this study—market orientation, IT investments, and mass customization—were examined for their effects on CRM performance and partnership quality, and for the mediating effects of CRM performance and partnership quality on the relationships between the CRM elements and customer lock-in. The results of this study suggest that the CRM elements positively affect CRM performance and partnership quality, but only CRM performance mediates the relationship. The differences in performance also suggest that the infusion of ICT influences a business's ability to retain its customers, especially when focused on customer network effect. For businesses either entering or engaged in e-business, the results of this study will add to their understanding of CRM.

REFERENCES

Amit, R. and Zott, C. Value creation in e-business. *Strategic Management Journal*, 22, 6/7 (2001), 493–520.
Babin, B.J. and Griffin, M. The nature of satisfaction: An updated examination and analysis. *Journal of Business Research*, 41 (1998), 127–136.
Berry, L.L. and Parasuraman, A. *Marketing Service*. New York: Free Press, 1991.
Cannon, J. P. and Perreault, W. D. Buyer-seller relationships in business markets. *Journal of Marketing Research*, 36, 4 (1999), 439–460.
Chen, P. and Hitt, L.M. Measuring switching costs and the determinants of customer retention in internet-enabled businesses: A study of the online brokerage industry. *Information System Research*, 13, 3 (2002), 255–274.
Chou, T. C.; Dyson, R. G.; and Powell, P. L. An empirical study of the impact of information technology intensity in strategic investment decisions. *Technology Analysis & Strategic Management*, 10, 3 (1998), 325–339.
Cohen, W.M. and Levinthal, D. Absorptive capacity: A new perspective on learning and innovation. *Administrative Science Quarterly*, 35 (1990), 128–152.

Day, G.S. The capabilities of market-driven organizations. *Journal of Marketing*, 58, 4 (1994), 37–52.

Day, G.S. Managing marketing relationships. *Journal of the Academy of Marketing Science*, 28 (2002), 24–31.

Desphande, R. and Farley, J.U. Measuring market orientation: Generalization and synthesis, *Journal of Market Focused Management*, 2, 1 (1998), 213–232.

Deshpande, R.; Farley, J.U.; and Webster, F.E. Jr. Corporate culture, customer orientation, and innovativeness. *Journal of Marketing*, 57, 1 (1993), 23–37.

Desppande, R. and Farley, J.U. Measuring market orientation: Generalization and synthesis. *Journal of Market Focused Management*, 2, 1 (1998), 213–232.

Dewan R.; Jing, B.; and Seidmann, A. Adoption of internet-based product customization and pricing strategies. *Journal of Management Information Systems*, 17, 2 (2000), 9–28.

Doms, M.; Dunne, T.; and Troske, K.R. Workers, wages, and technology. *Quarterly Journal of Economics*, 112 (1997), 253–290.

Gerbing, D.W. and Anderson, J.C. An updated paradigm for scale development incorporating unidimensionality and its assessment. *Journal of Marketing Research*, 25, 2 (1988), 186–192.

Gilmore, J., and Pine, J. The four faces of mass customization. *Harvard Business Review*, 75, 1 (1997), 91–101.

Granovetter, M. and Soong, R. Threshold models of interpersonal effects in consumer demand. *Journal of Economic Behavior and Organization*, 7 (1986), 83–99.

Han, J.K.; Kim, N.; and Kim, H.B. Entry barriers: a dull-, one-, or two-edged sword for incumbents? Unraveling the paradox from a contingency perspective. *Journal of Marketing*, 65, 1 (2001), 1–14.

Jones, M. A. and Suh, J. Transaction-specific satisfaction and overall satisfaction: An empirical analysis. *Journal of Services Marketing*, 14, 2 (2000), 147–159.

Kalakota, R. and Robinson, M. *e-Business 2.0: Roadmap for Success*. Boston: Addisson-Wesley, 2001.

Katz, J. and Tassone, A. The polls: Public opinion trends-privacy and information technology. *Public Opinion Quarterly*, 54 (1990), 125–143.

Klemperer, P. Markets with consumer switching costs. *Quarterly Journal of Economics*, 102, 2 (1987), 375–394.

Kohli, A. and Jaworski, B. J. Market orientation: The construct, research propositions, and managerial implication. *Journal of Marketing*, 54 (1990), 1–18.

Kohli, R.; Piontek, F.; Elington, T.; VanOsdol, T.; Shepard, M.; and Brazel, G. Managing customer relationships through e-business decision support applications: A case of hospital-physician collaboration. *Decision Support Systems*, 32 (2001), 171–187.

Kolekofski, K.E. Jr. and Heminger, A.R. Beliefs and attitudes affecting intentions to share information in an organizational setting. *Information & Management*, 40 (2003), 521–532.

Kotha, S. Mass customization: Implementing the emerging paradigm for competitive advantage. *Strategic Management Journal*, 16 (1995), 21–42.

Li, E.Y.; McLeod, R. Jr.; and Rogers, J.C. Marketing information systems in fortune 500 companies: A longitudinal analysis of 1980, 1990, 2000. *Information & Management*, 38, (2001), 307–322.

Luneborg, J.L. and Nielsen, J.F. Customer-focused technology and performance in small and large banks. *European Management Journal*, 21, 2 (2003), 258–269.

Mercer Market Survey. Available at www.mercer.com. 2000.

Moorman, C. and Rust, R.T. The role of marketing. *Journal of Marketing*, 63 (1999), 180–197.

Narver, J.C. and Stanley, F. S. The effect of market orientation on business profitability. *Journal of Marketing*, 54 (1990), 20–35.

Oliver, R. L. and DeSarbo, W.S. Response determinants in satisfaction judgments. *Journal of Consumer Research*, 14, 4 (1988), 495–507.

Pedhazur, E.J., and Schmelkin, L. *Measurement, Design, and Analysis: An Integrated Approach* Hillsdale, NJ: Lawrence Erlbaum Associates, 1991.

Peppers, D., and Rogers, M. *Enterprise One-to-One: Tools for Competing in the Interactive Age*. New York: Doubleday, 1999.

Peppers, D.; Rogers, M.; and Dorf, R. *The One-to-One Fieldbook*. New York: Currency, 1999.

Pine, B.J. *Mass Customization: The New Frontiers in Business Competition*. Boston: Harvard Business School Press, 1993.

Pitta, D.A. Marketing one-to-one and its dependence on knowledge discovery in databases. *Journal of Consumer Marketing*, 15, 5 (1998), 468–480.

Porter, M. and Millar, V. How information gives you competitive advantage. *Harvard Business Review*, July (1985), 149–160.

Reichheld, F. F. and Teal, T. *The Loyalty Effect* (Boston: Harvard Business School Press, 1996).

Roberts, J.H. Developing new rules for new markets. *Academy of Marketing Science*, 28, 1 (2000), 31–44.

Romano, N.C., Jr. and Fjermestad, J. Electronic commerce customer relationship management: A research agenda. *Information Technology and Management*, 4 (2003), 233–258.

Ryals, L. and Knox, S. Cross-functional issues in the implementation of relationship marketing through customer relationship management. *European Management Journal*, 19 (2001), 534–542.

Scott Morton M. (Ed.). *The Corporation of the 1990s: Information Technology and Organizational Transformation* (New York: Oxford University Press, 1991).

Silveira, G. D.; Borenstein, D.; and Fogliatto, F. S. Mass customization: Literature review and research directions. *Journal of Personal Selling & Sales Management*, 72 (2001), 1–13.

Storey, C. and Easingwood, C. J. Types of new product performance: evidence form the consumer financial services sectors, *Journal of Business Research*, 46 (1999), 193–203.

Swift, R.S. *Accelerating Customer Relationships* (Upper Saddle River: Prentice-Hall, 2001).

Vandermerwe, S. How increasing value to customers improves business results. *Sloan Business Review*, 42, 1 (2000), 27–37.

Venkatraman, N. IT-enabled business transformation: From automation to business scope redefinition. *Sloan Management Review*, 35, 2 (1994), 73–87.

Weber, Y. and Pliskin, N. The effects of information systems integration and organizational culture on a firm's effectiveness. *Information & Management*, 30 (1996), 81–90.

Winer, R.S. A framework for customer relationship management. *California Management Review*, 43, 4 (2001), 89–105.

Zauberman, G. The intertemporal dynamics of consumer lock-in. *Journal of Consumer Research*, 30 (2003), 405–419.

Zineldin, M. Beyond relationship marketing: Technologicalship marketing. *Marketing Intelligence and Planning*, 18 (2000), 9–23.

PART IV

CRM IN BUSINESS-TO-CUSTOMER COMMERCE

CHAPTER 9

WHAT MAKES CUSTOMERS SHOP ONLINE?

NA LI AND PING ZHANG

Abstract: *Electronic commerce customer relationship management (e-CRM) has become a fundamental research area, as business-to-customer e-commerce (B2C) is growing at a phenomenal rate. Among the many issues eCRM addresses, one question is often asked: "What makes customers shop online?" Thorough understanding of this issue will help an electronic store become more competitive. A good number of studies have been conducted to answer this question. These studies seem to take diverse perspectives and investigate various aspects of the phenomenon, yet few have drawn coherent pictures of the dynamics. The objective of this chapter is to draw such a picture. To fit the theme of advances in MIS, we conduct an analytical review of the IS literature on B2C online shopping behavior at the level of the individual. We develop a classification of research variables and a framework to provide an overview of the state of the art of this area and to point out limitations and directions for future research. The results show that one's online shopping intention, behavior, and satisfaction are significantly associated with one's beliefs about and affective reactions to e-commerce/e-stores and one's attitudes toward online shopping. In addition, external environment, demographics, personal characteristics, and e-store characteristics have significant effects on customers' shopping intention, behavior, and satisfaction, either directly or mediated by beliefs, affect, and attitudes. Needed for future research are a common theoretical framework, widely accepted instruments, and consistency in terminology to allow comparing results across studies and to accumulate knowledge. We also call for more research effort in customer satisfaction and affective reactions, which have not received adequate attention despite their fundamental roles in customers' online shopping.*

Keywords: *Electronic Commerce Customer Relationship Management, eCRM, Online Shopping, Internet Shopping, Consumer Belief, Affective Reaction, Consumer Attitude, Consumer Intention, Consumer Behavior, Satisfaction, Empirical Study.*

INTRODUCTION

Business-to-consumer (B2C) electronic commerce has emerged in recent years as an important way of doing business. According to ePayments Resource Center (2004), the total B2C e-commerce revenues for the United States increased from $75 million in 1999 to $750 million in 2003. Similarly, Europe's B2C revenues grew from U.S. $25 to $60 million and Japan's from $25 to $250 million between 1999 and 2003. However, online shopping is far from being a popular act, even among people who are experienced Internet users and spend long hours online. For example, according to the USC Annenberg School Center for the Digital Future, 75.9 percent of

Americans were Internet users in 2003. They spent an average of 12.5 hours/week online. And 96.7 percent of them had more than one year of Internet experience (USC Annenberg School Center for the Digital Future 2004). However, only 43 percent of American adults purchased online in 2003, spending an average of $95.14 per month (USC Annenberg School Center for the Digital Future 2004). While B2C e-commerce has not been widely accepted in the broad sense, there is significant room for its growth, once the B2C shareholders find effective ways to attract and sustain more customers to conduct more transactions online. The question is: What factors lead customers to shop online?

This is a key question to be answered in the e-commerce customer relationship management (e-CRM) area. Abundant studies have been conducted in recent years to investigate customers' online shopping behaviors. Most of them have attempted to reveal factors influencing or contributing to online shopping beliefs, attitudes, intentions, and behaviors. Romano and Fjermestad (2003) have identified five major perspectives that researchers may adopt to approach various issues surrounding e-CRM. These include e-CRM markets, e-CRM business models, e-CRM knowledge management, e-CRM technology, and e-CRM human factors. These areas are not mutually exclusive and may influence one another directly or indirectly. Generally each study of customers' online shopping behaviors takes one or more of the five perspectives. As a result, these studies investigate various factors in diverse ways and reveal different aspects of the phenomenon. For example, Case, Burns, and Dick (2001, p. 873) suggested that "Internet knowledge, income, and education level are especially powerful predictors of Internet purchases among university students" according to an online survey of 425 U.S. undergraduate and MBA students. Ho and Wu (1999) discovered positive relationships between online shopping behavior and five categories of factors: e-stores' logistical support, product characteristics, Web sites' technological features, information characters, and home page presentation. Jarvenpaa et al. (2000) empirically revealed positive associations between consumer trust in Internet stores and perceived store reputation and size. Higher consumer trust reduces perceived risks associated with Internet shopping and generates more favorable attitudes toward shopping at a particular store, which in turn increases one's willingness to patronize that store.

These studies have all made important contributions to our understanding of the dynamics of the online shopping phenomenon. However, there is a lack of coherent understanding of the impact of most, if not all, possible factors related to online shopping behaviors. This makes comparisons of different studies difficult, applications of research findings limited, and the prospect of synthesizing and integrating the empirical literature elusive.

This chapter synthesizes the representative studies of consumer online shopping behavior based on an analytical literature review. To be consistent with the theme of advances in MIS, we focus on the IS literature. To draw validated results, we emphasize empirical studies, especially those using quantitative methods. In doing so, we attempt to provide a comprehensive picture of the state of the art of this area and point out limitations and directions for future research. We approach the research question mainly from the e-CRM human factors perspective, since what interests us here is human behavior. Variables related to e-CRM markets, business models, and technology are also investigated, because they influence (potential) customers' perceptions, attitudes, and behaviors in various ways.

RESEARCH METHOD

Journal and Article Selection

Published research articles were selected from nine journals for the period of January 1998 to December 2003: *Communications of the ACM* (CACM), *Decision Support Systems* (DSS), *Inter-*

Table 9.1

Quantitative Empirical Research Method

ID	Method Name and Description	Examples
1	Experiment: Includes lab and field experiments; manipulates independent variable; controls for intervening variables; conducted in controlled settings or in a natural setting of the phenomenon under study	Chau et al. (2002); Devaraj et al. (2002)
2	Field study: No manipulation of independent variables, involves experimental design but no experimental controls, is carried out in the natural settings of the phenomenon of interest.	Gefen et al. (2003); Huang (2003)
3	Survey: Involves large numbers of observations; the research uses an experimental design but no controls.	Bhattacherjee (2001); Lee et al. (2003)

national Journal of Electronic Commerce (IJEC), *International Journal of Human–Computer Studies* (IJHCS), *Information Systems Research* (ISR), *Journal of the Association for Information Systems* (JAIS), Journal of Management Information Systems (JMIS), *MIS Quarterly* (MISQ), and *Information and Management* (IM). Six of them (CACM, ISR, JMIS, MISQ, DSS, and IM) are commonly considered top or outstanding journals in the IS discipline (Mylonopoulos and Theoharakis 2001; Whitman et al. 1999; Hardgrave and Walstrom 1997). Although not ranked in many journal assessments due to its recent inception, JAIS is included in this study owing to its unique position as the flagship research journal for the Association for Information Systems (AIS), and its perceived high quality and rising status in recent journal rankings studies (Lowry et al. 2004). IJEC is included because it is the only journal specifically dedicated to electronic commerce (Ngai and Wat 2002). The coverage of a six-year period is considered well suited for this type of research (Vessey et al. 2002).

We conducted an exhaustive search in the nine journals to identify research articles that satisfy the following criteria: (1) examines the relationship of at least one of the customer factors identified in our framework (see below) with other factors; and (2) employs quantitative empirical method.

Alavi and Carlson's research method framework (Alavi and Carlson 1992) is used in this study for its wide acceptance in the IS community (Pervan 1998; Romano and Fjermestad 2001; Zhang and Li 2004). Owing to the objective of the current study, only quantitative empirical strategies are adapted. Table 9.1 excerpts the descriptions and examples for quantitative empirical methods from Alavi and Carlson (1992). Studies focusing purely on development of instruments are not included in this paper, because they usually do not investigate relationships among different constructs, while studies developing/validating instruments and investigating relationships among constructs at the same time are included.

Research Framework

A research framework can be very useful for synthesizing existing studies, and thus for making sense of the empirical evidence and demonstrating gaps and future directions. The development of a framework may take both top-down (theory-driven) and bottom-up (evidence-driven) approaches and several iterations. In this study, we first present a theoretically driven framework that in general agrees with the empirical evidence at a higher level. Then we conduct an in-depth examination of the selected empirical papers to enhance and refine the framework to a detailed level that can guide our understanding and future research directions.

Figure 9.1   **Research Framework of Online Customer Behavior**

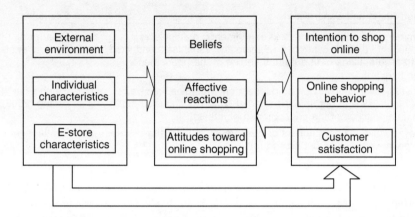

Figure 9.1 shows the research framework for this study. It is developed based on theoretical work in individual psychology, IS, and an abstract-level examination of the collected studies. The framework resembles the key components and relationships in the theory of reasoned action (TRA) (Fishbein and Ajzen 1975), theory of planned behavior (TPB) (Ajzen 1991), and many studies on technology acceptance and individual reactions and behavior toward technology. This makes sense, because consumer online behavior is human behavior in a particular context.

The box on the far right in Figure 9.1 includes three outcome variables: intention to shop online, online shopping behavior, and customer satisfaction. Broadly speaking, online shopping behavior refers to consumers' actions of visiting/revisiting e-stores, placing orders to buy products, or signing contracts to accept and use services via the Internet. Products are anything tangible, such as software, hardware, books, clothing, food, and so on (Liang and Lai 2002; Bellman et al. 1999; USC Annenberg School Center for the Digital Future 2004), while banking/financial service, insurance, brokerage, and electronic newspapers are typical examples of B2C e-commerce service (Bhattacherjee 2001a; Bhattacherjee 2001b; Kim et al. 2002; Liao and Cheung 2002; Lu and Li, 2002). Intention is the cognitive representation of a person's readiness to conduct a specified behavior (Fishbein and Ajzen 1975). In the B2C commerce context, it refers to the strength of one's willingness to perform consuming behavior online. Intention is considered to be the immediate antecedent of behavior (Fishbein and Ajzen 1975). Abundant studies on both technology acceptance and consumer online shopping have employed behavioral intention instead of actual behavior as (one of) the final dependent variable(s) (e.g., Gefen et al. 2003; Liang and Lai 2002). Satisfaction was originally defined by Locke (1976, p. 1300) in the job performance context as "a pleasurable or positive emotional state resulting from the appraisal of one's job." Later the definition was extended by Oliver (1981, p. 29) to the consumption context as "the summary psychological state resulting when the emotion surrounding disconfirmed expectations is coupled with the consumer's prior feelings about the consumption experience." Both definitions emphasize a "psychological or affective state related to and resulting from a cognitive appraisal of the expectation–performance discrepancy" (Bhattacherjee 2001b, p. 353).

Within the middle box are the customers' evaluative reactions (also referred to as beliefs), affective reactions, and attitudes toward online shopping phenomena. Theories (such as TRA and

TPB) and empirical evidence show that these reactions and attitudes are strong predictors of the outcome variables (e.g., Liang and Huang, 1998; Koufaris 2002; Henderson and Divett 2003; Bhattacherjee 2001b; Lee et al. 2003). A belief refers to a person's subjective evaluation of an object. It links a given object to an attribute (Fishbein and Ajzen 1975). In the B2C context, we define it as a (potential) customer's subjective evaluation of a relevant object such as the Internet as a shopping channel, a specific e-store or online shopping experience. Beliefs are expected to impact a (potential) customer's shopping intention, behavior, and satisfaction (Devaraj et al. 2003; Liang and Huang 1998; Han and Noh 1999–2000; Vellido et al. 2000, Lee et al. 2003).

Triandis (1980) proposed a model where affect impacts intention. Affect refers to "the feelings of joy, elation, or pleasure, or depression, disgust, displeasure, or hate associated by an individual with a particular act" (Triandis 1980, p. 211). Russell (2003) proposed a construct called perception of affective quality (PAQ), which refers to a person's "perception of the pleasant-unpleasant and activating-deactivating qualities of stimuli" (p. 148). Russell (2003) described an emotional episode to illustrate how PAQ changes one's affect and in turn impacts his or her perceptual-cognitive appraisal of an object that results in certain actions. Empirical studies provide evidence for the influence of affective reactions toward stimuli on intention/behavior (e.g., Griffith et al. 2001; Koufaris 2002). It is therefore reasonable to include customers' affective reactions as an antecedent of online shopping outcome. Affective reactions can be toward the Internet shopping channel, a specific e-store, or online shopping experience.

Attitude has been defined and measured very differently in various studies. In one definition, attitude "represents a summary evaluation of a psychological object captured in such attribute dimensions as good-bad, harmful-beneficial, pleasant-unpleasant, and likable-dislikable" (Ajzen 2001, p. 28). Attitude has also shown mixed impact on behavior and intention. TPB states that only specific attitudes toward the behavior in question can be expected to predict that behavior. Empirical studies in IS and online consumer behavior support this assertion (e.g., Karahanna et al. 1999; Khalifa and Limayem 2003; Tan and Teo 2000). Therefore we include attitude toward online shopping behavior in the middle box and expect it to predict the outcome variables. In the B2C e-commerce context, attitude refers to an individual's positive or negative feelings about performing online shopping behavior, including using the EC channel generally and using a specific e-store (e.g., Chen et al. 2002; Khalifa and Limayem 2003). According to the classic tripartite model of attitude structure, attitudes consist of affective, cognitive, and behavioral components (Breckler and Berman 1991). Based on this view, attitudes are assumed to be influenced by cognition as well as affect (Ajzen 2001). This indicates that within the middle box, beliefs and affective reactions could impact attitudes.

According to its definitions, satisfaction could be influenced by beliefs and affective reactions, since satisfaction results from a cognitive appraisal of the difference between expectation (in terms of beliefs and affective reactions) and performance (reflected by beliefs and affective reactions). This is supported by a number of empirical studies (e.g., Han and Noh 1999–2000; Lee et al. 2003). On the other hand, satisfaction may help to form or change a person's beliefs or intentions (e.g., Bhattacherjee 2001a; Bhattacherjee 2001b; Devaraj et al. 2002; Kim et al. 2002; Pavlou 2003). . This is represented by the arrow from the right box to the middle box.

The box on the left contains "external variables" (Ajzen and Fishbein 1980) that influence the outcome variables directly or indirectly through beliefs, affective reactions, and attitudes. External environment refers to those contextual factors that may impact online consumers' behavior but are not under the control of either the consumers or the e-store vendors. For example, the existing legal framework is an external environment factor that protects consumers from financial loss in online transactions. Other examples would be network speed, government support for e-commerce, offline competitors' performance, etc. (Liao et al. 2001; Khalifa and Limayem 2003; Ramaswami et al. 2000–2001). Individual characteristics include demographics and personality/ trait, propensity, lifestyle, etc. Electronic store characteristics refer to the objective features of e-stores, including the characters of electronic vendors, product/service on sale, services support-ing transactions, and e-stores' Web sites. Theoretical and empirical evidence has been found to support the impacts of these external variables on those in the middle and right boxes (e.g., Borchers 2001; Lee et al. 2000; Bellman et al. 1999; Bhatnagar et al. 2000; Li et al. 1999; Koufaris et al. 2002; Kimery and McCord 2002; Liang and Lai 2000; Kim et al. 2001; Cho et al. 2001, 2002, 2003; Cho and Fjermestad 2006).

Classification of Variables

Variables in each selected paper were classified according to a scheme developed by the authors— a refinement of the constructs in the research framework in Figure 9.1. The scheme was pretested with a small set of papers and evolved and refined during the rest of the coding process. The final coding scheme includes ten categories: external environment, consumer demographics, personal characteristics, e-store characteristics, beliefs about online shopping phenomena, affective reac-tions, attitudes toward online shopping behavior, intentions to shop online, shopping behavior, and satisfaction. Most categories consist of subcategories. For example, beliefs about online shopping (ID: 5) includes two types, beliefs about the Internet as a general shopping channel (5.1) and beliefs about a specific e-store or a specific online shopping experience (5.2). The latter subcategory (5.2) is further classified into six types: beliefs about e-store vendor, offerings (products and services), supporting service, Web site/technology, e-store as a whole, and online shopping experience. Table 9.2 shows descriptions and examples for each category and subcategory.

Noteworthy is the inconsistency of terminologies in the existing studies. Sometimes one term was used to refer to several constructs by different researchers. At other times one construct was referred to by several different terms. During our coding process, a variable was assigned to a category according to its nature instead of the name used in the original study. For example, Luo and Seyedian (2003–2004) treated "site value" as users' attitude toward Internet storefront sites. However, they defined it as the "extent to which users perceive a web site as useful, important, and valuable" and measured it in a corresponding way. This indicates that "site value" is consis-tent with beliefs about the Internet as a shopping channel. Therefore we assigned it into 5.1, "Beliefs about EC channel."

RESULTS

A total of 44 quantitative empirical papers focusing on online consumers' evaluative and affective reactions, attitudes, behaviors, and satisfaction issues were published over the period of 1998 to 2003 in the nine selected IS journals. Each paper is described briefly in the Appendix. Two such papers were published in 1998, two in 1999, eight in 2000, seven in 2001, 14 in 2002, and 11 in 2003. A few papers were published in issues comprising two years; they were treated as if pub-lished in the earlier year. For example, a paper from Han and Noh (1999–2000) was considered published in 1999. Though the collection basket size is fairly small, the increasing publication trend over the recent years indicates a growing interest in this research area.

About 68 percent of the selected studies (30 studies) employed survey methods. Surveys were conducted through telephone interviews, Web-based surveys, paper–and-pencil surveys, mail surveys, etc. Nine studies (20 percent) utilized experimental methods (including lab controlled

Table 9.2

Classification Scheme for Variables

ID	Category	Description	Examples
1	External environment	Contextual factors that may impact online consumers' behavior but are not under the control of either the consumers or the e-store vendors, e.g., the existing legal framework, network features, government support for e-commerce, off-line competitors' performance, etc.	Network speed (Liao et al., 2001)
2	Consumer demographics	Demographic information about customers, including age, gender, education, income, household size, region, nationality, knowledge, experience, etc.	Age, gender, household income, occupation (Chen and Hitt, 2002)
3	Personal characteristics	Personality/trait, propensities, product involvement, lifestyle, purpose of Internet use, need specificity, etc.	Need specificity, product involvement (Koufaris et al., 2001–2002); Trust propensity (Lee and Turban, 2001)
4	E-store characteristics	Objective features of e-stores, including characteristics about the vendors, products/service for sale, supporting services, and websites/technologies.	See below.
4.1	Vendor characteristics	Features of an e-store's vendor.	None.
4.2	Offering (product, service on sale) characteristics	Features of the products or services sold by e-stores, e.g., product variety, value (price, quality), technological complexity, ego-related level, expenditure level, etc.	Product price and quality (Devaraj et al., 2003)
4.3	Supporting service characteristics	Features of the service e-stores offer to support the B2C transaction process, including during-sale and after-sale service such as network externality, return process, facilitating conditions (transaction efficiency), etc.	Return process (quick/simple) (Devaraj et al., 2003)
4.4	Website/ Technology characteristics	Features of the websites/technologies of e-stores, including website structure, information presentation, navigation/searching mechanisms, decision making aids, efficiency, security, accessibility, etc.	Content presentation (Griffith et al., 2001); Ease of access of product information (measured by number of clicks to get certain information) (Shim et al., 2002)
4.5	E-store characteristics	Features of an e-store as a whole, such as loyalty incentives' availability, cost, reputation, etc.	Minimum deposit required to open an account, specific retention strategy controlled by e-stores (Chen and Hitt, 2002); Store reputation (Devaraj et al., 2003)

(continued)

Table 9.2 (continued)

ID	Category	Description	Examples
5	Beliefs about online shopping	An individual's subjective evaluation of objects in B2C e-commerce context. It could be subjective evaluation of the Internet as a shopping channel or of a specific e-store or a specific online shopping experience.	See below.
5.1	Beliefs about EC channel	An individual's subjective evaluation of the Internet as a shopping channel in terms of its usefulness, ease of use, convenience, security, risk, trust, uncertainty, transaction cost, time saving, technical features, etc.	Perceived risk (behavioral uncertainty; environmental uncertainty) (Pavlou, 2003); Perceived convenience of Internet shopping, perceived financial risk of Internet shopping (providing credit card information through the web) (Bhatnagar et al., 2000)
5.2	Beliefs about an e-store/online shopping experience	An individual's subjective evaluation of a specific e-store or an online shopping experience.	See below.
5.2.1	Beliefs about vendor	An individual's subjective evaluation of an electronic vendor. Includes customer's trust toward vendor, perceived risk with vendor, perception of cost to switch vendors, empathy, reliability, responsiveness, assurance, familiarity with vendor, etc.	Perceived risk with vendor, empathy (customer perceptions that the service provider is giving them individualized attention and has their best interests at heart) (Gefen, 2002)
5.2.2	Beliefs about offering (product, service on sale)	An individual's subjective evaluation of the products or services for sale in an e-store, e.g., perceived usefulness of products, perceived performance of the service, etc.	Perceived performance of online knowledge community at adoption (Khalifa and Liu, 2003); Product quality (Lee et al., 2003)
5.2.3	Beliefs about supporting service	An individual's subjective evaluation of the service an e-store offers to support the B2C transaction process, including during-sale and after-sale service, etc.	Time to receive product (Lee et al., 2003)
5.2.4	Beliefs about website/ technology	An individual's subjective evaluation of an e-store's website or relevant technologies, e.g., perceived usefulness, perceived ease of use, tangibility, convenience, firmness, challenges, website design quality, etc.	Perceived firmness (including internal stability and external security) (Kim et al., 2002)
5.2.5	Beliefs about an e-store as a whole	An individual's overall subjective evaluation of an e-store that mixes beliefs about vendor, product, supporting service, and website/technology associated with this store.	Motivator of consumer purchases in terms of electronic store design quality (Liang and Lai, 2002)

5.2.6	Beliefs about specific online shopping experience	An individual's overall subjective evaluation of a specific online shopping experience at a specific e-store	Cost reduction, convenience in purchasing (Lee et al., 2003)
6	Affective reactions	An individual's primitive emotional reactions toward objects in B2C e-commerce context, e.g., the Internet as a shopping channel, a specific e-store or online shopping experience. It contains three dimensions, arousal, pleasure, and dominance.	See below.
6.1	Affective reactions to EC channel	It refers to an individual's primitive emotional reactions toward the Internet as a shopping channel.	Shopping enjoyment as a type of sociopsychological value (Lee et al., 2003)
6.2	Affective reactions to an e-store/online shopping experience	An individual's primitive emotional reactions toward a specific e-store or a specific online shopping experience.	See below.
6.2.1	Affective reactions to vendor	An individual's primitive emotional reactions toward an electronic vendor.	None.
6.2.2	Affective reactions to offering (e.g., product, service on sale)	An individual's primitive emotional reactions toward the products or services for sale in an e-store.	Consumer involvement with retailers' offerings (exciting, neat, appealing, fun, interesting) (Griffith et al., 2001)
6.2.3	Affective reactions to supporting service	An individual's primitive emotional reactions toward the service an e-store offers to support the B2C transaction process, including during-sale and after-sale service, etc.	None.
6.2.4	Affective reactions to website/ technology	An individual's primitive emotional reactions toward an e-store's website or relevant technologies.	Entertainment (perceived entertainment value of the site) (O'Keefe et al., 2000)
6.2.5	Affective reactions to an e-store as a whole	An individual's primitive emotional reactions toward an e-store as a whole.	Emotions experienced in a virtual shopping environment (including 3 dimensions: arousal, pleasure, and dominance) (Huang, 2003)
6.2.6	Affective reactions to specific online shopping experience	An individual's primitive emotional reactions toward a specific shopping experience at a specific e-store	Shopping enjoyment (reflects the customer experience at the video store: interesting, fun) (Koufaris, 2002)
7	Attitudes to online shopping behavior	An individual's positive or negative feelings about performing online shopping behavior, including using the EC channel generally and using a specific e-store.	See below.

Table 9.2 *(continued)*

ID	Category	Description	Examples
7.1	Attitudes to using EC channel generally	An individual's positive or negative feelings about using the Internet as a shopping channel	Attitude toward using online banking generally (Tan and Teo, 2000)
7.2	Attitudes to using a specific e-store	An individual's positive or negative feelings about performing online shopping behavior at a specific e-store.	Customer attitude toward the e-publishing site (operationalized as students' positive feelings toward repetitive use of the site) (Lu and Lin, 2002)
8	Intention to shop online	Consumers' willingness to shop online in general or at a specific e-store.	See below.
8.1	Intention to shop online generally	Consumers' willingness to use the Internet as a shopping channel in general, not limited to a specific e-store.	Acceptance of electronic channel (intention to purchase a particular product electronically) (Liang and Huang, 1998)
8.2	Intention to shop at a specific e-store	Consumers' willingness to re/visit or re/purchases at a specific e-store.	Willingness to purchase/ visit again/purchase again at a specific store (Liang and Lai, 2002); Customer loyalty (Lu and Lin, 2002)
9	Shopping behavior	Consumers' actions of visiting/revisiting e-stores, placing orders to buy products, or signing contracts to accept and use services.	See below.
9.1	Shopping online generally	Consumers' actions of visiting/revisiting e-stores, placing orders to buy products or signing contract to accept services via the Internet. Not limited to a specific e-store.	Frequency of e-commerce experience (Han and Noh, 1999–2000); Frequency of purchasing financial products online (not limited to a financial agent specifically) (Ramaswami et al., 2000–2001)
9.2	Shopping at a specific e-store	Consumers' visiting/revisiting e-stores, placing orders to buy products or signing contracts to accept and use services at a specific e-store.	Frequency of using a virtual store (Chen et al., 2002); Switching (a change of the major brokerage firm by a customer) (Chen and Hitt, 2002)
10	Satisfaction	Summary of the psychological state resulting when the emotion surrounding disconfirmed expectations is coupled with the consumer's prior feelings about the consumption experience (Oliver, 1981)	See below.

10.1	Satisfaction with EC channel	Summary of psychological state resulting from disconfirmation/confirmation of a customer's expectations about the Internet as a shopping channel by his/her evaluation of online shopping experience.	Satisfaction with general EC experience (Han and Noh, 1999–2000)
10.2	Satisfaction with an e-store/online shopping experience	Summary of psychological state resulting from the extent to which a consumers' evaluation of an overall online shopping experience/e-store confirms his/her expectations.	See below.
10.2.1	Satisfaction with vendor	Customer satisfaction with an e-store's owner.	None.
10.2.2	Satisfaction with offering (product, service on sale)	Customer satisfaction with the products or services for sale in an e-store	Price satisfaction (Cao et al., 2003–2004)
10.2.3	Satisfaction with supporting service	Customer satisfaction with the service supporting the transactions offered by an e-store, e.g., delivery process, return process, etc.	Satisfaction with fulfillment process (Cao et al., 2003–2004)
10.2.4	Satisfaction with website/technology	Customer satisfaction with the characters of an e-store's website or other features related to technology	Satisfaction with ordering process (Cao et al., 2003–2004)
10.2.5	Satisfaction with an e-store as a whole	Customer satisfaction with an e-store as a whole, not with a specific aspect such as product or website	Customer satisfaction with a specific Internet business (e-store) (Kim et al., 2002)
10.2.6	Satisfaction with a specific online shopping experience	Customer satisfaction with overall experience of patronizing an e-store	Satisfaction with overall experience of using an online banking division of one of the largest national banks in the US (Bhattacherjee, 2001b)

experiments and field experiments). Four were field studies. One study (Shim et al. 2002) combined both qualitative and quantitative methods, while quantitative methods including logistic regression were employed to explore the findings from existential phenomenology.

Results of Topical Coverage

Variables belonging to external environment, demographics, personal characteristics, and e-store characteristics were examined as independent variables in most studies. That is, these variables are proposed as predictors of or variables significantly correlated with constructs capturing consumers' cognitive and affective reactions and behaviors in B2C e-commerce context. These four factors fall into the left box in Figure 9.1. Intentions, behaviors, and satisfaction are treated as dependent variables in most studies. These three factors appear in the right box in Figure 9.1. They serve as the outcomes in most online customer behavior models. Occasionally, the influences of intentions on behaviors and impacts of satisfaction on intentions, behaviors, and beliefs are examined in such models. The other factors—online shopping beliefs, affective reactions, and attitudes—are treated as either dependent or independent variables in the 44 studies. Often such a variable is considered as a mediator in SEM or PLS models, thus it is both an IV and a DV. For example, Gefen and Straub (2000) hypothesized and confirmed that perceived ease of use of an e-store's Web site (belief) affected its perceived usefulness (belief), which in turn affected an individual's intention to buy books at this site. Beliefs, affective reactions, and attitudes fall into the middle box in Figure 9.1.

Table 9.3 summarizes the distribution of the variables investigated in the article collection. Note that the number of papers examining a certain type of variables may be less than the sum of its subcategories, because one paper may investigate multiple subcategories of one type of variables.

As Table 9.3 indicates, three out of the four factors in the left box in Figure 9.1—demographics, personal characteristics, and e-store characteristics—have been investigated in 15, 12, and 13 studies, respectively, while another IV factor, external environment, has been examined in seven studies.

Among the three factors in the middle box in Figure 9.1, consumer beliefs have received extraordinary attention. This type of variable has been studied in 38 papers. Beliefs about both the Internet as a shopping channel in general and a particular e-store or specific online shopping experience have been widely investigated. In contrast, affective reactions and attitudes toward online shopping behavior are less represented. They have been explored in only ten and five studies, respectively. Consumers' affective reactions to e-stores' vendors or supporting service haven't been touched upon yet by the collection of studies.

Among the three factors in the right box of Figure 9.1, intention to shop online has been studied by 26 papers. In most studies intentions were treated as the ultimate outcome in consumer online shopping models. Fourteen studies managed to measure consumers' actual shopping behaviors. Customer satisfaction has drawn the attention of 12 studies.

A detailed presentation of variables examined in each article is shown in Table 9.4.

Results of Significant Relationships

This section summarizes the significant relationships among the ten types of variables empirically supported by the 44 studies. We are particularly interested in findings that attempted to reveal factors predicting or significantly correlating with the variables in the right and middle boxes in Figure 9.1. Since we focus here on the direct and primary factors, we do not present moderators or moderating relationships in this section but rather in the discussion section.

Intention to Shop Online. Twenty-six out of the 44 empirical studies confirmed significant relationships between an individual's intention to shop online and other constructs. As expected, intention has been found to be a good predictor of online shopping behavior (e.g., Khalifa and Limayem 2003; Suh and Han 2003; Pavlou 2003).

Many studies in the collection attempted to identify antecedents of behavioral intentions. A number of studies found that a prospective consumer's subjective beliefs about the Internet as a shopping channel in general significantly impact one's intention to shop online (Devaraj et al. 2003; Khalifa and Limayem 2003; Liang and Huang 1998; Liao and Cheung 2001). These beliefs pertain to many aspects of the EC channel, such as efficiency, time saving, security/risks associated with transaction, uncertainty, price, transaction cost, customer service, comparative shop-

Table 9.3

Variables Investigated in the Collection

ID	Category	Variable Type	No. of Papers Examining this Variable
1	External environment	IV	7
2	Demographics	IV	15
3	Personal characteristics	IV	12
4	E-store characteristics	IV	13
4.1	Vendor characteristics		0
4.2	Offering (product, service on sale) characteristics		6
4.3	Supporting service characteristics		2
4.4	Website/technology characteristics		7
4.5	E-store characteristics		6
5	Beliefs about online shopping	IV/DV	38
5.1	Beliefs about EC channel		13
5.2	Beliefs about an e-store / online shopping experience		30
5.2.1	Beliefs about vendor		8
5.2.2	Beliefs about offering (product, service on sale)		8
5.2.3	Beliefs about supporting service		0
5.2.4	Beliefs about website/technology		15
5.2.5	Beliefs about an e-store as a whole		8
5.2.6	Beliefs about an online shopping experience		5
6	Affective reactions	IV/DV	10
6.1	Affective reactions to EC channel		1
6.2	Affective reactions to an e-store/online shopping experience		9
6.2.1	Affective reactions to vendor		0
6.2.2	Affective reactions to offering (product, service on sale)		1
6.2.3	Affective reactions to supporting service		0
6.2.4	Affective reactions to website/technology		3
6.2.5	Affective reactions to an e-store as a whole		2
6.2.6	Affective reactions to a specific online shopping experience		3
7	Attitudes to online shopping behavior	IV/DV	5
7.1	Attitudes to using EC channel generally		2
7.2	Attitudes to using a specific e-store		3
8	Intention to shop online	DV/IV	26
8.1	Intention to shop online generally		7
8.2	Intention to shop at a specific e-store		19
9	Shopping behavior	DV	14
9.1	Shopping online generally		9
9.2	Shopping at a specific e-store		7
10	Satisfaction	DV/IV	12
10.1	Satisfaction with EC channel		4
10.2	Satisfaction with an e-store / online shopping experience		9
10.2.1	Satisfaction with vendor		0
10.2.2	Satisfaction with offering (e.g. product, service on sale)		1
10.2.3	Satisfaction with supporting service		0
10.2.4	Satisfaction with website/technology		1
10.2.5	Satisfaction with an e-store as a whole		1
10.2.6	Satisfaction with a specific online shopping experience		8

Notes:
IV–Independent variable; DV–Dependent variable.
Total number of papers in the collection: 44.

162

Table 9.4

Variables Investigated in Each Study

Authors (Year)	1 External environment	2 Demographics	3 Personal characteristics / disposition	4.1 Vendor characteristics	4.2 Offering characteristics	4.3 Supporting service characteristics	4.4 Website/Technology characteristics	4.5 E-store characteristics	5.1 Beliefs about EC channel	5.2 Beliefs about an e-store/shopping experience	6.1 Affective reactions to EC channel	6.2 Affective reactions to an e-store/ shopping experience	7.1 Attitude to using EC channel generally	7.2 Attitude to using a specific e-store	8.1 Intention to shop online generally	8.2 Intention to shop at a specific e-store	9.1 Purchasing online generally	9.2 Shopping at a specific e-store	10.1 Satisfaction with EC channel	10.2 Satisfaction with an e-store/shopping experience
Bellman et al. (1999)		×	×		×				×								×			
Bhatnagar et al. (2000)		×															×			
Bhattacherjee (2001a)								×		×				×		×				×
Bhattacherjee (2001b)										×										×
Cao et al. (2003–2004)					×															×
Chau et al. (2002)	×	×	×					×		×		×								
Chen and Hitt (2002)		×	×		×		×					×		×		×		×		
Chen et al. (2002)																		×		
Devaraj et al. (2002)					×	×	×	×	×	×					×				×	
Devaraj et al. (2003)		×							×	×					×					
Featherman et al. (2003)										×				×						
Gefen and Straub (2000)										×				×						
Gefen (2002)										×				×						

Study	C1	C2	C3	C4	C5	C6	C7	C8	C9	C10	C11	C12	C13	C14	C15	C16	C17	C18	C19	C20
Gefen et al. (2003)													X					X		
Grifith et al. (2001)		X						X					X				X			
Han and Noh (1999–2000)	X	X						X				X				X			X	X
Henderson and Divett (2003)							X					X		X						
Huang (2003)			X					X		X				X	X					
Khalifa and Liu (2003)								X			X			X	X					
Khalifa and Liu (2002–2003)								X			X			X	X					
Khalifa and Limayem (2003)	X					X			X			X		X	X	X				
Kim et al. (2000)							X	X			X	X		X	X	X	X			
Kim et al. (2002)							X	X			X	X		X	X	X				X
Koufaris (2002)		X	X								X	X		X	X	X			X	
Koufaris et al. (2001–2002)		X	X								X	X		X	X	X				
Lee and Turban (2001)			X			X		X												
Lee et al. (2003)							X	X	X									X		
Liang and Huang (1998)		X				X		X				X	X			X				
Liang and Lai (2002)		X	X			X		X						X	X				X	
Liao and Cheung (2001)	X	X					X	X	X			X		X						
Liao and Cheung (2002)								X	X					X	X					
Lu and Lin (2002)								X				X		X	X			X		
Luo and Seyedian (2003–2004)		X				X	X	X										X		
O'Keefe et al. (2000)	X	X				X			X											
Parthasarathy and Bhattacherjee (1998)	X	X			X															
Pavlou (2003)								X					X	X	X	X	X		X	X
Ramaswami et al. (2000–2001)	X	X				X		X				X					X			
Ranganathan and Ganapathy (2002)								X												
Salam et al. (2003)					X X		X	X												
Shim et al. (2002)														X						X
Slyke et al. (2002)		X				X														
Suh and Han (2003)		X				X		X			X	X		X	X	X			X	
Tan and Teo (2000)		X X									X	X								
Vellido et al. (2000)								X				X								

ping, relative life content, asset specificity, etc. Attitude toward online shopping behavior has been confirmed to be another antecedent of Internet shopping intention (Khalifa and Limayem 2003; Tan and Teo 2000). Objective e-store features such as product price and Web site design factors (e.g., information content, download time, safety) are significantly associated with shopping intention (Devaraj et al. 2003; Liao and Cheung 2001). In addition, external environment (e.g., social influences from family, media, etc.), personal needs, as well as Internet experience would enhance one's intention to adopt online shopping (Devaraj et al. 2003; Khalifa and Limayem 2003; Tan and Teo 2000).

Similarly, a prospective customer's willingness to patronize a specific Internet store is significantly associated with one's beliefs about this store in terms of its vendor, offering, supporting service, Web site, and one's overall shopping experience in the store. This has been verified by a good number of studies (e.g, Bhattacherjee 2001a; Bhattacherjee 2001b; Chen et al. 2002; Gefen 2002; Liao and Cheung 2002). Perceived usefulness of the product/service offered for sale is an important motivator of shopping intention (Bhattacherjee 2001a; Bhattacherjee 2001b). The intention could be damaged by perceived risks related to e-store performance, finance, time, psychology, social image, and privacy (Featherman et al., 2003). Customer trust toward the vendor or store may enhance shopping intention directly or indirectly by reducing perceived risk (Gefen 2002). Perceived e-store/Web site design quality (e.g., PU, PEOU, transaction accuracy, security, tangibles, etc.) is another fundamental factor users consider when deciding which e-store to shop (Chen et al. 2002; Gefen and Straub 2000; Gefen 2002; Liang and Lai, 2002; Liao and Cheung 2002). Affective reactions toward an e-store also predict a customer's shopping intention. Positive shopping enjoyment, emotions experienced in a virtual shopping environment, and perceived control may increase shopping intentions (Huang 2003; Koufaris 2002; Koufaris et al. 2001–2002). Besides beliefs and affective reactions, researchers discovered that customer attitude toward patronizing a certain e-store is a strong antecedent of shopping intention (Lu and Lin 2002; Chen et al. 2002).

Both general and specific online shopping intention might be enhanced due to higher customer satisfaction (e.g., Bhattacherjee 2001a; Bhattacherjee 2001b; Devaraj et al, 2002; Kim et al. 2002). For example, Devaraj et al. (2002) found that consumer satisfaction with EC channel had a positive impact on one's EC channel preference, which was measured through four items pertaining to one's intentions to shop online and one's recommendation of an EC shopping channel to others. According to its nature, EC channel preference is considered as online shopping intention.

Online Shopping Behavior. Fourteen empirical studies have identified antecedents of or variables significantly correlated with customers' online shopping behavior. Generally, whether one buys products or service online is influenced by external environment, demographics, personal characteristics, e-store features, beliefs about online shopping, and behavioral intention. People who have a wired lifestyle and those who have more experience with the Internet and online shopping are more open to purchasing on the Internet (Bellman et al. 1999; Bhatnagar et al. 2000). Further, people who like being first to use new technologies and who agree that the Internet improves productivity are more likely to shop online (Bellman et al. 1999). Chen and Hitt (2002) revealed that product variety is significantly correlated with reduced switching and attrition behaviors in the online brokerage industry. Better facilitating conditions such as transaction efficiency would attract more customers to patronize e-stores (Khalifa and Limayem 2003). Beliefs about the Internet as a shopping channel in terms of security, risk, trust, convenience, control, Web site features (e.g., ease of use), and customer service have been confirmed to be strong predictors of shopping behaviors (Han and Noh 1999–2000; Vellido et al. 2000). Of course, intention to shop online is another predictor (Khalifa and Limayem 2003) of shopping behavior. In addition, competitors' performance, which is an external environment factor, plays an important role in predicting consumers' online shopping behavior. For example, Ramaswami et al. (2000–2001) confirmed that less satisfaction with the performance of an offline financial service agent would lead to greater disagreement between consumer and the agent, which in turn would encourage the customer to buy financial products online.

Customers still have many decisions to make, even if they have decided to buy a certain product or service online. Which specific store to shop? How much to spend? How often to shop? As expected, behavioral intention is a good predictor of shopping behavior at a specific e-store (Suh and Han 2003, Pavlou 2003). Despite that, Liang and Lai (2002) proposed and validated that better e-store features such as lower product price, better Web site design, and better store reputation motivate customer shopping behavior at a specific store. Similarly, Parthasarathy and Bhattacherjee (1998) found that network externality (i.e., providing a manual, a tutorial, a user guide to help purchasers use the product) attracts customers. Moreover, empirical studies confirmed that customer beliefs about a store Web site (e.g., PU, PEOU) and product attributes (e.g., usefulness and compatibility) have significant impact on one's shopping behavior (Henderson and Divett 2003; Parthasarathy and Bhattacherjee 1998). Personal factors such as special needs and external/interpersonal influence (e.g., influence from mass media, advertising, friends, colleagues, etc.) would motivate one to buy products or service at a particular e-store (Liang and Lai 2002, Parthasarathy and Bhattacherjee 1998). Sometimes certain shopping behavior could be predicted by other types of shopping behavior. For instance, Parthasarathy and Bhattacherjee (1998) conducted a study to understand consumers' postadoption behavior in the context of online communication service. They found that discontinuers use the service less extensively during their initial adoption period than continuing adopters; while those who turn to other similar service providers later adopt the service earlier and use it more extensively than those who stop using this type of service completely.

Customer Satisfaction. The results of 12 out of the 44 empirical studies illustrate significant relationships between online customer satisfaction and other constructs. Most studies treated satisfaction as a dependent variable and tried to identify its antecedents. It has been verified that customers' satisfaction with general B2C e-commerce channel is influenced by one's general beliefs about the Internet as a shopping channel (e.g., perceived ease of use, transaction cost, time saved, etc.) (Devaraj et al. 2002; Han and Noh 1999–2000; Lee et al. 2003), affective reaction toward the EC channel (Lee et al. 2003), and personal disposition such as perceived importance of contextual marketing, and perception of the importance of customer-orientation strategy (Luo and Seyedian 2003–2004).

Customer satisfaction with shopping experience at a specific e-store has been found to be significantly associated with product price (Cao et al. 2003–2004), Web site/technology features or other e-store characteristics (Shim et al. 2002), one's beliefs about this e-store or shopping experience obtained at this site (Bhattacherjee 2001a; Bhattacherjee 2001b), affective reactions to the e-store website/technology (Kim et al. 2002), and satisfaction with price and ordering process (Cao et al. 2003–2004). Beliefs about an e-store/shopping experience include evaluative perceptions about the product, Web site, expectation disconfirmation, and desire disconfirmation (Khalifa and Liu 2002–2003). For instance, Bhattacherjee (2001b) verified that customer satisfaction with one's overall experience of an online banking division (OBD) was positively associated with the perceived usefulness of this OBD and the extent of confirmation of one's expectation.

On the other hand, satisfaction has been found to have significant influences on customers' shopping intention as discussed in the preceding section (e.g., Bhattacherjee 2001a; Bhattacherjee 2001b; Devaraj et al. 2002; Kim et al. 2002). Furthermore, customer satisfaction with past transactions could even impact one's beliefs about an e-store, such as trust in the retailer (Pavlou 2003).

Beliefs about Online Shopping Phenomenon. Several studies observed that beliefs about both the Internet as a shopping channel and a specific e-store or shopping experience are associated with external environment (e.g., social disturbance factor), demographics (e.g., e-commerce experience), personal characteristics (e.g., purpose of Internet use), product characteristics (e.g., technological complexity, ego-related level, expenditure level, etc.), and satisfaction with shopping experience (Han and Noh 1999–2000; Luo and Seyedian 2003–2004; O'Keefe et al. 2000; Bhatnagar et al. 2000; Chau et al. 2002; Pavlou 2003).

Different aspects of beliefs about the Internet as a shopping channel are significantly related. Four studies found this type of connection (Devaraj et al. 2002; Han and Noh 1999–2000; Liang and Huang 1998; Salam et al. 2003). For example, perceived online transaction cost is significantly associated with perceived uncertainty (including product uncertainty and process uncertainty) and asset specificity (including site specificity, physical asset specificity, human asset specificity, brand name specificity, and temporal specificity) (Liang and Huang 1998). Perceived inconvenience of online shopping reduces the expectation of e-commerce usefulness (Han and Noh 1999–2000).

Similarly, ten studies support the strong relationship between different aspects of beliefs about a specific e-store or shopping experience (e.g., Bhattacherjee 2001b; Chen et al. 2002; Gefen and Straub, 2000). For instance, perceived usefulness is positively predicted by perceived ease of use of an e-store or its website (Gefen and Straub 2000). Customer trust toward an e-store vendor is significantly associated with perceived risk of conducting transactions with this vendor and perceived reputation of the vendor, negatively and positively, respectively (Gefen 2002; Pavlou 2003). A customer's desires before adopting an electronic service and one's perceived performance of the service at adoption together predict his/her desire disconfirmation (Khalifa and Liu, 2002–2003).

Affective reactions to online shopping phenomenon

Traditionally, affective reaction consists of three dimensions: arousal, pleasure, and dominance (Russell and Pratt 1980; Mehrabian and Russell 1974; Huang 2003). In this collection of studies, all three are studied to some extent, yet few studies cover all three at the same time except Huang (2003). Pleasure received more attention than the other two dimensions. It has been called perceived entertainment value (Chau et al. 2002; O'Keefe et al. 2000) and shopping enjoyment (Koufaris et al. 2001–2002; Koufaris 2002). Empirical studies confirmed that it is associated with personal characteristics (e.g., purpose of Internet use and product involvement) and beliefs about e-stores (e.g., perceived information load and positive challenges of the website) (Chau et al. 2002; O'Keefe et al. 2000; Koufaris et al. 2001–2002; Koufaris 2002; Huang 2003). Huang (2003) observed that arousal (measured as stimulated-relaxed, excited-calm, frenzied-sluggish) experienced in a virtual shopping environment is associated with an individual's arousal-seeking tendency (i.e., liking arousal by change or by new stimuli). He also demonstrated that dominance (controlling-controlled, dominant-submissive, autonomous-guided) is significantly related to perceived information load of an e-store's website.

Figure 9.2   **A Refined Model**

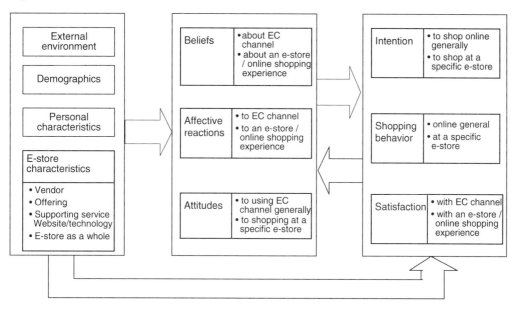

Attitudes Toward Online Shopping Behavior. Three studies discovered antecedents of customers' attitudes toward using or purchasing at a specific e-store (Chen et al. 2002; Lu and Lin 2002; Suh and Han 2003). All these antecedents fall into the subcategory of beliefs about an e-store/online shopping experience. Chen et al. (2002) observed that perceived usefulness and ease of use of an e-store and the compatibility of its use with existing values, beliefs, and needs positively influence a potential customer's attitude toward using this store. Lu and Lin (2002) found that a user's beliefs about the content (referring to the product/service offered by an e-store), context (i.e., effectiveness of the Web site's interface), and infrastructure (i.e., efficiency of a collection of assets) of an electronic newspaper site positively impact one's attitude toward using this site. Suh and Han (2003) validated that a customer's trust in an e-store would predict positive attitude toward using this store.

A Refined Model

The findings of this study support the research framework depicted in Figure 9.1. The foregoing examination of the existing studies provides more details for the research model. A refined model is shown in Figure 9.2.

   As discussed in the preceding section, external environment, demographics, personal characteristics, and e-store characteristics have been examined as independent variables in most studies. Significant impacts of these factors on individual's online shopping intentions, behaviors, and satisfaction are confirmed by these studies. These influences are either direct or mediated by (potential) customers' beliefs, affective reactions, and attitudes. Some studies explore only the impacts of beliefs, affective reactions, and attitudes on intention, behavior, and satisfaction without touching those variables in the left box (e.g., Khalifa and Liu 2002–2003). However, this does not deny the external factors' input roles. In the other direction, outcome variables in the right box, such as satisfaction, could have fundamental impacts on a customer's beliefs about online shopping. In addition, significant associations exist between variables within the same box. For example, intention to shop online is a good predictor of shopping at a specific e-store.

DISCUSSION

Before we discuss the implications of this study and the future directions of this research area, it is important to acknowledge the study's limitations.

The first limitation is the source of the selected papers, which may introduce bias into the study results. Due to the nature of B2C e-commerce research, relevant studies are published across various journals in multiple disciplines, such as information systems, marketing, management, advertising, etc. Including all the studies in this area is close to infeasible. To focus on the information systems perspective and still have a good set of representative studies, we used a journal basket approach and did an exhaustive search of nine primary IS journals for publications in most recent years, yielding a total of 44 quantitative empirical papers. Selection of this basket of papers might introduce bias into analysis due to its limited coverage and disciplinary perspectives. The second limitation of the current study is the omission of moderating variables and relationships in the analysis. As a first attempt to draw an overview of the research area and to control the scope of the study, we tried to focus on the main factors and their relationships. Moderators are important and give the picture richness that warrants future investigation.

Despite the limitations, we believe that the findings presented in this chapter, representing one of the few studies that synthesize existing work on consumer online shopping behavior, do offer interesting insight into the state of the art of this research stream and have several important implications that may guide future research in this area.

Moderating Effects

A few studies in the collection explored moderating effects. All significant moderators belong to "external factors" that fall into the left box in Figures 9.1 and 9.2 (Liang and Huang 1998; Luo and Seyedian 2003–2004; Koufaris et al. 2001–2002; Lee and Turban 2001). Shopping experience, online customer tenure (i.e., new vs. repeat), and trust propensity are good examples of such moderators. For example, Koufaris et al. (2001–2002) discovered that customer tenure moderates the positive impact of the perceived control one has experienced in an e-store on his/her intention to return to this e-store. Lee and Turban (2001) revealed that one's trust propensity positively moderates the relationship between one's perceived integrity of Internet merchants and his/her trust in online shopping. Though not included in analysis of the current study, moderators serve an important role in understanding the dynamics of online customer behaviors. Therefore we call for future examination in this direction.

Theoretical Models

The collected studies took different perspectives and utilized different theoretical models. There is little consensus on consistent theoretical models to describe and predict online shopping intention, behavior, satisfaction, and other relevant constructs. This lack of a common theoretical framework suggests the need to develop an integrative model of the phenomenon in order to promote systematic investigation of its components and the online shopping process. By identifying common elements and developing our model based on IS literature, we hope to have taken a step toward promoting this type of integration and synthesis of relevant literature.

Terminology

Terminology usage in the existing studies is inconsistent. Sometimes a single term is used to refer to several different constructs by different researchers. At other times, one construct could be referred to by several different terms. For example, pleasure experienced in a virtual shopping environment (Huang 2003), perceived entertainment value (Chau et al. 2002; O'Keefe et al. 2000), and shopping enjoyment (Koufaris et al. 2001–2002; Koufaris 2002) all refer to the valence dimension of affective reaction toward an e-store. In contrast, the same term, compatibility, has been used to stand for different constructs. In Chen et al. (2002) and Parthasarathy and Bhattacherjee (1998) it refers to the degree to which using a virtual store/service is consistent with the customer's existing values, beliefs, ideas, experience, and needs, while in Vellido et al. (2000) it represents control and convenience of shopping experience. This phenomenon indicates that research in online customer behavior is still fairly new and developing. Unification of terminologies is needed.

Instruments

The ten factors and the diverse instruments to measure these variables used by different studies indicate that online shopping is a multidimensional and multidisciplinary phenomenon. Our examination shows that various studies have different ways of operationalizing seemingly identical constructs. This methodological issue needs to be addressed in future research, so that widely accepted and validated instruments can be employed for measuring consumer online shopping behavior and other relevant constructs. Addressing this issue will make comparing and synthesizing results across studies more feasible and easy.

Student Subjects

A good number of studies have, for convenience, employed university students as subjects (e.g., Gefen 2002; Lee and Turban 2001). These papers do provide important and interesting evidence to help us understand online shopping behaviors. However, the use of student subjects might introduce bias into the studies. University students belong to a specific population that typically has more Internet/computer experience, better Internet/computer skills, and higher education levels than "normal" people, yet they may not be financially established, or have the same purchasing power as those with full-time jobs. Further, demographic variables such as Internet experience, Web skills, education, and household income are significantly associated with a (potential) customer's reactions, attitudes, intentions, and behaviors in B2C e-commerce (Devaraj et al. 2003; Koufaris 2002; Liao and Cheung 2001). Therefore it might be questionable to generalize the results from a study using student sample in e-commerce context. Realizing this problem, some researchers have employed "normal" customers as subjects (e.g., Cao et al. 2003–2004; Koufaris 2002). We call for more such studies.

Affective Constructs

Affect, mood, and emotion are fundamental aspects of human beings. Many psychologists argue that it is impossible for a person to have a thought or perform an action without engaging, at least unconsciously, his or her emotional systems. Especially in the marketing and consumer behavior area, neglecting the role of affective constructs may leave the picture incomplete or ignore "normal" online shopping behavior, in line with the psychologists' argument that neglecting affect in behavior studies means not looking at the normal behavior people have. Compared with cognitive beliefs (38 empirical studies examined belief variables in the collection), affective reactions have been paid less attention (10 studies). Therefore we call for more research effort in investigating the role affect-related constructs play in customers' online shopping behaviors.

Impacts and Antecedents of Customer Satisfaction

Satisfaction could significantly improve customers' trust in and loyalty to an e-store and thus bring this store more transactions and profit (Bhattacherjee 2001a; Bhattacherjee 2001b; Devaraj et al. 2002; Kim et al. 2002; Pavlou 2003). While a number of papers attempt to reveal antecedents of online customer satisfaction (e.g., Bhattacherjee 2001a; Bhattacherjee 2001b), more studies are needed to further explore the impacts and antecedents of this construct.

CONCLUSION

In an effort to provide a comprehensive and coherent understanding of customers' online shopping behavior, which is a key issue of e-CRM, this study has investigated and synthesized representative quantitative empirical studies in the IS literature over the period from 1998 to 2003. In this chapter, we first present a theoretically driven framework to describe customers' online shopping behavior, which agrees with the collection of the 44 empirical papers at a higher level. Ten categories of factors are identified: external environment, consumer demographics, personal characteristics, e-store characteristics, beliefs about online shopping phenomena, affective reactions, attitudes toward online shopping behavior, intentions to shop online, shopping behavior, and satisfaction. Through an analytical review of the 44 papers, we develop a classification scheme of these factors and assign the variables investigated in the empirical studies to corresponding categories. Further, based on the significant relationships amongst the variables verified in the empirical studies, the original framework is refined and a more detailed one is proposed (see Figure 9.2).

This research framework helps us get a broader view of customers' online shopping behavior. It has significant implications for both practitioners and academic researchers. Important "external" factors and psychological constructs that may directly or indirectly impact customers' intention, behavior, and satisfaction are revealed in this chapter. These findings would help the electronic store owners, e-commerce Web site designers, and other EC shareholders to target more appropriate consumer groups, to improve product and service quality, and to design better e-commerce Web sites. Thus they could attract more online transactions and establish more successful e-CRM.

This study also identifies where there might be gaps in the research stream and potential opportunities in future research. By analyzing the variables under investigation in the empirical studies, we discover that customer satisfaction and affective reactions toward EC channel or specific e-stores have not been given enough attention, though they play fundamental roles in our understanding of customers' online shopping behavior. In addition, we recognize important methodological issues in this research area. A common theoretical framework, widely accepted instruments, and consistency in terminology are much needed to compare results across studies and to accumulate knowledge in this subfield.

In summary, we believe that the current study provides beneficial implications for both academic research and industry practice based on an insightful review of the existing work on consumer online shopping phenomena.

APPENDIX 9.1

FORTY-FOUR PAPERS EXAMINED IN THIS STUDY

Authors (Year)	Journal	Type	Description of study
Bellman et al. (1999)	CACM	Survey	Using 1997's WVTM data; 10,180 respondents
Bhatnagar et al. (2000)	CACM	Survey	Using 1997's GVU data; 645 respondents
Bhattacherjee (2001a)	DSS	Survey	Online brokerage OLB user; 122 usable responses
Bhattacherjee (2001b)	MISQ	Survey	122 online banking users
Cao et al. (2003–2004)	IJEC	Survey	Using data about 9 book e-retailers from BizRate.com (weekly average ratings of customer satisfaction) and a databases of market-basket prices
Chau et al. (2002)	CACM	Experiment	2 identical experiments in U.S. (119 subjects) and HK (150 subjects)
Chen and Hitt (2002)	ISR	Field study	Using web site traffic data to measure switching costs for online service providers; using "clickstream" data on over 2,000 individuals who utilize the 11 largest online broker sites provided by Media Metrix; also use additional data from Gomez Advisors, an online market research firm, to determine the attributes of the sites studied
Chen et al. (2002)	IM	Survey	Online survey, 253 responses
Devaraj et al. (2002)	ISR	Experiment	134 subjects; subjects purchased similar products through conventional as well as EC channels and reported their experiences in a survey after each transaction
Devaraj et al. (2003)	CACM	Experiment	134 respondents
Featherman et al. (2003)	IJHCS	Experiment	Two computer lab usability tests utilizing vendors shopping trial demonstration software; 214 and 181 subjects respectively
Gefen and Straub (2000)	JAIS	Experiment	202 MBA students at a U.S. university
Gefen (2002)	JAIS	Survey	Online book purchase; 160 students subjects
Gefen et al. (2003)	MISQ	Field study	213 responses; experienced online shoppers who were undergraduate and graduate business students at a leading business school in the mid-Atlantic region of the United States
Griffith et al. (2001)	IJEC	Experiment	Between-subjects research design; 3 treatment conditions: (1) Print content presentation vs. physical medium interface: $n = 103$; (2) Online replication content presentation vs. Web-based physical-medium interface: $n = 112$; (3) Media vivid content presentation vs. Web-based physical-medium interface: $n = 121$.
Han and Noh (1999–2000)	IJEC	Survey	Survey using questionnaire; regular mail, e-mail, f2f interview; simple random sampling from a finite population in Korea; 325 subjects, who were business owners, employees, students, homemakers, and others; people's opinions about general EC
Henderson and Divett (2003)	IJHCS	Field study	247 participants completed the survey; electronically recorded indicators of use in the form of deliveries, purchase value, and number of log-ons to the system; recorded for the month the participants completed the questionnaire and 6 further months.
Huang (2003)	IM	Field study	115 web users including students, staff, and faculty from a large university
Khalifa and Liu (2003)	JAIS	Survey	Online service-online knowledge community; two stages: at adoption, 131 responses; post-adoption, 107 responses

(continued)

APPENDIX 9.1 *(continued)*

Authors (Year)	Journal	Type	Description of study
Khalifa and Liu (2002–2003)	IJEC	Survey	2 rounds: (1) 356 new members of an online knowledge community for electronic business practitioners; (2) 131 respondents of the first survey a week after their membership registration
Khalifa and Limayem (2003)	CACM	Survey	Longitudinal study consisting of 2 online surveys: 1,410 and 705 responses, respectively
Kim et al. (2000)	IJHCS	Experiment	2 consecutive experiments; compare subjects' reactions in different shopping sites with different link structure; 172 and 67 subjects for each, respectively
Kim et al. (2002)	ISR	Survey	In Korea; 4 domains: virtual mall (4,644 subjects), stock brokerage (6,582 subjects), search portal (3,462 subjects), online game (1,991 subjects); 30 trained subjects to assess objective features of architectural quality
Koufaris (2002)	ISR	Survey	An online bookstore; 280 responses who were all new customers of the bookstore
Koufaris et al. (2001–2002)	IJEC	Survey	An e-commerce company; 332 customers
Lee and Turban (2001)	IJEC	Survey	405 subjects who were undergraduate students in Hong Kong
Lee et al. (2003)	JAIS	Survey	65 responses; undergraduate students in Hong Kong
Liang and Huang (1998)	DSS	Survey	5 products; 85 subjects familiar with the Internet
Liang and Lai (2002)	IM	Experiment	3 e-bookstores in Taiwan; 3 experts; 30 student subjects
Liao and Cheung (2001)	IM	Survey	Internet users in Singapore, 312 responses
Liao and Cheung (2002)	IM	Survey	323 responses; Singapore; e-retail banking
Lu and Lin (2002)	IM	Survey	145 undergraduate students in Taipei; e-publishing web site
Luo and Seyedian (2003–2004)	IJEC	Survey	Northeastern United States; 180 useful responses
O'Keefe et al. (2000)	IJHCS	Experiment	3 experiments in 3 countries: U.S. (122 subjects), HK (150 subjects), UK (44 subjects)
Parthasarathy and Bhattacherjee (1998)	ISR	Survey	443 responses from randomly selected subscribers of a mailing list
Pavlou (2003)	IJEC	Survey	2 studies: 1. three experiential exploratory surveys, 103 students subjects; 2. online survey using online consumers as population, 155 responses
Ramaswami et al. (2000–2001)	IJEC	Survey	154 respondents; financial service
Ranganathan and Ganapathy (2002)	IM	Survey	214 online shoppers in Illinois
Salam et al. (2003)	CACM	Survey	Using 2 separate data sets of the 1997 GVU Center's Web Survey data, 3,987 and 5,048 respondents, respectively
Shim et al. (2002)	JAIS	Mixed	2 phases: (1) existential phenomenology (23 respondents); (2) Logistic regression (89 individual firms). Findings from Phase 1 were explored with quantitative methods in Phase 2.
Slyke et al. (2002)	CACM	Survey	511 subjects ranging in age from 17 to 48 years
Suh and Han (2003)	IJEC	Survey	Internet banking adoption in Korea; 2001; 502 responses
Tan and Teo (2000)	JAIS	Survey	Internet banking adoption; online questionnaire survey, Singapore, 454 responses
Vellido et al. (2000)	IJEC	Survey	Using data from the GVU's ninth WWW user survey, "Internet Shopping (Part 1) Questionnaire"; 2,180 subjects

REFERENCES

Ajzen, I. Nature and operation of attitudes. *Annual Review of Psychology*, 52 (2001), 27–58.

Ajzen, I. The theory of planned behavior. *Organizational Behavior and Human Decision Process*, 50 (1991), 179–211.

Ajzen, I. and Fishbein, M. *Understanding Attitudes and Predicting Social Behavior*. Englewood Cliffs, NJ: Prentice-Hall, 1980.

Alavi, M. and Carlson, P. A review of MIS research and disciplinary development. *Journal of Management Information Systems*, 8, 4 (1992), 45–62.

Bellman, S.; Lohse, G.; and Johnson, E. Predictors of online buying behavior. *Communications of the ACM*, 42, 12 (1999), 32–38.

Bhatnagar, A.; Misra, S.; and Rao, H.R. Online risk, convenience, and Internet shopping behavior. *Communications of the ACM*, 43, 11 (2000), 98–105.

Bhattacherjee, A. An empirical analysis of the antecedents of electronic commerce service continuance. *Decision Support Systems*, 32 (2001a), 201–214.

Bhattacherjee, A. Understanding information systems continuance: An expectation-confirmation model. *MIS Quarterly*, 25, 3 (2001b), 351–370.

Borchers, A. Trust in Internet shopping: A test of a measurement instrument. In *Proceedings of the 7th Americas Conference on Information Systems*, 2001, 799–803.

Breckler, S.J. and Berman, J.S. Affective responses to attitude objects: Measurement and validation. *Journal of Social Behavior and Personality*, 6, 3 (1991), 529–544.

Cao, Y.; Gruca, T.S.; and Klemz, B.R. Internet pricing, price satisfaction, and customer satisfaction. *International Journal of Electronic Commerce*, 8, 2 (2003–2004), 31–50.

Case, T.; Burns, O.M.; and Dick, G.N. Drivers of on-line purchasing among U.S. university students. In *Proceedings of the 7th Americas Conference on Information Systems*. 2001, 873–878.

Chau, P.Y.K.; Cole, M.; Massey, A.P.; Montoya-Weiss, M.; and O'Keefe, R.M. Cultural differences in the online behavior of consumers. *Communications of the ACM*, 45, 10 (2002), 138–143.

Chen, L.; Gillenson, M.L.; and Sherrell, D.L. Enticing online consumers: An extended technology acceptance perspective. *Information and Management*, 39 (2002), 705–719.

Chen, P. and Hitt, L. Measuring switching costs and the determinants of customer retention in Internet-enabled businesses: A study of the online brokerage industry. *Information Systems Research*, 13, 3 (2002), 255–274.

Cho, Y. and Fjermestad, J. Using electronic customer relationship management to maximize/minimize customer satisfaction/dissatisfaction. In N.C. Romano Jr. and J. Fjermestad, (eds.), *Advances in Management Information Systems: Special Issue on Customer Relationship Management*, 2006.

Cho, Y.; Im, I.; Hiltz, S.R., and Fjermestad, J. The effects of post-purchase evaluation factors on online vs. offline customer complaining behavior: implications for customer loyalty. *Advances in Consumer Research*, 29 (2002), 318–326.

Cho, Y., Im, I.; Fjermestad, J.; and Hiltz, S.R. The impact of product category on customer dissatisfaction in cyberspace. *Business Process Management Journal*, 9, 5 (2003), 635–651.

Cho, Y.; Im, I.; Hiltz, R.; and Fjermestad, J. Causes and outcomes of online customer complaining behavior: Implications for customer relationship management (CRM). In *Proceedings of the 7th Americas Conference on Information Systems*, 2001, 900–907.

Davis, F.D.; Bagozzi, R.P.; and Warshaw, P.R. User acceptance of computer technology: A comparison of two theoretical models. *Management Science*, 35, 8 (1989), 982–1003.

DeLone, W.H. and McLean, E.R. Information systems success: The quest for the dependent variable. *Information Systems Research*, 3, 1 (1992), 60–95.

Devaraj, S.; Fan, M.; and Kohli, R. Antecedents of B2C channel satisfaction and preference: Validating e-commerce metrics. *Information Systems Research*, 13, 3 (2002), 316–333.

Devaraj, S.; Fan, M.; and Kohli, R. E-loyalty—elusive ideal or competitive edge? *Communications of the ACM*, 46, 9 (2003), 184–191.

ePayments Resource Center. Electronic transactions statistics (available at www.epaynews.com/statistics/, accessed on August 8, 2004).

Featherman, M.S. and Pavlou, P.A. Predicting e-services adoption: A perceived risk facets perspective. *International Journal of Human-Computer Studies*, 59 (2003), 451–474.

Fishbein, M. and Ajzen, I. *Belief, Attitude, Intention, and Behavior: An Introduction to Theory and Research*. Reading, MA: Addison-Wesley, 1975.

Gefen, D. and Straub, D. The relative importance of perceived ease of use in IS adoption: A study of e-commerce adoption. *Journal of the Association for Information Systems*, 1, 8 (2000), 1–28.

Gefen, D. Customer loyalty in e-commerce. *Journal of the Association for Information Systems*, 3 (2002), 27–51.

Gefen, D.; Karahanna, E.; and Straub, D.W. Trust and TAM in online shopping: An integrated model. *MIS Quarterly*, 27, 1 (2003), 51–90.

Griffith, D.A.; Krampf, R.F.; and Palmer, J.W. The role of interface in electronic commerce: Consumer involvement with print versus on-line catalogs. *International Journal of Electronic Commerce*, 5, 4 (2001), 135–153.

Han, K.S. and Noh, M.H. Critical failure factors that discourage the growth of electronic commerce. *International Journal of Electronic Commerce*, 4, 2 (1999–2000), 25–43.

Hardgrave, B. and Walstrom, K. Forums for MIS scholars. *Communications of the ACM*, 40, 11 (1997), 119–124.

Henderson, R. and Divett, M.J. Perceived usefulness, ease of use and electronic supermarket use. *International Journal of Human-Computer Studies*, 59 (2003), 383–395.

Ho, C. and Wu, W. Antecedents of consumer satisfaction on the Internet: An empirical study of online shopping. In *Proceedings of the 32nd Hawaii International Conference on System Sciences*, 1999.

Huang, M.H. Modeling virtual exploratory and shopping dynamics: An environmental psychology approach. *Information and Management*, 41 (2003), 39–47.

Jarvenpaa, S.L.; Tractinsky, N.; and Vitale, M. Consumer trust in an Internet store. *Information Technology and Management*, 1 (2000), 45–71.

Karahanna, E.; Straub, D.W.; and Chervan N. L. Information technology adoption across time: A cross-sectional comparison of pre-adoption and post-adoption beliefs. *MIS Quarterly*, 23, 2 (1999), 183–213.

Khalifa, M. and Liu, V. Determinants of satisfaction at different adoption stages of Internet-based services. *Journal of the Association for Information Systems*, 4, 5 (2003), 206–232.

Khalifa, M. and Liu, V. Satisfaction with Internet-based services: The role of expectations and desires. *International Journal of Electronic Commerce*, 7, 2 (2002–2003), 31–49.

Khalifa, M. and Limayem, M. Drivers of Internet shopping. *Communications of the ACM*, 46, 12 (2003), 233–239.

Khalifa, M.; Limayem, M.; and Liu, V. Online consumer stickiness: A longitudinal study. *Journal of Global Information Management*, 10, 3 (2002), 1–15.

Kim, E.B.; Eom, S.B.; and Yoo, S. Effective user interface design for online stores in the Asia Pacific region: A survey study. In *Proceedings of the 7th Americas Conference on Information Systems*, 2001, 867–872.

Kim, J.; Lee, J.; Han, K.; and Lee, M. Businesses as buildings: Metrics for the architectural quality of internet businesses. *Information Systems Research*, 13, 3 (2002), 239–254.

Kim, J. and Yoo, B. Toward the optimal link structure of the cyber shopping mall. *International Journal of Human-Computer Studies*, 52 (2000), 531–551.

Kimery, K.M. and McCord, M. Third-party assurances: The road to trust in online retailing. In *Proceedings of the 35th Hawaii International Conference on System Sciences*, 2002.

Koufaris, M.; Kambil, A.; and LaBarbera, P.A. Consumer behavior in Web-based commerce: An empirical study. *International Journal of Electronic Commerce*, 6, 2 (2001–2002), 115–138.

Koufaris, M. Applying the technology acceptance model and flow theory to online consumer behavior. *Information Systems Research*, 13, 2 (2002), 205–223.

Lee, J.; Pi, S; Kwok, R.C.; and Huynh, M.Q. The contribution of commitment value in internet commerce: An empirical investigation. *Journal of the Association for Information Systems*, 4 (2003), 39–64.

Lee, K.O. and Turban, E. A trust model for consumer Internet shopping. *International Journal of Electronic Commerce*, 6, 1 (2001), 75–91.

Li, H.; Kuo, C.; and Russell, M.G. The impact of perceived channel utilities, shopping orientations, and demographics on the consumer's online buying behavior. *Journal of Computer-Mediated Communication*, 5, 2 (1999).

Liang, T. and Huang, J. An empirical study on consumer acceptance of products in electronic markets: A transaction cost model. *Decision Support Systems*, 24 (1998), 29–43.

Liang, T. and Lai, H. Effect of store design on consumer purchases: An empirical study of on-line bookstores. *Information and Management*, 39 (2002), 431–444.

Liao, Z. and Cheung, M.T. Internet-based e-banking and consumer attitudes: An empirical study. *Information and Management*, 39 (2002), 283–295.

Liao, Z. and Cheung, M.T. Internet-based e-shopping and consumer attitudes: An empirical study. *Information and Management*, 38 (2001), 299–306.

Locke, E.A. The nature and causes of job satisfaction. In M.D. Dunnette, ed., *Handbook of Industrial and Organizational Psychology* (New York: Holt, Reinhart and Winston, 1976), 1297–1349.

Lowry, P.B.; Romans, D.; and Curtis, A. Global journal prestige and supporting disciplines: A scientometric study of information systems journals. *Journal of Association for Information Systems*, 5, 2 (2004), 29–77.

Lu, H. and Lin, J.C. Predicting customer behavior in the market-space: A study of Rayport and Sviokla's framework. *Information and Management*, 40 (2002), 1–10.

Luo, X. and Seyedian, M. Conceptual marketing and customer-orientation strategy for e-commerce: An empirical analysis. *International Journal of Electronic Commerce*, 8, 2 (2003–2004), 95–118.

Mehrabian, A. and Russell, J. A. *An Approach to Environmental Psychology* (Cambridge, MA: MIT Press, 1974).

Mylonopoulos, N. and Theoharakis, V. On-site: Global perceptions of IS journals. *Communications of the ACM*, 44, 9 (2001), 29–33.

Ngai, E.W.T. and Wat, F.K.T. A literature review and classification of electronic commerce research. *Information and Management*, 39 (2002), 415–429.

Novak, T.P.; Joffman, D. L.; and Yung, Y. F. Measuring the customer experience in online environments: A structural modeling approach. *Marketing Science*, 19, 1 (2000), 22–42.

O'Keefe, R.M.; Cole, M.; Chau, P.Y.K.; Massey, A.; Montoya-Weiss, M.; and Perry, M. From the user interface to the consumer interface: Results from a global experiment. *International Journal of Human-Computer Studies*, 53 (2000), 611–628.

Oliver, R.L. Measurement and evaluation of satisfaction processes in retail settings. *Journal of Retailing*, 57, 3 (1981), 25–48.

Parthasarathy, M. and Bhattacherhee, A. Understanding post-adoption behavior in the context of online services. *Information Systems Research*, 9, 4 (1998), 362–379.

Pavlou, P. Consumer acceptance of electronic commerce: Integrating trust and risk with the technology acceptance model. *International Journal of Electronic Commerce*, 7, 3 (2003), 101–134.

Pedersen, P.E. Behavioral effects of using software agents for product and merchant brokering. *International Journal of Electronic Commerce*, 5, 1 (2000), 125–141.

Pervan, G.P. A review of research in group support systems: Leaders, approaches and directions. *Decision Support Systems*, 23 (1998), 149–159.

Picard, R.W. Does HAL cry digital tears? Emotions and computers. In D. G. Stork, ed., *Hal's Legacy: 2001's Computer as Dream and Reality*. Cambridge, MA: MIT Press, 1997, 279–303.

Ramaswami, S.N.; Strader, T.J.; and Brett, K. Determinants of on-line channel use for purchasing financial products. *International Journal of Electronic Commerce*, 5, 2 (2000–2001), 95–118.

Ranganathan, C. and Ganapathy, S. Key dimensions of business-to-consumer web sites. *Information and Management*, 39 (2002), 457–465.

Ratchford, B.T.; Talukdar, D.; and Lee, M. A model of consumer choice of the Internet as an information source. *International Journal of Electronic Commerce*, 5, 3 (2001), 7–21.

Romano, N.C. and Fjermestad, J. Electronic commerce customer relationship management: A research agenda. *Information Technology and Management*, 4 (2003), 233–258.

Romano, N.C. and Fjermestad, J. Electronic commerce customer relationship management: An assessment of research. *International Journal of Electronic Commerce*, 6, 2 (2001), 61–113.

Russell, J. A. Core affect and the psychological construction of emotion. *Psychological Review*, 110, 1 (2003), 145–172.

Russell, J.A. and Pratt, G. A description of the affective quality attributed to environments. *Journal of Personality and Social Psychology*, 38 (1980), 311–322.

Salam, A.F.; Rao, H.R.; and Pegels, C.C. Consumer-perceived risk in e-commerce transactions. *Communications of the ACM*, 46, 12 (2003), 325–331.

Shim, J.P.; Shin, Y.B.; and Nottingham, L. Retailer web site influence on customer shopping: An exploratory study on key factors of customer satisfaction. *Journal of Association for Information System*, 3 (2002), 53–76.

Slyke, C.V.; Comunale, C.L.; and Belanger, F. Gender differences in perceptions of web-based shopping. *Communications of the ACM*, 45, 7 (2002), 82–86.

Suh, B. and Han, I. The impact of customer trust and perception of security control on the acceptance of electronic commerce. *International Journal of Electronic Commerce*, 7, 3 (2003), 135–161.

Tan, M. and Teo, T.S.H. Factors influencing the adoption of Internet banking. *Journal of the Association for Information Systems*, 1, 5 (2000).

Te'eni, D. and Feldman, R. "Performance and satisfaction in adaptive websites: An experiment on searches within a task-adapted website." *Journal of the Association for Information Systems*, 2, 3 (2001).

Triandis, H.C. Values, attitudes, and interpersonal behavior. In H.E. Howe, ed., *Nebraska Symposium on Motivation, 1979: Beliefs, Attitudes and Values*. Lincoln: University of Nebraska Press, 1980, 195–259.

USC Annenberg School, Center for the Digital Future. The digital future report: Surveying the digital future—Year four: ten years, ten trends. 2004 (available at http://www.digitalcenter.org/downloads/DigitalFutureReport-Year4-2004.pdf, accessed on August 10, 2004).

Vellido, A.; Lisboa, P.J.G.; and Meehan, K. Quantitative characterization and prediction of on-line purchasing behavior: A latent variable approach. *International Journal of Electronic Commerce*, 4, 4 (2000), 83–104.

Vessey, I.; Ramesh, V.; and Glass, R.L. Research in information systems: An empirical study of diversity in the discipline and its journals. *Journal of Management Information Systems*, 19, 2 (2002), 129.

Whitman, M.; Hendrickson, A.; and Townsend, A. Research commentary. Academic rewards for teaching, research and service: Data and discourse. *Information Systems Research*, 10, 2 (1999), 99–109.

Zhang, P. and Li, N. An assessment of HCI research in MIS: Topics and methods. *Computers in Human Behavior*, 20, 2 (2004), 125–147.

CHAPTER 10

TOWARD ACHIEVING CUSTOMER SATISFACTION IN ONLINE GROCERY SHOPPING

Lessons Learned from Australian and Swiss Cases

SHERAH KURNIA AND PETRA SCHUBERT

Abstract: *Online grocery shopping is expected to grow significantly in the next few years. It is important for online merchants to ensure customer satisfaction in order to increase customer loyalty and attract new customers. However, few studies have been undertaken to assess the performance of online stores in terms of meeting customers' expectations. The study described in this chapter employs the Extended Web Assessment Method (EWAM), an evaluation tool specifically created for the assessment of electronic commerce applications. It was used to assess a number of online grocers in Australia and Switzerland and to identify their strengths and weaknesses. General expectations of customers in online grocery shopping and opportunities to improve customer satisfaction were explored and highlighted. In general, the findings show that Web sites in both countries do not fully meet the expectations of customers.*

Keywords: e-Commerce, Customer Relationship Management, Web Shops, Web Applications, Web Assessment

INTRODUCTION

The advance of the Internet technology has enabled businesses to easily reach consumers in dispersed geographical locations. Despite some concerns with security issues, the use of online shopping has been increasing in the last few years (Australian Retailers Association 2000, Park et al. 1998, Morgan 1998). An Internet business application that has received much attention in the last few years is online grocery shopping (Morganosky and Cude 2000; MSNBC News 2004). Consumers can purchase grocery products anywhere, any time, and the products can then be delivered to or picked up by the purchasers (Ellis 2003). Despite the failure of the first few online grocers around the world—Webvan, Publix Super Markets, and ShopLink, to name a few—online grocery shopping is projected to experience a significant growth in the next few years (Allen and Fjermestad 2001, MSNBC News 2004, Anonymous 2001).

Online grocery shopping has many potential benefits to consumers, particularly in terms of convenience and time saving (Park et al. 1998, Anderson et al. 2000, Barnett and Alexander 2003). Convenience and time saving have become important issues for consumers in grocery shopping, since there have been more women participating in the labor force, more dual-income and thus higher-income households, and more single-parent and elderly households with various resource constraints (Park et al. 1998; Turner 2001). Thus, online grocery shopping enables consumers to avoid typical problems of traditional shopping such as searching for a parking space, looking for products on frequently changing store shelves, failing to obtain assistance from the staff, particularly in specialty departments, and standing in a long checkout line (Anderston 2001; Pastore 2001). Retailers will also reap significant benefits, since online grocery shopping will lead to more efficient use of personnel, simplification of building infrastructure, lower costs, and more rapid gain in profitability (Pastore 2001; Australia Retailers Association 2000; Slonae 2000). In addition, through the establishment of long-term relationships with customers, there is an opportunity for online retailers to enjoy a stable cash flow (Allen and Fjermestad 2001). Therefore, online grocery shopping has been an attractive retail channel in many regions, notably the United States, United Kingdom, Europe, and Australia (Schuster and Sporn 1998; Morgan 2000; Morganosky and Cude 2000; Ellis 2003; MSNBC News 2004).

While it may look easy for supermarkets or other grocers to offer online grocery shopping service facilitated by the Internet, many factors need to be addressed carefully for successful operation of an online business (Anderson et al. 2000; Van der Heijden 2000). Besides issues related to business models, value proposition, and organizational set-up, one of the most important factors is the overall design of the Web site as the primary interface with the consumer in online shopping. Consumers need to feel comfortable and confident with the online systems, from getting the information about the products, ordering, paying, tracking to receiving the products (Barnett and Alexander 2003; Freeman 2003). Nevertheless, in general, few Internet merchants have ever tried to assess their Web sites from a consumer perspective to reveal weaknesses and initiate improvements. This may contribute to some failures reported in the literature (see, for example, Mahajan and Srinivasan 2002; Helft 2001; and Bulkeley 2004). It is therefore crucial for supermarkets or any grocers wishing to offer a successful online service to recognize the importance of the overall design of Web sites that facilitate online grocery shopping. Poorly designed Web sites may help account for the slow uptake of online grocery shopping in many regions (Schuster and Sporn 1998; Kutz 1998; Kurnia and Chen 2003; Kurnia 2003). Given the fact that grocery products, particularly fresh items such as fruit and vegetables, have attributes that can be discovered only through the senses, online grocers face many challenges in achieving a desirable level of customer satisfaction (Cho et al. 2003).

Despite the failures of early online grocers in the late 1990s, there has been a significant growth in the online grocery industry, particularly in the last two years. Various online retailers have been established around the world, including Australia and Switzerland. Although only six online grocers were assessed in this study, Alexander and Barnett (2004) identified 40 online grocers across Australia. In the United States, many online retailers such as Safeway Inc., Albertsons Inc., Peapod LLC (Chicago and the East Coast), and Freshdirect.com (New York) have experienced a tremendous growth in their online business with an increasing number of customers and are expanding their business coverage (MSNBC 2004). This indicates that the market for online grocery shopping exists and that it has the potential to grow.

Although it is believed that online grocery shopping will not take over the overall market, as it will make up only a very small percentage of the overall business, the annual growth expected from online shopping is significant for retailers (MSNBC 2004). In order to survive and grow, it is crucial for online grocers to increase customer satisfaction with online grocery shopping, since customer satisfaction will lead to increased customer loyalty and the ability to attract new customers (Cho et al. 2002). This is consistent with the view that the commercial environment has shifted from a transaction-based to a relationship-based economy (Romano and Fjermestad 2003).

Therefore, online grocers also need to manage their relationships with customers, which they can do in each phase of the business transaction.

In this chapter, we demonstrate the usefulness of evaluating online grocers' Web sites based on the perception of consumers in order to identify their strengths and weaknesses. Various online grocers' Web sites in Australia and Switzerland were assessed using the Extended Web Assessment Method (EWAM) tool. The current tool was developed at the University of Applied Sciences Basel in Switzerland and is now widely used in research, teaching, and consulting (Schubert 2003). Since the assessment was based on consumers' expectations, and on strengths and weaknesses identified in each phase of the market transaction, it can be used by online grocers to design strategies that can improve customer relationship management. Our objective is to assist practitioners to develop better online shops in the grocery sector in order to promote the growth of online grocery shopping through increased customer satisfaction (Cho et al. 2002). Using the framework proposed by Allen and Fjermestad (2001), we systematically discuss some lessons learned from this study in terms of product, place, price, and promotion.

In the next section, we provide a basic description of the EWAM tool, including the theoretical background and data collection and analysis procedures. We then describe the Web assessment conducted in this study and present selected findings. Finally, we present a comparative analysis, discuss some lessons learned, and draw conclusions.

THE EXTENDED WEB ASSESSMENT METHOD (EWAM)

The Web Assessment Method has been in use for several years (Selz and Schubert 1998; Schubert and Selz 1999; Schubert 2003) and has been statistically tested with empirical data (Stamm 2003). It is a sound method based on scientific principles but also oriented to offer e-shop operators advice for improvement of their services. The method defines an evaluation grid with a set of criteria for appraising the quality and success of existing e-commerce applications. In addition to a rigorous focus on consumer perspectives, success in implementing an offer of products and services is considered with reference to the specific features of the electronic medium.

The Web Assessment Model examines the three classic transaction phases of electronic markets: information, agreement, and settlement. A fourth element, the community component, is integrated as a link between the actual purchase transaction and the necessary trust relationship in the virtual realm. Where marketing aspects are concerned, the Web Assessment Model focuses on the special features inherent in the Internet.

The Web Assessment Method, developed in 1997, represents a step toward an all-embracing evaluation of e-commerce applications from the customer's point of view. The method was fundamentally revised in the summer of 2000. Besides taking account of new research findings, especially in the Internet marketing field, it also incorporated the Technology Acceptance Model established for the acceptance of information systems (Davis 1985).

Evaluation Criteria

The Extended Web Assessment Method defines an evaluation grid made up of a set of criteria with which to appraise the quality and success of e-commerce applications. A successful e-commerce application must meet the needs of the user in accordance with "perceived usefulness" (Criteria USEF1–USEF15) and "ease of use" (Criteria EOU1–EOU8). Under the heading "trust" (Criteria TRUST1–TRUST2), questions about the subjective norm (Fishbein and Ajzen 1975) are also taken into account. Trust is the sine qua non of e-commerce, for business will not be trans-

Figure 10.1 **Two-Step Assessment: (1) Importance Rating, (2) Web Site Evaluation**

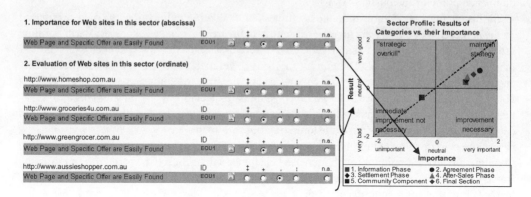

acted in situations where there is no trust. A success or quality feature must be assigned to one of these categories. The list of criteria can be found in the online questionnaire [http://www.e-business.fhbb.ch/ewam]. Evaluation of an e-commerce application with EWAM begins by assigning the concerned Web site to a sector. During evaluation, the reference sector for benchmarking will be identified.

The success and quality criteria are formulated in general terms and are valid in every sector, but are differentiated by their importance ratings. In order to take due account of the differences between the individual sectors, criteria are given weights corresponding to the different sector profiles and their relevance in the sector. Thus, for instance, being up to date with information is of greater importance for a supplier of financial information (e.g., stock brokerage, real-time share prices) than for a supplier of consumer goods. On the other hand, the choice of generic services (EOU 5) (e.g., tracking a parcel) is of less importance for an enterprise that distributes digital goods (e.g., software) than for one that delivers books. Specific and high-quality analyses necessitate precise recording of the level of importance per criterion and per sector. The importance per criterion is recorded on a scale of "unimportant" (–2), "less important" (–1), "important" (+1), and "very important" (+2).

An EWAM criterion is first assigned to a criteria category ("ease of use," "usefulness," or "trust"). Within these three categories the criterion is allotted to one of the four transaction phases of electronic markets (information, agreement, settlement, and after-sale), to the community component, or to the category "final section" which concerns all phases.

Like ServQual (Parasuraman et al. 1988), an instrument for assessing service quality, EWAM is based on a double evaluation for each criterion. Figure 10.1 shows the two steps of an evaluation. In the first step, the assessor declares the subjective importance of an attribute. The next step is an evaluation of all the Web sites in the concerned sector. The aggregation of the importance ratings of the assessors (Step 1) is an important prerequisite for the generation of results. In cases where importance is low (–2), the actual evaluation values (Step 2) are almost annihilated. The lower the importance value of a criterion, the smaller the impact of this attribute on the overall score. Unlike ServQual, where each of the two questions is compared for every single assessor, EWAM aggregates the importance ratings for multiplication with the evaluations. This procedure has the advantage of leveling out extreme values for expectations and taking into account the different experience levels of the assessors.

The EWAM Tool: Data Collection and Analysis

Data are collected over the Internet with an online questionnaire (the EWAM tool). An assessor conducting an evaluation with the EWAM tool begins by recording the URL of the Web site under examination and assigning it to a sector. The scale of the possible choices is so arranged that the assessor must decide on a positive or negative statement with each value. The scale has four values (+2, +1,–1,–2). The alternative value "N/A" (i.e., not applicable) can be used if a criterion is not relevant or not available in a particular context. The criteria are formulated in such a way that a positive (negative) evaluation will lead to a positive (negative) result. "I strongly agree" always scores +2, "I slightly agree," +1, "I slightly disagree,"–1, and "I strongly disagree,"–2. "N/A" scores zero, which is disregarded in further calculations (e.g., averages). The criterion "cost benefits passed on to the client (USEF2)" can be evaluated only when the business has a physical counterpart where prices differ from those offered on the Web site.

THE WEB ASSESSMENT STUDY OF THE SWISS AND AUSTRALIAN GROCERY SECTOR

The participants in this study were students enrolled in electronic commerce classes at the University of Melbourne, Australia, and the University of Applied Sciences in Basel, Switzerland, in the years 2003 and 2002 respectively. In Australia, each Web site to be evaluated was assigned to four tutorial classes. A tutorial class consisted of 20 students on average. In Switzerland, there was only one class of 25 students, where each student evaluated all four Web sites. Although the participation was voluntary, the students were encouraged to perform the evaluation, since the participation meant extra practice in preparation for a subsequent assignment. The number of responses for the Web sites varied from 5 to 56. Although for a few Web sites the number of participants was quite low, a subsequent qualitative evaluation by the authors revealed the plausibility and usefulness of the results.

In Australia, six operational Web sites were identified at the beginning of this study and all were included in this study. Two of the Web sites belong to the two major Australian retailers (Coles and Woolworths), while the other four are pure online players without physical stores. At present, Woolworths offer the online grocery shopping service to approximately 200 suburbs in Sydney, under the name 'Woolworths (Safeway) HomeShop.' Coles supermarkets offer the online service to consumers in 25 suburbs in Melbourne and 41 in Sydney under the banner 'Colesonline' (Colesonline 2003). The online retailers, including ShopFast, Groceries4U, AussieShopper, and GreenGrocer, have been established to serve more specific regions of Australia. ShopFast, for example, delivers to Sydney, Central Coast, and Wollongong, while AussieShopper focuses on the Brisbane area, GreenGrocer operates in both Sydney and Melbourne, and Groceries4U serves consumers in the Adelaide metropolitan area.

The Swiss study included the two large Swiss retailers (Coop and Migros), the shop of the Spar-Group Switzerland, and the shop of a Swiss grocery group called Bon appétit Groupe AG (LeShop). Coop, Migros, and Spar operate a close-meshed grid of physical stores and offer online shopping as an additional customer service. In contrast, LeShop is a pure online player and was the first company offering grocery products online in Switzerland. Since spring of 2002, when data were collected for the Swiss grocery stores, the Swiss online market has seen some important changes. First, Spar shut down its online shop in August 2002 for a lack of demand, while LeShop was sold to private investors at the end of 2002. Then, at the beginning of 2004, LeShop almost had to shut down its operations but was rescued by a group of investors. A couple of months later,

Table 10.1

The Importance of Each Category Used in the Study

	Importance Grocery (Range: −2/+2)	
Phase/Component	Australia	Switzerland
1. Information Phase	0.97	0.84
2. Agreement Phase	1.44	1.50
3. Settlement Phase	0.99	0.59
4. After-Sales Phase	1.02	1.38
5. Community Component	−0.44	−0.88
6. Final Section	1.23	1.13

LeShop and Migros merged into one joint online store, which at the time of writing this chapter was run by the former LeShop crew.

For the evaluation of the Web sites, the students used the EWAM tool, as described in the previous section. Before the evaluation process started, the students were thoroughly instructed in the use of the tool. The training of the assessors is an important learning process that confronts them with the basics of high-quality e-commerce services. Data were submitted by the students online and analyzed centrally by the authors. For each Web site, a personal Web assessment report was produced. Specific sector assessments compare companies in the same sector against one another.

IMPORTANCE RATINGS

In this section, we first examine the importance of categories for the grocery sector as rated by the participants in Australia and Switzerland (Table 10.1). Six Web sites for the grocery sector were assessed in Australia and four in Switzerland. Details of these sites are provided in the next sub-section. The rating is based on a four-point scale: from unimportant (−2) to very important (+2).

The results show that the perceived importance of criteria for both countries is very similar and that all phases except for the community component were perceived to be important. A closer look at the results reveals that the accessibility of the Web site, structure of the contents, quality of information, and price benefits are important criteria which the participants emphasized for the information phase. Other items, including ordering procedure, tracking and tracing, and access to customer support, were found to be crucial in the agreement, settlement and after-sales phases, respectively. In addition, the availability of the system, the design of the user interface, and the trustworthiness were also cited as important by most participants.

The above findings suggest that customers or users in general have a high quality expectation toward the Web sites in the grocery sector. The main reason might be the novelty of buying groceries online which results into a perceived uncertainty that is still high (Barnett and Alexander 2003; Kinsey and Senauer 1996; Slonae 2000). Consumers are very sensitive to ordering groceries online, since there is a high chance of not getting the grocery items in the expected quality, especially for perishable products such as fruit and vegetables (Barnett and Alexander 2003). This is consistent with the findings of previous studies exploring the slow uptake in online grocery shopping adoption in a number of regions (Schuster and Sporn 1998; Kutz 1998; Kurnia and Chen 2003, Kurnia 2003). Consequently, items such as trustworthiness were rated paramount and significantly more important than, for example, in a different study of the book retail industry. A number of online grocers, however, believe that with their training qualification and in-

Figure 10.2   **Summary of the Overall Web Evaluation (Australia)**

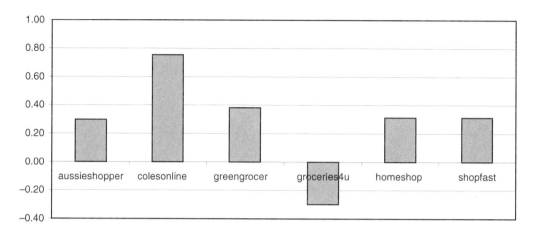

Overall Score with Importance Weighting

frastructure (such as refrigerated delivery truck) they are better at picking and transporting products than customers (MSNBC 2004). Therefore, with an improved trust level of consumers, the number of consumers who are willing to purchase groceries online can be expected to increase.

Furthermore, the agreement phase is perceived to be more important in the grocery than in other sectors, with the order procedure being especially important. Grocery shopping involves searching and selecting a comparatively large number of products. A smart and easy-to-use order procedure that supports the customer in making selections and filling the shopping cart is thus crucial for a satisfactory shopping experience. On the other hand, our study shows that the availability of recommendation systems is more important for other than grocery items, which is not surprising, given that groceries are everyday items with a rather stable need. In the same way, the community component is perceived to be not so important for the grocery sector.

Australian Results

Six Australian Web sites were found to be operational at the time of this study. They included: http://www.homeshop.com.au, http://www.groceries4u.com.au, http://www.greengrocer.com.au, http://www.aussieshopper.com.au/, http://www.shopfast.com.au/, and http://www.colesonline.com.au/.

Figure 10.2 depicts the summary of the overall evaluation of the six Web sites. The score is based on a four-point scale from –2: very bad to +2: very good. As shown in the figure, Colesonline appears to be the best site in the sector, whereas Groceries4U Web site has the worst evaluation result. Other Web sites require significant improvements in order to achieve a quality comparable to that of Colesonline, which is the best-practice Web site in this sector.

Figure 10.3 summarizes the company profile for all Web sites evaluated in this study, indicating the score obtained in each phase. It shows that the best-practice company was rated much higher than other companies in most of the categories involved in this study, particularly in the agreement phase, after-sales phase, and the final section. The performance of other sites evalu-

Figure 10.3 **Summary of the Company Profile (Australia)**

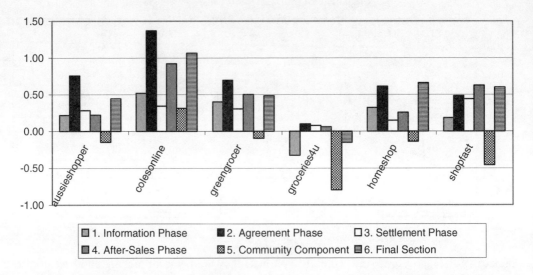

Company Profile with Importance Weighting

Legend:
- 1. Information Phase
- 2. Agreement Phase
- 3. Settlement Phase
- 4. After-Sales Phase
- 5. Community Component
- 6. Final Section

ated varied across all categories. For these Web sites, the highest score was obtained for the agreement phase and the final section, but it was scored less than one by the participants. Thus, most participants were not satisfied with these sites in general. These observations were confirmed by the subsequent qualitative analyses conducted by the authors, as discussed below.

First, from the qualitative analysis, it was found that Colesonline, as the best-practice, has a pleasant user interface with information about various aspects (for example items on specials, clearance aisle, information and support, payment and pricing policy) organized in a logical way. Furthermore, the use of hypermedia to describe products is consistent and appropriate. In addition, the site enables consumers to make use of their experience in shopping at the physical supermarket by organizing products by aisles. Therefore, most assessors gave a relatively high rating for most of the criteria in the information phase of Colesonline. Groceries4U, on the other hand, contains too much information on its main page, not all of which is needed by consumers before they start to shop online. Moreover, the arrangement of the information on the site is inconsistent and confusing. Besides, many pictures that describe the products are not available. Furthermore, the use of flashing images to indicate new items can be irritating to some consumers. All this further explains why most of the assessors were unsatisfied with Groceries4U in the information phase.

For the settlement phase, the subsequent qualitative analysis discovered that the ordering procedure actually highlights the strength of Colesonline. The Web site provides consumers with a very clear procedure. The 'Buy' button is located next to each item and the 'Shopping Basket' is always apparent to consumers, so that they can fill in or modify the quantity of each product as required in case of a change of mind during the process. This provides additional explanation why Colesonline received the highest rating for the settlement phase. At the other extreme, the analysis discovered that Groceries4U's unclear ordering procedure particularly frustrates consumers. One way to put items in the shopping basket is to enter the quantity ones wishes to buy from the list of products and then click the 'Buy' button. This button, however, may not be apparent to consumers if the list is long, since it is located far at the bottom of the list. Likewise, the 'Shopping Basket' is not readily viewable to consumers, since they need to click on the 'Go to Shopping Cart' button that is also located at the bottom of the list of products. Finally, in this way of selecting products, the shopping trolley is not updated instantly, which is likely to confuse the consumers. This suggests that Groceries4U needs to undertake major improvements in the agreement phase.

In the settlement phase, the results of the assessment demonstrate that Colesonline is no longer in the lead. The qualitative analysis discovered that all Web sites actually allow customers to pay using mobile EFTPOS and online payment with credit cards or customer account. AussieShopper also allows customers to pay with cash or check upon delivery. Besides, unlike other Web sites, it enables customers to track and trace their orders by providing the driver's contact number. This explains why AussieShopper was rated favorably for the 'integration of generic service' and 'tracking and tracing' criteria in this phase compared to other Web sites. However, the analysis could explain why Colesonline received the lowest rating for the 'tracking and tracing' criterion.

For the after-sales phase, the qualitative analysis revealed that while other Web sites simply provide the company contact details for customer inquiries, Colesonline offers a 'Customer Care Center.' This is intended to help customers with any queries regarding Colesonline, offering the best technical and nontechnical assistance possible through a trained staff. A contact number and the operating hours of the Customer Care Center are provided. This increases consumers' confidence in the accessibility and performance of customer support provided by Colesonline. Therefore, Colesonline was rated high in the after-sale phase. Groceries4U was rated lowest in this phase. The possible explanation emerging from the subsequent analysis was that Groceries4U has various contact persons and numbers to deal with general enquiries, customer service, and technical assistance and provides no information on their availability. This may reduce the consumers' confidence in terms of the accessibility and performance of the customer support, which does not seem to be well integrated. Other Web sites have a stable performance in this phase as they provide reasonable customer support details.

For the final section, Colesonline once again received the highest rating. Many of the issues discussed in the information and agreement phases are related to the last phase. The analysis also discovered that the performance of Colesonline and Shopfast in this section is very comparable, and therefore some assessors may favor Colesonline while some prefer Shopfast. Due to its provision of the Customer Care Center and the fact that it is operated by one of the largest retail chains in Australia, Colesonline was rated very high for the 'trustworthiness of the Web site' criterion. In addition, Colesonline offers a personal shopping list to consumers and therefore received the highest rating for the personalization function.

Figure 10.4 compares the assessment figures with the perceived user expectations for both the best-practice and sector profiles. The ideal situation is achieved when all the categories lie on or above the diagonal, as shown on the figure. Consistent with the above findings, the figure depicts that for Colesonline, three phases—the agreement phase, after-sales phase, and final section—lie exactly on the diagonal and are within the 'maintain strategy' zone. This indicates that these three categories have a good performance, as the users' expectations meet the actual assessment. Two other items—the information and settlement phases—are below the diagonal but still within the 'maintain strategy' zone. A further analysis indicates that Colesonline particularly has a high performance for accessibility of the Web site and products (scored at 1.73), quality of the content (1.26), models and method of pricing (1.16), access to customer support (1.16), availability of the

Figure 10.4 **Strategy Evaluation for the Best Practice and Sector Profile (Australia)**

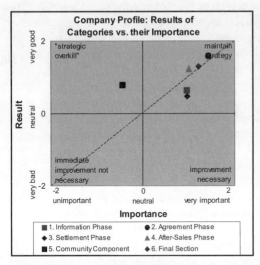
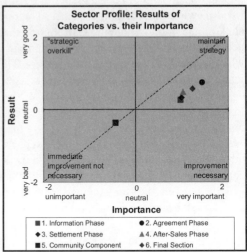

system (1.45) and trustworthiness of the Web site (1.40). The community component of Colesonline, however, has a reasonably good performance, although this component is not considered as important. Therefore, this item lies on the 'strategic overkill' zone in Figure 10.4. These findings are consistent with the qualitative analysis.

In regard to the sector profile, all items except for the community component are situated in the 'maintain strategy' zone, but they are quite far below the diagonal. This implies that there are still opportunities to improve most of the Australian Web sites in the grocery sector, although the sites have a reasonable performance. The community component lies on the diagonal and is situated in the 'immediate improvement not necessary" zone. This means that, although the community component of the sector profile does not have a high score, it was not rated as important either. Therefore, no immediate improvement is required for this.

In summary, based on the results of the Web evaluation of the Australian sites, the study reveals that the majority of the Web sites still require some improvements in many areas, as they still lag behind the performance of the best-practice company. The lack of maturity of Web sites in this sector could be a factor contributing to the slow acceptance of online grocery shopping in Australia. Therefore, by improving the Web sites, particularly in the specific areas identified in this study, the acceptance of online grocery shopping by Australian consumers could likely be improved.

Swiss Results

Four Swiss Web sites were assessed: http://www.shop.coop.ch, http://www.leshop.ch, http://www.migros-shop.ch, and http://www.spar.ch.

Figure 10.5 summarizes the overall evaluation of the Web sites included in the Swiss grocery sector. Migros appears to be the best site in the sector and Spar the worst. Other Web sites require significant improvements in order to achieve a quality comparable to that of Migros, which is the best-practice Web site in this sector. The two large-scale companies Migros and Coop reached

Figure 10.5 **Summary of the Overall Web Evaluation (Switzerland)**

Overall Score with Importance Weighting

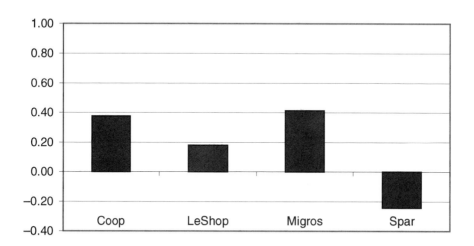

nearly the same overall result. The customer choice between them likely depends on personal preferences toward the real-world brand (the vendor), product range, and price level. In Switzerland, a kind of "religious war" between Migros and Coop followers can be observed which seems to translate also to the online realm.

Figure 10.6 summarizes the company profile for all Web sites evaluated in this study, indicating the score obtained in each phase. It shows that in Switzerland, the best-practice company does not stand out as much as it does in Australia. The companies were more evenly rated.

Overall, the Swiss results are better than the Australian results. Most participants seem to be satisfied with the sites in general. These observations were confirmed by the subsequent qualitative analyses conducted by the authors as well as the qualitative remarks supplied by the Swiss assessors.

In the information phase the analyzed Web sites show varying results. Important criteria in this phase are the possibility of finding and locating the Web site, the presentation of products, information about special offers, and the quality and quantity of the information provided. All four Swiss Web sites can be found easily on the Web. The assessors criticized that the two leaders in the retail sector, Migros and Coop, do not point out the existence of an online shop on their general company Web site. They recommended that LeShop as a pure online player should work harder to move to a higher place in search engines, because as a pure online shop it has not got the same name recognition as the other three retailers.

In the shops of Coop, Migros, and LeShop, the range is presented very "originally and clearly." Products are arranged with reference to product categories or in the same order as in the physical stores. Migros and Coop give detailed descriptions of the products, which was positively emphasized by the assessors. Nearly all products are illustrated with graphics, which facilitates their recognition by inexperienced shoppers. Spar, on the other hand, does not offer pictures; this fact was often mentioned as missing and "rather boring." Information about delivery time is given by all Web shops. Navigation within the Web sites of Coop, Migros, and LeShop is easy, clear, and logically built. The Spar Web site is confusing; one of the assessors even called it "malicious."

Figure 10.6 **Summary of the Company Profile (Switzerland)**

Company Profile with Importance Weighting

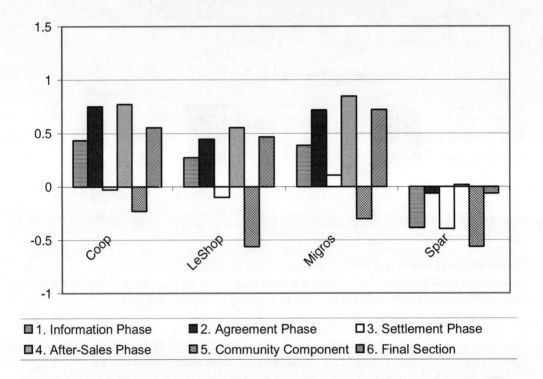

1. Information Phase   2. Agreement Phase   3. Settlement Phase
4. After-Sales Phase   5. Community Component   6. Final Section

For the agreement phase the shops of Migros, Coop, and LeShop received a good evaluation. The ordering process is transparent and interactive. LeShop offers the possibility of payment by invoice and bank transfer, while Coop even offers the possibility of cash payment. The assessors welcome the choice among these three payment methods. The results for Spar differ: Some assessors praise the "clear and simple" structure of the payment process, while others describe "the navigation and subnavigation [as] not well designed." Moreover, some of the virtual sections did not contain any products.

In the Migros shop, customers are able to define a personal shopping list which is very helpful in selecting everyday items. Coop additionally makes the customers shopping proposals based on the transaction profiles. Furthermore, it must be mentioned that buying grocery products online does not lead to direct price advantages for the customer. The shipping costs are reduced or dropped if a purchase reaches a certain amount, which saves the customer from walking to the store and fetching his purchase personally.

For the settlement phase, in all shops—except Coop, where cash payment is possible—payment has to be made in advance by credit card or bank transfer or later by invoice. Payment by credit card is the most widely used method in Swiss online shopping in general. The assessors do not criticize it, nor do they praise it as a particularly beneficial payment method. Coop allows for a very precise selection of the delivery time (+/–30 minutes). In contrast, Migros indicates a large-scale delivery period, which the assessors criticized. On the other hand, they appreciate the short delivery time provided by Migros: depending on the delivery region, orders can be placed until 10.00 in the morning and the goods will be delivered shortly after 4.00 on the same day. LeShop offers a longer delivery period, because delivery is limited by the Swiss postal service (LeShop's fulfillment partner). Spar delivers within a period of three hours by courier but only within very limited delivery areas. The charge for delivery (between 10 and 15 Swiss Francs) was acceptable to the assessors. Migros is the only vendor that offers order tracking. Since this function is not considered very important, the assessors do not criticize its lack in the other shops. In the grocery sector, purchase order tracking seems to be a so-called nice-to-have feature which does not lead to a real advantage for the customer.

For the after-sales phase only few comments were made. This is a positive result, because the assessors had to use the customer service very rarely. In those cases where calling the customer service was necessary, assessors praised the "friendly and competent telephone support" (provided by LeShop). One example was a question for LeShop customer support regarding the handling and return of delivery boxes, for which a deposit had to be paid. In the case of Coop and Migros, customers appreciated the integration of the payback programs ("SuperCard" and "Cumulus") into the online shop. This makes it possible to collect shopping points no matter which channel (electronic or brick-and-mortar) a customer is using. For low-quality products and for products that do not meet customer expectations completely, LeShop offers a money-back strategy. This offer is very helpful to ensure that only high-quality and fresh products are delivered. Calling customer service by phone or e-mail will be unavoidable if the customer forgets his password. It is found a nuisance that in all evaluated shops customer service is available only during (extended) business hours. For the customer who wants to shop late in the evening this is not very helpful.

Looking at the importance of the EWAM criteria, it becomes obvious that the community component is not very important in the grocery sector. Accordingly, there were few comments about it. The assessors did not expect community functions.

For the final section, Migros once again received the highest rating. User guidance is intuitive und well structured in all evaluated shops. The graphical design of the user interface is a matter of taste. The assessors repeatedly praised the facility to overview purchase orders at the end of the shopping process on the LeShop Web site. In the case of Coop and Migros some assessors felt insecure during the payment process because the payment module does not have the same look and feel as the other pages of the shop. All vendors make little use of the possibilities for hyperlinks. The presentation of suitable recipes, the offer of a nutrition consultation or of search possibilities for further information do exist, but they appear to be copied from a paper version of the product catalog.

In the shops of Coop and Migros, the trisection of the screen into range, product, and shopping cart was rated as good. The permanent display of the shopping cart as well as the opportunities to change its contents in the shops of Coop, LeShop, and Migros were positively noted. In these three shops it is also possible to save a personal shopping cart and to open it again if required and generate a new purchase order from it. The assessors rate this personalization method as very useful. Further differences between the analyzed online shops can be observed in the area of trustworthiness of the shops. The high trustworthiness of Coop and Migros is based on their high name recognition, since they have been established vendors for decades. Le Shop, on the other hand, as a young and pure online grocer, first had to stand the test on the market for grocery products.

Figure 10.7 shows a comparison of the best-practice example of Migros with the average sector profile. In regard to the sector profile, all items except for the community component are

Figure 10.7   **Strategy Evaluation for the Best Practice and Sector Profile (Switzerland)**

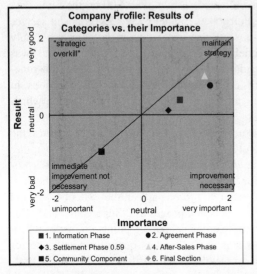 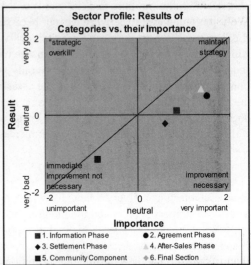

situated in the "maintain strategy" zone, but they are slightly below the diagonal. This implies that there are still opportunities for an average improvement of Swiss Web sites in the grocery sector.

Looking at the details of the study, the results show that the more important phases are better realized than the less important ones in all shops. This is an indication that Swiss online merchants have a pretty good idea of what is important for their clientele. The position in regard to the diagonal varies highly among the different shops. The further away from the diagonal the values are, the greater the disproportion between the target value (importance rating) and the conceived situation (assessment rating). This is most noticeable for Spar, where almost all elements are in the lower right quadrant.

In summary, based on the results of the Web evaluation of the Swiss sites, the study reveals that the majority of the Web sites do meet user expectations up to a certain point. The best-practice company does not stand out as far as in the Australian sample.

COMPARATIVE ANALYSIS AND FINDINGS

Using the EWAM tool, this study indicates that online grocers in Australia and Switzerland have not fully met the expectations of consumers. The study further shows that the performance of Swiss online grocers in various transaction phases has been more consistent across the sample sites compared to the Australian case. In Australia, the best-practice site was rated much higher than other sites in almost all transaction phases.

Although Australia and Switzerland differ in many respects, the results of the study demonstrate that consumers' expectations in online grocery shopping are consistent in both regions. The study shows the importance of having a pleasant, easy-to-use user interface with no information overload on the pages. Furthermore, the availability of the images of products was found to be important in the information phase. Both studies also indicate the importance of having a good position in search engines, particularly for pure online players.

However, the studies indicate that in general, online grocers in Australia and Switzerland have not met the expectations of consumers. All the Web sites assessed, except Colesonline, were rated below 0.5 by the assessors. The structure of the contents, the quantity and quality of information of most Web sites in the studies are still far below consumers' expectations. In particular, most Web sites are unable to pass price benefits on to consumers.

The analysis of the importance ratings also indicates that the importance varies among the different phases and components of the transaction process. Other studies showed that these ratings also vary between different industries (Schubert and Dettling 2001). In order to improve the design of a Web site, it could be useful to analyze the importance rating in the relevant sector and concentrate design activities on the most important phases or on specific criteria.

For the agreement phase, the studies demonstrate the importance of having a transparent ordering procedure and a clear status of the purchase process at any time. The majority of Web sites assessed have a reasonable performance in this phase.

For the settlement phase, the choice of preferred payment method is crucial. Credit card, customer account, cash or check upon delivery should be accepted. The ability to track and trace orders is considered a 'nice-to-have' feature but may not be necessary, as demonstrated by the Swiss study. However, precise selection of the delivery date and time is important in both cases. The importance of the settlement phase was rated higher in Australia than in Switzerland. Since Australia is a big continent and everything is spread over a relatively larger geographic location than in Switzerland, it would be more important for consumers in Australia to be able to track their orders as well as to be informed about the exact delivery time, so that they can plan their activities accordingly. It would be more troublesome for Australian than for Swiss customers to return products, for example, because of the geographical factor.

For the after-sales phase, both studies show the importance of having an online Customer Care Center (as in the case of Colesonline) with a contact number as well as the details of the hours of operation. Most of the Web sites assessed have a reasonable performance in this phase.

For the final section, this study shows that trustworthiness of the sites plays a crucial role. Colesonline, which is operated by one of the largest retail chains in Australia, and Coop and Migros, which have a high name recognition because they are established Swiss vendors, received high rating in general. The study further shows that customers appreciate the integration of brick-and-mortar payback programs ("SuperCard" and "Cumulus" demonstrated in the Switzerland study) into the online shop. Last but not least, the ability for consumers to recall their personal shopping list for consecutive sessions was found to be an attractive and useful feature.

Most online grocers evaluated in this study still need to better understand and be aware of all of the above expectations of consumers in order to improve their Web sites in the various phases of the buying process.

LESSONS LEARNED

Below are several lessons learned from assessing the various aspects of transactional support of Australian and Swiss shopping environments. They are discussed based on the framework proposed by Allen and Fjermestad (2001).

Product

Product is concerned with the content of a market space—that is, what is being sold (Allen and Fjermestad 2001). In the context of online shopping, products are now replaced with information about products. Internet technology has lowered the cost of collecting and disseminating product information to a larger customer base. Likewise, customers' searching costs have been significantly decreased. Customers can now perform product evaluation and price comparison across many online sellers quickly and easily before deciding to purchase (Rayport and Sviokla 1994).

However, some grocery products, particularly highly perishable ones such as fruit and vegetables, are considered as sensory products. These products have some attributes that can be discovered only through our senses such as touch, taste, and smell (Cho et al., 2003). Such products require sophisticated information to assist buyers to make a sound decision. Therefore Web interface and design is a paramount in the online grocery shopping. Image-based systems and highly interactive communication tools may be necessary as part of decision support systems to achieve customer satisfaction and to manage customer relationships (Cho et al. 2003; Romano and Fjermestad 2003). Through an online system that enables a dialog between customers and online grocers, uncertainty about products can be reduced and customer satisfaction increased.

None of the online grocers in this study have offered any interactive tools to enhance customer relationship and maintain customer loyalty. Such tools may increase the convenience experienced by customers while shopping online and, therefore, the possibility that they will return to the same site for the next purchase (Rayport and Sviokla 1994). Thus, online grocers should consider implementing interactive tools in order to improve customer satisfaction.

Place

There are two aspects related to place: 'context,' which refers to how products are sold, and 'infrastructure,' which enables transactions to occur by allowing buyers and sellers to meet (Rayport and Sviokla 1994). As demonstrated in this study, consumers expect online grocers to provide a good searching facility in order to find products and a simple ordering procedure to allow customers to carry out their shopping tasks quickly. Most online grocers assessed in this study have a good performance in this respect.

Although this study revealed that the availability of a recommendation system is important in online grocery shopping, the ability of online grocers to provide personalization of contents is still limited. Personalization would include monthly summaries of expenses or one-to-one marketing—particularly products on special that may interest a particular consumer based on his/her buying patterns. These features would add value for online customers, since it would assist them in the purchasing process (Pastore 2001). In this study, only Coop and Colesonline have shown the capability to offer a simple personalization function by generating shopping proposals based on customers' profiles. Thus, it is also important for online grocers to offer additional value to online consumers in order to retain them or to increase their number. At the current stage, customers do not obtain much extra value apart from convenience and time saving, and they may not have access to nutritional information by shopping online as opposed to visiting a supermarket. In fact, this information is very valuable for customers with health constraints. In addition, online grocers can make the shopping easier for consumers if their Web sites can generate a shopping list based on the meals customers plan to have.

In addition, quality of customer service is also important for sensory products. Cho et al. (2002) revealed that satisfactory responses from the online merchants on any problem with the product normally lead to enhanced customer loyalty. Online grocers, for example, need to provide the assurance of accurate customers' order fulfillment and delivery. In general, online grocery customers will not tolerate even a 1 percent mistake in their order, since it will require them to visit the local supermarket for exchange or return, which means that the objective of online shopping for convenience and time saving will not be fulfilled. Online grocers should provide high-quality customer service to deal with such problems so that the benefits obtained by online grocery customers will not be eroded. Therefore, as indicated in this study, the availability and performance of customer support as assessed in the after-sales phase plays a major role in this context.

It is also important to increase the customers' level of trust in the ability of online grocers to pick and deliver high-quality products accurately. Trust has been recognized as one of the important human factors in customer relationship management (Romano and Fjermestad 2003; Komiak and Benbasat 2004). To increase trust, online grocers need to develop appropriate strategies to improve existing online customer satisfaction and to change the consumers' habit of visiting stores physically, which has been proved not to be an easy task (Allen and Fjermestad 2001; Black 2001).

Price

The Internet has increased price competition due to price transparency that can be easily obtained by buyers and low search cost in comparing prices offered by various retailers. This aspect also affects customer loyalty, since customers can quickly shift to another merchant when they are not satisfied with the prices offered. In addition, Cho et al. (2003) revealed that for sensory products like groceries, the impact of price differences on customer dissatisfaction are higher than for nonsensory products. Therefore, online grocers should standardize their prices in order to increase customer satisfaction. Currently, various online grocers still offer differing prices for the same products.

Generally, consumers expect to have low-cost or free delivery to offset their inability to take the products immediately after shopping online. This still remains one of the challenges faced by grocery retailers, particularly for those who also run physical stores, since online customers actually introduce extra costs related to picking and packing goods as well as delivery, in addition to the costs associated with running the brick-and-mortar operations (Anderson et al. 2000). Therefore, online grocers need to enhance their distribution and order processing capabilities in order to improve delivery performance and lower the costs involved (Romano and Fjermestad 2003). This, in turn, has the potential to improve their customer relationship systems and accelerate the adoption of online grocery shopping.

Although the original intention of offering online grocery shopping was to provide convenience and time savings for consumers at some extra cost, price has been discovered to have a large impact on the use of this new way of shopping for groceries (Pastore 2000). The fact that all Australian and Swiss online grocers in this study are still unable to offer low costs to consumers is therefore one of the important reasons why online grocery shopping has not been widely adopted in these regions. Only if online grocers are able to offer at least the same price as local supermarkets can they expect to grow significantly. Customers are normally willing to pay extra only for the convenience and other value-added features offered by online merchants (Allen and Fjermestad 2001). Online merchants will thus be able to lock in customers by providing additional features that make shopping easier.

Promotion

There are many ways organizations can promote and encourage potential buyers to purchase their products. The Internet enables merchants to have both 'reach' and 'richness,' since they can reach more buyers by offering a wider selection of products and can disseminate rich information about their products online (Evans and Wurster 1999). Customers' information collected by the merchants can be used to offer personalized information or products to customers (Allen and Fjermestad 2001). For example, based on a customer's shopping profile, the merchant can offer a one-to-one advertisement on a favorite product of a particular customer. This advertisement can also be made available during a transaction for cross-selling purposes.

For some customers, however, privacy concerns due to lack of trust still remain an issue that may limit the promotion of particular products. This issue has been recognized as one of the most critical human factors in customer relationship management (Komiak and Benbasat 2004; Romano and Fjermestad 2003).

Researchers have suggested a number of reasons for the failure of those early online grocers, which include the ambition to grow too fast without adequate capability in handling a large volume of orders, the high spending on advertising, poorly run operations, inability to meet customers' expectations, and the lack of critical mass due to small size of target market (Black 2001; MSNBC 2004). Therefore, by giving attention to various issues discussed in this section, online grocery retailers will be able to meet consumers' expectations, improve their customer relationship systems, increase their target market, and improve their operation efficiency accordingly. Moreover, through establishing a larger customer base and long-term relationships, online grocers will experience consistent cash flow, which may outweigh the delivery costs as a result of better utilization of resources and the high volume of transactions. All this will enable online grocers to avoid the failure of the past and increase their maturity level.

CONCLUSIONS AND LIMITATIONS TO THIS STUDY

EWAM is one of the oldest evaluation methods of its kind. It lays down a conceptual framework for the evaluation of commercial Web sites that in its basic form, the Web Assessment Method, has already proved itself in operation for several years. In this study, we have demonstrated the usefulness of the EWAM tool in assessing various Swiss and Australian Web sites within the grocery sector. Strengths and weaknesses of various Web sites of Australian and Swiss grocers have been highlighted, valuable lessons have been learned, and opportunities to improve customer satisfaction in each phase of transaction have been outlined. As discussed comprehensively in this chapter, most of the Web sites in both countries still lack an acceptable degree of sophistication. Their designers still need to better understand consumers' expectations and improve the performance of their Web sites accordingly in order to increase the consumers' satisfaction level. This, in turn, can accelerate the use of online shopping. However, since some grocery products have attributes that are difficult to examine online, online grocery operations face many challenges to enhance customer relationship management and increase customer satisfaction.

An empirical study with a limited sample set, such as this study, can reflect only a partial and somewhat biased picture of current practice in the analyzed sector. The bias exists because the students share similar opinions of e-commerce and they are homogeneous (since they attended the same electronic commerce class, their opinions tend to be less universal than if they were hand picked at random). Furthermore, the participants of this study are not representative of the hundreds of thousands of Web users in Australia and Switzerland. Nevertheless, since the EWAM tool is a highly knowledge-requiring process, one cannot ask a random sample of people to do the assessments. In addition, although the Web sites chosen for evaluation were not very diverse, the number of serious players in the online world is still limited. Therefore, the limited number of participants and the Web sites assessed in this study should not invalidate the findings obtained. These findings have been confirmed by the subsequent qualitative evaluations, as described in this chapter, and the lessons learned from this study have been consistent with findings reported in the literature.

REFERENCES

Allen, E. and Fjermestad, J. E-commerce marketing strategies: An integrated framework and case analysis *Logistics information management*, 14, 1–2 (2001) 14–23.

Anderson, E.J.; Philpott, A.B.; Discenza, J.H.; Haley, K.B.; Palmer, J.W. Web site usability, design, and performance metrics. *Information Systems Research*, 13, 2 (2002), 151–167.

Barnes, Stuart J. and Vidgen, Richard, An evaluation of cyber-bookshops: The WebQual method. *International Journal of Electronic Commerce*, 6, 1 (2001), 6–25.

Barnett, M. and Alexander, P. Can e-grocers survive the last mile? *The 4th International We-B Conference*, Perth, Western Australia, 2003, CD ROM.

Black, J. Business Week Online—Online Extra: Why online grocers won't all go hungry, 2001 (available at www.businessweek.com/magazine/content/01_20/b3732699.htm, accessed on September 1, 2004).

Cho, Y.; Im, I.; Fjermestad, J.; and Hiltz, R. The impact of product category on customer dissatisfaction in cyberspace, *Business Process Management Journal*, 9, 5 (2003), 635–651.

Cho, Y.; Im, I.; and Hiltz, R. The effects of post-purchase evaluation factors on online vs. offline customer complaining behaviour: Implications for customer loyalty. *Advances in Consumer Research*, 29 (2002), 318–326.

Davis, F.D. Jr. A technology acceptance model for empirically testing new end-user information systems: Theory and results. Doctoral Thesis, Sloan School of Management: Massachusetts Institute of Technology, 1985.

Ellis, C. Lessons from online grocers, *MIT Sloan Management Review*, 44, 2 (2003), 8.

Evans, P. and Wurster, T.S. Getting real about virtual commerce, *Harvard Business Review*, November (1999), 84–94.

Fishbein, M.; Ajzen, I. *Belief, Attitude, Intention and Behavior: An Introduction to Theory and Research*, Reading, MA: Addison-Wesley, 1975.

Freeman, M. The current state of online supermarket usability in Australia. In *The 14th Australasian Conference on Information Systems*, Perth, Western Australia, 2003, CD-ROM.

Kinsey, J. and Senauer, B. Consumer trends and changing food retailing formats. *American Journal of Agricultural Economics*, 78, 5 (1996), 1187–91.

Komiak, S.X. and Benbasat, I. Understanding customer trust in agent-mediated electronic commerce, web-mediated electronic commerce, and traditional commerce. *Information Technology and Management*, 5, 1–2 (2004), 181–207.

Koufaris, M., Applying the technology acceptance model and flow theory to online consumer behavior. *Information Systems Research*, 13, 2 (2002), 205–223.

Kurnia, S. and Chien, J.A-W. The acceptance of online grocery shopping. In *The 16th Bled Electronic Commerce Conference*, Bled, Slovenia, 2003, CD-ROM.

Liu, C.; Arnett, K.P.; and Litecky, C., Design quality of websites for electronic commerce: Fortune 1000 webmaster's evaluations. *International Journal of Electronic Commerce & Business Media*, 10, 2 (2000), 120–129.

Mahajan, V. and Srinivasan, R. The dot.com retail failures of 2000: Were there any winners? *Journal of the Academy of Marketing Science*, 30, 4 (2002), 474–486.

Mich, L.; Franch, M.; and Gaio, L. Evaluating and designing Web site quality. *IEEE Multimedia*, January–March 2003, 34–43.

Morganosky, M. and Cude, B. Consumer response to online grocery shopping. *International Journal of Retail and Distribution Management*, 28, 1 (2000), 17–26.

MSNBC News, Online groceries keep expanding quietly, 2003 (available at www.msnbc.msn.com/id/4993549/, accessed on September 1, 2004).

Parasuraman, A.; Zeithaml, V.; and Berry, L. SERVQUAL: A multi-item scale for measuring consumer perceptions of service quality. *Journal of Retailing*, 64, 1 (1988), 12–40.

Pastore, M. Online grocery sector needs a little marketing, 2001 (available at www.clickz.com/stat/markets/retailing/article.php/753121, accessed on August 20, 2004).

Rayport, J.F. and Sviokla, J.J. Managing in the marketspace. *Harvard Business Review* (November 1994), 141–150.

Romano, N. C. Jr. and Fjermestad, J. Electronic commerce customer relationship management: A research agenda. *Information Technology and Management*, 4, 2–3 (2003), 233–258.

Schubert, P. and Dettling, W. Web site evaluation: Do Web applications meet user expectations? Music, consumer goods and e-banking on the test bed. In *The 14th International Bled Electronic Commerce Conference*, 2001, CD-ROM

Schubert, P. and Selz, D. Web assessment—measuring the effectiveness of electronic commerce sites going beyond traditional marketing paradigms. In *The 32nd Hawaii International Conference on System Sciences*, Hawaii. Los Alamitos, CA: IEEE Computer Society Press, 1999, CD-ROM

Schubert, P. Extended Web Assessment Method (EWAM)—Evaluation of electronic commerce applications from the customer's viewpoint, *International Journal of Electronic Commerce*, 7, 2 (2003), 51–80.

Schuster, A. and Sporn, B. Potential for online grocery shopping in the urban area of Vienna. *Electronic Markets*, 8, 2 (1998), 13–16.

Selz, D. and Schubert, P. Web assessment—A model for the evaluation and assessment of successful electronic commerce applications. In *The 31st Hawaiian International Conference on System Sciences*, Hawaii. Los Alamitos, CA: IEEE Computer Society Press, 1998, pp. 222–231.

Spiliopoulou, M., Web usage mining for Web site evaluation. *Communications of the ACM*, 43, 8 (2000), 127–134.

Turner, J. Online grocers try to extend their shelf life, The Christian Science Publishing Society, 2001 (available at www.csmonitor.com/cgi-bin/durableRedirect.pl?/durable/2001/02/12/fp16s2–csm.shtml, accessed on August 20, 2002).

Yoo, B. and Donthu, N. Developing a scale to measure the perceived quality of an internet shopping site (SITEQUAL), *Quarterly Journal of Electronic Commerce*, 2, 1 (2001), 31–46.

EDITORS AND CONTRIBUTORS

Rainer Alt is a project manager and a senior lecturer at the Institute of Information Management, University of St. Gallen, Switzerland. He received his master's degree in business administration from the University of Erlangen-Nuremberg in Germany and his Ph.D. from the University of St. Gallen. Before assuming his current position, he was with Roland Berger Strategy Consultants in Germany.

Michael R. Bartolacci is an assistant professor of information sciences and technology at Penn State Berks/Lehigh Valley College. Dr. Bartolacci holds a Ph.D. in industrial engineering with a concentration in information systems from Lehigh University. He has published in journals such as the *INFORMS Journal of Computing* and the *Asian Journal of Information Technology*. Dr. Bartolacci's special research interests include the modeling of telecommunications and electronic commerce, and online customer relationship management systems.

Walter Brenner is professor of information systems at the University of St. Gallen, Switzerland, and managing director of the Institute of Information Management. After earning his graduate degree, his doctorate degree and his venia legendi from the University of St. Gallen, he worked for several years for the Alusuisse-Lonza AG based in Basel, Switzerland, among other positions as the Head of Application Development. From 1993 until 1999 he was professor of business administration and information management at the TU Bergakademie Freiberg, Germany and subsequently professor of information management and business administration at the University of Essen, Germany. His research focus is on integrated information management, customer relationship management and innovative technologies.

Adrian Bueren is a researcher at the Institute of Information Management of the University of St. Gallen, Switzerland. He is a member of the Competence Center Customer Knowledge Performance (CC CKP), in which large European companies do joint research on customer relationship management and knowledge management. His research focuses on content management in customer-oriented business processes, especially in the financial services industry. He earned a master's degree in business administration at the University of St. Gallen.

Ja-Shen Chen is an associate professor in the Business Administration Department at Yuan Ze University, Taiwan. He received his Ph.D. in decision sciences from Rensselaer Polytechnic Institute, New York. His current research focus is the investigation of empirical studies, as well as modeling techniques, on e-commerce and e-business management, especially in the areas of customer relationship management and supply chain management. He has been a principal investigator for a number of academic and industrial funded projects and also has published in journals and conference papers in the decision sciences and information management areas.

Russell K.H. Ching is a professor in the College of Business Administration and chair of the Management Information Science Department at California State University, Sacramento. Dr. Ching received his doctorate from the University of Arkansas, Fayetteville, where he studied in computer information systems. His research in CRM, e-business, and organizational absorptive capacity has been published in various journals and international conference proceedings.

Yoon C. Cho is an assistant professor in the College of Business Administration, Hawaii Pacific University, Honolulu, HI. He earned a Ph.D. in management from Rutgers, The State University of New Jersey, and an M.B.A. from Cornell University. Her current interests are in electronic commerce marketing including CRM, customer satisfaction/dissatisfaction, and complaining behavior.

Jerry Fjermestad is an associate professor in the School of Management at NJIT. He received his B.A. in chemistry from Pacific Lutheran University, an M.S. in operations research from Polytechnic University, an M.B.A in operations management from Iona College, and an M.B.A. and Ph.D. from Rutgers University in management information systems. He has taught courses on management information systems, decision support systems, systems analysis and design, electronic commerce, and data warehousing, and graduate seminars in information systems. His current research interests are in collaborative technology, decision support systems, data warehousing, electronic commerce, global information systems, customer relationship management, and enterprise information systems. Dr. Fjermestad has published in the *Journal of Management Information Systems, Group Decision and Negotiation, Journal of Organizational Computing and Electronic Commerce, Information and Management, Decision Support Systems, Logistics Information Management, International Journal of Electronic Commerce, Journal of Computer-Mediated Communication, Technology Analysis & Strategic Management,* and the *Proceedings of Hawaii International Conference on System Sciences.* He has also been a special issue editor for the *International Journal of Electronic Commerce, Group Decision and Negotiation, Logistics Information Management,* and *Business Process Management Journal.* Jerry is on the editorial board of the *Journal of Enterprise Information Management* and the *International Journal of Enterprise Systems* and is an associate editor of the *International Journal of e-Collaboration.*

Malte Geib is a researcher at the Institute of Information Management at the University of St. Gallen, Switzerland. He is a member of the Competence Center Customer Knowledge Performance, in which large European companies do joint research on customer relationship management and knowledge management. His research focuses on customer relationship management and customer knowledge transfer in networked enterprises, especially in the financial services industry. Malte has worked as software engineer for IBM Germany and as a consultant for Deutsche Telekom AG, Deutsche Telekom Immobilien, and Bausparkasse Schwäbisch-Hall. He earned a degree as master of science in information systems from the University of Muenster, Germany, and has lectured at the University of Muenster, the University of St. Gallen, and the University of Tartu, Estonia.

Na (Lina) Li is a doctoral student at the School of Information Studies, Syracuse University. She earned her master and bachelor degrees in information management from Peking University, Beijing, China. Her research interests include motivational, affective, cognitive, behavioral, and performance aspects of human–technology interaction, user interface evaluation, and software learning/training. Her research has appeared or will appear in *Computers in Human Behavior,*

CACM, Proceedings of Americas Conference on Information Systems (AMCIS), and *Proceedings of the International Conference on Information Systems (ICIS)*.

Lutz M. Kolbe has headed the Competence Center Customer Knowledge Performance (CC CKP) since July 2002, and he teaches at AACSB-accredited University of St. Gallen, Switzerland. His research interests are customer relationship management and security management as well as advanced technologies in the residential environment. After working as financial consultant, Lutz studied information management at Brunswick Technical University, Germany, where he received a master's degree. He went on working on his dissertation at Freiberg Technical University, Germany, and the University of Rhode Island, United States. He received his Ph.D. in 1997, then worked at Deutsche Bank in Frankfurt and New York, where he became managing director in 2001.

Sherah Kurnia is a lecturer at the Department of Information Systems, the University of Melbourne. She obtained her doctorate in computing from Monash University, Australia, after completing a research project on the adoption of efficient consumer response in Australia, as an example of an electronic commerce enabled interorganizational system. Her research interests are in the area of electronic commerce, supply chain management, adoption of inter-organizational systems, and technological innovations in general, including mobile technologies and the use of information technology in developing countries. She is regular contributor to the *International Journal of Supply Chain Management* and has published a paper in the journal of *Strategic Information Systems*. She is the regional editor for the special issue on mobile business of the *Korean Journal of e-Business*.

Mary J. Meixell is an assistant professor of decision sciences in the School of Management at George Mason University. Before joining GMU, Dr. Meixell worked in materials and supply chain management in the telecommunications and automotive industries. She holds a Ph.D. in industrial engineering from Lehigh University, an M.S. degree in transportation from M.I.T, and a B.S. in civil engineering from Penn State. Her research is in supply chain and logistics management, on the bullwhip effect in manufacturing supply chains, on modeling demand scenarios in technology markets, and on operational performance in collaborative business environments.

Thomas Puschmann is a senior consultant at The Information Management Group (IMG), Switzerland. He received his master's degree in management sciences from the University of Konstanz and his Ph.D. from the University of St. Gallen. In his current position he is responsible for business networking, customer relationship management, and portals.

Nicholas C. Romano, Jr. is assistant professor of management science and information systems at Oklahoma State University (OSU.) He received a B.S. in biology (1986), and B.S. in MIS (1988), M.S. in MIS (1992), and Ph.D. in MIS (1998) from the University of Arizona. Prior to joining OSU in 2001 he was a assistant professor of MIS at the University of Tulsa and research scientist at the University of Arizona's Center for the Management of Information. He has been a technical consultant for GroupSystems.COM and worked for IBM as a systems programmer. He served as a visiting scholar at the University of Arizona in the summer of 2000, 2001, 2002, 2003 and 2004. His research interests involve collaborative systems and include technology-supported learning, group support systems design, use and facilitation, knowledge creation and management, collaborative project and process management, electronic customer relationship management, and information systems accessibility Dr. Romano has published papers in a number of scholarly journals, conference proceedings, and practitioner journals, including the *Journal of Management Information Systems, International Journal of Electronic Commerce, Journal of the American Society for Information Science, Information Systems Frontiers, Proceedings of the Hawaii International Conference on Systems Sciences, Proceedings of the Conference of the Association of Management*, and *Proceedings of the Americas Conference on Information Systems*. Dr. Romano has also co-guest-edited special issues of the *International Journal of Electronic Commerce, Business Process Management Journal, Journal of Enterprise Information Management* (formerly *Logistics Information Management–LIM*), and *Information Systems Frontiers* and is currently co-guest-editing an edition of the *Advances in Management Information Systems* monograph series, a special issue on universal accessibility for the Information Society on Accessibility, a special issue of the *Journal of Organizational Computing and Electronic Commerce*, and a special issue of the *International Journal of Electronic Collaboration*. Dr. Romano has served as the program review chair for the 2001, 2002, 2003, and 2004 AMCIS Conference, served as the proceedings editor in 2004, and will serve in both roles for AMCIS 2005. He is a member of the Web Academic Conference Management System Steering Committee, which oversees future development and implementation of the AIS Document Review System for IS conferences. Dr. Romano is founder and co-chair of minitracks on Computer-Supported Collaborative Learning Requiring Immersive Presence, Customer Relationship Management, and IS/IT Accessibility for AMCIS and the HICSS. Dr. Romano served as the program co-chair for the ISOneWorld Conference in 2003 and 2004 and also co-chaired a minitrack on CRM in 2002 and 2003. He is section editor of the *ISWORLD Journal* pages located at: Hyperlinkhttp://www.osu-tulsa.okstate.edu/nromano/wwwroot/iswjsp/. Dr. Romano also serves as an associate editor for the *Journal of Information Systems Technology (JIST)* and reviews regularly for *JMIS, IJEC, Management Science, DSS*, and other IS and related discipline journals.

Ragnar Schierholz is a researcher at the Institute of Information Management of the University of St. Gallen, Switzerland. He is a member of the Competence Center Customer Knowledge Performance (CC CKP), in which large European companies do joint research on customer relationship management and knowledge management. His research focus is on the application of mobile business technology in the field of customer relationship management (CRM). Earlier he worked as an IT consultant for IBM Germany, Lotus Professional Services Germany, and as an IT service engineer for ONEstone GmbH Germany. He earned degrees as master of science in computer science from Western Michigan University, Kalamazoo, United States, and as Diplom-Wirtschaftsinformatiker (equivalent to a master of science in information systems) from the University of Paderborn, Germany.

Petra Schubert is a full professor in e-business at the University of Applied Sciences in Basel (FHBB). She received her doctorate in information systems from the University of St. Gallen. Her research interests include the study of management of e-commerce applications, specifically personalization and virtual communities. Dr. Schubert authored one of the first books on virtual communities of transactions and is a regular minitrack chair for this topic at HICSS and AMCIS. She has written and co-edited several books, including *Digital Success, Successfully Planning and Realizing E-Business, Fulfillment in E-Business, Procurement in E-Business*, and *E-Business Integration*. She is a member of the editorial board of the *Electronic Commerce Research Journal (ECRJ)* and the *International Journal of Enterprise Information Systems (IJEIS)* and a regular reviewer for *Electronic Markets* and the *International Journal of Electronic Commerce (IJEC)*.

Carl-Erik Wikström is a partner and director in the Finnish IT company Mepco Ltd, which specializes in providing its customers with implementation and integration services of Microsoft Business Solutions CRM software products. Mr. Wikström has 20 years of experience in consulting and project management in several CRM projects in small and medium-sized companies in Finland. He is currently a doctoral student in the Finnish doctoral program INFWEST.IT Hyperlinkhttp://www.infwest.it.jyu.fi/. His research interests are in IS success, CRM, and organizational change. Mr. Wikström received his predoctoral degree in 1994 with the paper "An investigation of factors influencing the success of customer-oriented marketing information systems."

Ping Zhang is associate professor at the School of Information Studies, Syracuse University. Dr. Zhang earned her Ph.D. in information systems from the University of Texas at Austin, and her M.Sc. and B.Sc. in computer science from Peking University, Beijing, China. Her research appears or will appear in journals such as *Behaviour & Information Technology*, *CACM*, *CAIS*, *Computers in Human Behavior*, *DSS*, *IJHCS*, *IJEC*, *Journal of American Society for Information Science and Technology*, *JAIS*, *e-Service Journal*, and *IEEE Computer Graphics and Applications*, among others. Dr. Zhang received the Best Paper awards at the Americas Conference on Information Systems (2001) and the International Academy for Information Management (1997), and an excellence in teaching award from the University of Texas at Austin (1994). She is an associate editor for *IJHCS* and a guest editor for special issues of *JAIS*, *JMIS*, *IJHCS*, *IJHCI*, and *BIT*. She is the founding chair of AIS SIGHCI.

SERIES EDITOR

Vladimir Zwass is the Distinguished Professor of Computer Science and Management Information Systems at Fairleigh Dickinson University. He holds a Ph.D. in Computer Science from Columbia University. Dr. Zwass is the Founding Editor-in-Chief of the *Journal of Management Information Systems*; one of three top-ranked journals in the field of Information Systems, the journal has recently celebrated twenty years in publication. He is also the Founding Editor-in-Chief of the *International Journal of Electronic Commerce,* ranked as the top journal in its field. Dr. Zwass is the author of six books and several book chapters, including entries in the *Encyclopaedia Britannica,* as well as of a number of papers in various journals and conference proceedings. He has received several grants, consulted for a number of major corporations, and is a frequent speaker to national and international audiences. He is a former member of the Professional Staff of the International Atomic Energy Agency in Vienna, Austria.

INDEX